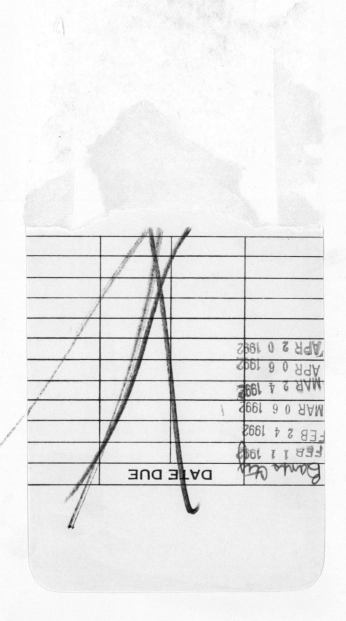
D0365676

THE HUNGRY FUTURE

Books by René Dumont

False Start in Africa   1966

La Culture du Riz dans le Delta du Tonkin   1935

Misère ou Prospérité Paysanne?   1936

Le Problème Agricole Français   1946

Les Leçons de l'Agriculture Américaine   1949

Voyages en France d'un Agronome   1951

Economie Agricole dans le Monde   1953

La Nécessaire Révolution Fourragère   1955

Révolution dans les Campagnes Chinoises   1957

Evolution des Campagnes Malgaches   1960

Terres Vivantes   1961

Reconversion de l'Économie Agricole:
 Guinée, Côte d'Ivoire, Mali   1961

Sovkhoz, Kolkhoz, ou le Problématique Communisme   1964

Cuba, Socialisme et Développement   1964

Développement Agricole Africain   1965

Chine Surpeuplée, Tiers-Monde Affamé   1965

The Hungry Future

René Dumont
and Bernard Rosier

Translated from the French by
Rosamund Linell and R. B. Sutcliffe

Foreword by Thomas Balogh

PRAEGER PUBLISHERS
New York • Washington

BOOKS THAT MATTER

Published in the United States of America in 1969
by Praeger Publishers, Inc.
111 Fourth Avenue, New York, N.Y. 10003

Second printing, 1970

English translation © 1969, by André Deutsch Ltd.

Library of Congress Catalog Card Number: 69-11861

Printed in the United States of America

To the children of backward countries who never
attain their full promise,
or who have died of kwashiorkor,
because the fish meal which might have saved them
has fed the chickens gorged by the rich.

In the last two decades or so the world has seen, in rapid and almost bewildering sequence, convincing and cumulative evidence of the advance in man's control over his natural environment. This remarkable development has taken many forms: heart-transplants, chemotherapy, antibiotics and the birth-control pill are examples of its constructive aspects; while hydrogen bombs and nerve gases represent the reverse, and destructive, side of the coin. But man's increasing domination of his natural environment has not been matched by similar progress in his control of his own nature and of his social and political environment. This yawning, and ever-widening, gap between human effectiveness in the physical sciences and the puniness of human achievement in the socio-political arena threatens the world with an alternative of catastrophes: annihilation on the one hand; or, on the other, the survival of islands of opulent frustration amidst starvation. It is this tragic paradox of our age which Professor Dumont treats in the most important of all his works which, like its predecessors, breaks much new ground.

The first fact to note is the suddenness with which this menacing cloud has appeared above the world's horizon. Before the war, the prosperous North Atlantic countries were much preoccupied with the threat of a decline in their populations, even to the extent of prophesying extinction and race-suicide. To counteract these dangers, therefore, they took steps to subsidize large families. At that time it was thought that, with increasing income, the population pattern of the rest of the world would automatically evolve in the same way as that of countries which had already successfully achieved industrialization. The net increase in the population of the developing countries was not an obvious menace, for if their birth rate was high, so was their death rate. And, if the North Atlantic example was any indication, a falling trend in the death rate would, after some delay, be duly followed by a decline in the birth rate, as a result of an organic social development. Unfortunately, this comforting expectation has been violently falsified by the medical revolution which was in no way organically connected with social progress. While the death rate collapsed, the birth rate rose – often quite sharply – as a result of medical advances which eliminated, or at least substantially checked, chronic or parasitic illness. Until 1700 or so the world population fluctuated around an unchanging level. It then began to grow, but the national rate of growth was hardly ever above 2 per cent, and mostly half of that. It is now moving towards 3 per cent, with large areas well in excess of that figure.

Moreover, for a number of years, the strong religious beliefs and social and psychological prejudices dating from a pre-scientific era have prevented rational attitudes in facing this tendency and have even inhibited discussion of the problem. In Marxist countries Malthusian analysis was presented as heretical unbelief in men's power to expand production under 'socialism'. During the valuable time thus lost, population continued to soar unabated. Gradually, however, a decisive change in attitudes has been brought about by the weight of the evidence of overpopulation coming to light: the spread of erosion as the growing population pressed against the marginal land; the exhaustion of the productive surplus by the investment needed for the expanding numbers; the increasing unemployment; the seething urban proletariat; and, in some acutely affected areas, the threat of famine. With this new awareness of the dangers involved, birth control under various euphemistic guises has gained increasingly wide acceptance.

It is devoutly to be hoped that the increase in numbers will be checked, for the need for such control is made clearer than ever before by Professor Dumont's ruthless dissection of the causes of the agricultural failures both in the East and the West. He uses his unparalleled knowledge and authority to clear away the hypocrisy which has bedevilled most multilateral aid reviews and the political subterfuge which has prevented most bilateral action from becoming effective. While many are those who cry havoc and call for increased aid, Professor Dumont goes much further. Like Professor Myrdal in his *Asian Drama*, he analyses the preconditions for success. Increased aid, increased trade: both, he concedes, are necessary but by themselves they are by no means enough. Indeed, a great number of people of goodwill, by stressing the magnitude of the needs and handing the bowl round instead of fearlessly analysing the requisites for successfully achieving social and economic development, are gravely imperilling international goodwill and willingness for sacrifice, rather than assisting what is perhaps one of the most important causes of our age, and one which certainly holds unlimited implications for all of us.

Professor Dumont does not fall into this easy trap. On the contrary, he tackles the root of the problem, which is not merely that more aid is needed but that the resources already available should be more effectively used. He underlines the need for a revolutionary change at national, regional, and international levels, in the present institutional arrangements for promoting economic and social development; and he demonstrates convincingly that one of the major causes of poverty in the 'poor' areas of the world is the defective social framework typical of so many developing countries, which frustrates all attempts at achieving the modernization of the economy or social progress. The need for urgent reform of antiquated systems of land tenure is a theme which recurs again and again in his detailed treatment of the problems inhibiting increased food production in the continents of Africa, Latin America, and Asia. But he does not blur the issues by presenting it as an easily achieved panacea. His chapter on the agriculture of the Socialist bloc nowhere underestimates the practical difficulties of redistributing land, and the same deep insight into the problems involved is reflected in his dispassionate analysis of the shortcomings of the lamentably few agrarian reforms so far attempted in Latin America, including those of the recently instituted Chilean programme, and even of the Mexican experience, despite its many commendable achievements.

He is quick to warn that sudden, ill-prepared structural changes can cause a drop in agricultural production; over-enthusiastic would-be reformers must therefore not lose sight of the fact that agrarian reform must be regarded first and foremost as an economic measure, with increased production as its principal aim. Nor can any master-recipe for success be suggested. Each situation must be examined in depth and a solution appropriate to the circumstances worked out. This means also that no solution can stand in isolation. The attack on underdevelopment must be a concerted one, and in making this analysis Professor Dumont rightly stresses the fundamental importance of a totally new approach to education and administration, placing the emphasis on technical proficiency. And inevitably, the argument constantly returns to the inescapable fact that no combination of methods, however successful in their own field of action, can do anything effective to stay the implacable advance of the ogre of famine unless they are accompanied by effective control of the rate of births. In this way, Professor Dumont tellingly centres our attention on some of the fundamental obstacles confronting current efforts to stimulate the economic and social development of the backward areas of the world. This is the nub of the problem. Further disillusionment by the developed world with the performance of the primitive economies, the persistence of inequality and the resultant growing resentment on the part of the 'Third World', will not only increasingly erode international aid, but will further undermine the already precarious stability of our world and widen the gap between our theoretical scientific knowledge and our pitifully inadequate practical achievements in applying that knowledge for the economic and social betterment of mankind.

The unique significance of this book is that it throws this fundamental problem into sharp relief.

THOMAS BALOGH

Balliol College, Oxford
    May, 1968

CONTENTS

INTRODUCTION

In the winter of 1958–59 I took part in a mission[1] sponsored by the United Nations Economic and Social Council at the request of the Indian government. The object of the mission was to evaluate the results obtained by community development on democratic lines in India. In the report particular emphasis was laid on the numerous economic factors hindering agricultural development in India.

Working in conjunction with our North American colleagues from the Ford Foundation, we estimated that in 1966 the country would require at the very minimum 110 million tons of cereal grains and dried pulses. This really is a minimum for a population of 500 million when reductions are made for seed, the needs of livestock and industry, and losses due to bad storage. India had a harvest of 88 million tons in 1964, which was a very good year climatically, and of 71 million tons in 1965, a year of severe drought. We should therefore emphasize that, contrary to official statements (famine being no great hardship when it is suffered by others), India is now in a state of chronic famine, varying in severity with the hazards of the monsoons; the situation seems to us bound to deteriorate.

In an article I wrote for the *New Statesman* (December 19, 1959) I referred to India's agricultural defeat. 'The Indians should have admitted their defeat; then they could have corrected their policy and improved the situation. The government chooses to try to minimize the seriousness of the famine, which has already taken hold, in an attempt to lighten its heavy burden of responsibility.'[2]

Thus, in 1959, we forecast that famine would strike India towards the end of the third Five Year Plan; it was with great sadness that we

[1] Our report, *Community Development Evaluation Mission in India,* was published in New Delhi by the Indian government in November 1959. I wrote Chapter IV and Margaret Read and M. G. Coldwell wrote the other chapters.
[2] Cf. Also G. Penchenier, 'Inde, opération survie', *Le Monde Diplomatique,* March 1966.

saw ourselves proved right. My young friend Bernard Rosier[3] and I now maintain that there is a serious threat of widespread famine in most of the Third World before 1980. So serious is the danger that we are forced to conclude that none of the policies of international cooperation and aid to underdeveloped countries carried out so far have succeeded in reaching their objectives; we even have cause to wonder whether they have not failed altogether.

These policies, though not useless, have been proved quite inadequate: the gap between the rich and the poor countries has grown steadily wider with the course of time. Towards the end of the eighteenth century, average *per capita* incomes in the poorest countries and the rich countries were in the ratio of 1:8, using Southern India and the United Kingdom as examples. In 1966, the ratio between the 60 dollars per year in some tropical African countries and the 3,600 dollars in the United States was 1:60.

If existing trends were to continue, before the end of the century the ratio would be 1 to over 100. We will hazard another guess: the ratio will never reach this differential. Long before this the gulf between the increasingly wasteful overconsumption of the affluent peoples and the deprivation of the starving poor will provoke violent reprisals which may even destroy our civilization. And the Western countries, watching China's nuclear progress with great alarm, are very likely to be the sufferers. Should the situation reach breaking point, intervention will be so long overdue as to be useless. But at present the vast production potential of the Atlantic bloc still offers great scope for action.

No campaign against hunger can be regarded as meaningful, however, unless it acknowledges that effective world solidarity must be established between the affluent countries and the poorest countries -- the new proletariat. This forces the issue into a political context. Besides, the West should not be afraid to come out in opposition to those leaders who have a vested interest in scarcity as a safeguard of their own power. The West should also admit that it lost the first battle against hunger; it is now in the position of France in June 1940. If it revises its strategy, it could still win the 'war for develop-

[3] Bernard Rosier wrote Parts I and II of this book, sections 7 and 8 of Chapter XII, and section 1 of Chapter XIII.

ment'. A recognition of the extreme seriousness of the situation will provide the initial foundation for the campaign; it should be not only humanitarian but also political. We hope that our brief essay will make some contribution to bringing this into effect.

The 'war for development' will be long; it will last for over a century. It will affect the lives of our grandchildren and our great-grandchildren. It will soon deserve complete, exclusive priority and the vast majority of our means and resources. Perhaps the survival instinct, in the usual absence of altruism, can push the West into action.

In the first part of this book, Bernard Rosier shows that the population explosion in the Third World is an absolutely unprecedented phenomenon; he shows the inherent limitations on the possible rate of growth of our food production, even in the face of our greatest efforts. Non-agricultural foodstuffs will be extremely important at some future date; but in the immediate future, they can do nothing to avert the threat of famine, which is imminent unless the birth rate is rapidly reduced.[4] In the second part, he draws attention to the high agricultural potential of the West, which cannot be further exploited unless it widens its outlets to supply currently unprofitable markets.

In the third part, I give an analysis of the agricultural problems of the socialist bloc, which would be solved more easily by more thorough destalinization in both the economic and the political spheres. In the fourth part, I show how the Third World should, initially, try to be self-reliant and how its corrupt, privileged minorities, who do not attach enough importance to the common good, impede progress.

In conclusion, the fifth part emphasizes the necessity for completely new forms of intervention whereby world solidarity can be made a concrete reality, and sketches out various possible measures. There is no attempt to predict any future developments, as the future will be the result of involved and confused conflicts of interests and ideologies, and one cannot possibly know how these

[4] At the current growth rate of 3.1 per cent per year, a population multiplies by twenty in a hundred years, and by 20^8 or 25,000 million in eight hundred years. At the present rate, in 2766, the population of Tunisia would be 33 million times the size of the world's population in 1966.

will be resolved. If our lack of understanding, our self interest and our prejudices remain unaltered, then atomic suicide on a world scale is a possibility that cannot be dismissed.

Our children must fight for the future of man and for their own survival. The rich countries will be the best provided with resources for this fight. More difficulties and problems will arise than any previous generation has had to face. Yet since it is only in the face of challenge that life takes on its full meaning, the future will be exciting, especially if the new generations can see the issues in their full dimensions and will fight to improve the lives of the people of the Third World. They will have to choose between a happy world and an overpopulated one.[5]

[5] In particular we should like to thank M. Aubrac of the FAO (Food and Agriculture Organization of the United Nations), M. Baron of the Laboratory of Human Nutrition of the Institut national de la santé et de la recherche médicale, M. Brette and M. Wotling of the Société de chimie organique et biologique, M. de Casabianca of the Institut de recherche agronomique tropicale, M. Scheid of the Institut d'Etudes politiques de Paris, M. Sebillotte and M. Séverac of the Institut national agronomique, and Mlle Soudan of the Institut scientifique et technique des pêches maritimes.

PART ONE Food and Population

CHAPTER ONE
The population explosion in the Third World

1. FAMINE, EPIDEMIC AND WAR: THE NATURAL REGULATORS OF WORLD POPULATION.

Alfred Sauvy[1] has argued that if industrial revolution and modern medicine were unknown, but more or less adequate food supplies and 'normal' living conditions were available to all, the natural rate of human population increase would be about 1 per cent per year on average. But Cipolla[1] points out that if the human race were descended from a single man and woman 10,000 years before Christ, and if their descendants had multiplied at the rate of 1 per cent per year,[2] the population of the world would now fill a sphere millions of kilometres in diameter. As it is, man has existed for far longer than 10,000 years but the present population could still occupy a sphere one kilometre in diameter.

The increase in world population has been relatively small because food supply has never been 'adequate' and living conditions have never been 'normal'. In fact, throughout human history, the great majority of men have lived in want; indeed they have frequently been decimated by famines, some of them serious enough to effect a dramatic adjustment in the size of the world's population in relation to the available food resources. Such famines happened not only in far-off times and places: between A.D. 1000 and the nineteenth century France was the victim of 150 serious famines – one every six years.

[1] There are two essential works on this subject: Alfred Sauvy, *Malthus et les deux Marx*, Editions Denoel, Paris, 1963; Carlo Cipolla, *The Economic History of World Population*, Penguin Books, London, 1962.
[2] The rate produced by a high birth rate of 40 to 45 per 1,000 and a high death rate of 30 to 35 per 1,000.

The ravages of famine would prepare the way for fatal and uncontrollable epidemics that attacked whole districts at irregular intervals, like the notorious Black Death which several times spread destruction throughout Europe.[3]

Finally, and all too often, war has added its onslaughts to those of natural disasters, its destructive capacity increasing with the 'progress' of military skill. The destruction wrought by war for food frequently caused famine, which in turn gave rise to epidemics.

Famine, epidemic and war, these three great curses of mankind, acted as extremely effective brakes on world population growth, regulating it to match available resources. For 10,000 years before the eighteenth century, population expansion took place at the very low average rate of less than 0.1 per cent per year, tracing a very uneven curve. It is thus impossible to understand human history, particularly demographic history, without recognizing the bitter struggle that man has waged ever since the beginning of life for subsistence and survival.

Agriculture, the basis of our modern system of food production, made its appearance in human history at a comparatively recent date. In fact, archaeological research dates its discovery to the Neolithic period. It is therefore less than 10,000 years old, whereas the story of mankind goes back about a million years.

For hundreds of thousands of years, man, like the higher forms of animal, probably lived on wild fruit, roots, leaves and larvae; then, as rudimentary tools were gradually developed, on fishing and hunting. This foraging economy could only be practised by nomadic peoples – it is still carried on today by some tribes, such as the Pygmies of Equatorial Africa and the Bushmen of Malaysia. It entails a life of wandering and searching – through hills and valleys – for an uncertain and meagre food supply. It places a distinct restriction on population growth.

Natural resources are limited, particularly in certain parts of the world. It was probably in an infertile region, such as the Near East, that agriculture was first practised under the combined stimulus of the pressing requirements of small communities and of discoveries by their most intelligent members. Agriculture is in essence

[3] Sixty per cent of the population of Marseilles died of plague as late as 1720.

the process by which the seeds of edible plants are sown intentionally. This process brought about the agricultural revolution of the Neolithic Age, and was then gradually disseminated throughout the world by migration, reaching Europe in about 1500 B.C. With the agricultural revolution, the human race embarked on a new epoch in its history.

With the gradual sophistication of agriculture, man no longer simply used nature, but began positively to exploit it for his own ends. Where he had formerly gathered, he now produced – or rather, he cultivated as well as gathered. His function as a cultivator gradually came to replace his function as a gatherer, although such a transformation was inevitably a slow one.[4]

Yet this new process was to have profound effects on human history: as agriculture increased the quantity of goods which could be derived from nature, it encouraged man to settle, at least for short periods. Moreover, it encouraged the new farmers to establish some form of social organization which would enable them to enjoy the fruits of their work – the harvest which must be stored – in peace. As it offered an effective means of combating famine – this, of course, was its main purpose – the agricultural revolution gave rise to an increase in population which in turn demanded further progress. The earliest forms of agriculture, traces of which can still be found today, were too crude to satisfy growing demand.

Goaded on by sheer necessity, man embarked on a ceaseless search for ways of improving the efficiency of his work, that is, of increasing his control over nature. He attempted to increase and perfect his use of cultivated plants and domesticated animals. Progress was slow, experimental and uneven, varying by continent and people, and by geographical, social, and historical situation.

The principal achievements of agriculture have had significant consequences for the evolution of our society. The use of animals, particularly of horses and oxen, represented a significant advance, particularly in the realm of transportation. The farm worker's and artisan's constant improvements in agricultural implements (from the hoe to the plough, from the yoke carried on the farmer's shoulders

[4] This 'foraging' type of economy still exists to some extent in many societies and, as we have said, it still forms the basis of some societies' livelihood, as with the Pygmies and the Bushmen.

to the waggon and cart) prepared the way for sophisticated machines. The close interrelation between agriculture and stock-breeding resulted in a decisive step forward. Primitive cultivators would use a small plot of land cleared by burning; having exhausted its fertility they moved on to cultivate another area. In a non-intensive agricultural system, the land could be kept fertile with the use of animal manure and, consequently, one plot could be kept under continuous cultivation, particularly by following the familiar corn/fallow rotation.

These techniques, however, were the heritage of only a few European and Asian peoples. Even today most African peasants do not know that agriculture should be carried on in conjunction with stock-breeding; many do not know how to preserve and improve the fertility of their land, many do not use domesticated animals, and the majority have only the crudest implements.

After the sixteenth century, and above all in the eighteenth the people of north-western Europe experienced far-reaching changes, particularly in their system of agriculture. These changes sparked off the industrial revolution, history's second great economic revolution, which completely overthrew the established pattern of society and its demographic evolution.

2. INDUSTRIAL AND DEMOGRAPHIC REVOLUTION

The industrial revolution was taking place in England at the end of the eighteenth century. Europe had been well in advance of the other continents in the economic field ever since the end of the Middle Ages, due to the conjunction of a large number of favourable circumstances. The birth of modern science (under the stimulus of Galileo, Kepler, Descartes, Pascal, Bacon, and others), important technological inventions, the great geographical discoveries – all these factors greatly influenced the evolution of Western society, notably in England, the Low Countries, France and northern Italy. The intellectual ferment of the times encouraged that reassessment of generally accepted ideas without which no progress is possible. With intensive commercial activity between Europe and colonial markets, a prosperous and important merchant class developed, eager to make innovations and invest in new and even risky projects. Manufacturing, particularly textile manufacturing, began to expand on a large scale.

All these new trends intensified the demands on agriculture. As cities expanded, demand grew both for foodstuffs and for wool for manufacturing. Profiting from trade and inflation, the merchant class grew richer. In the rural areas they began to take the place of the great noble landowners of the Middle Ages; they reorganized the great farm holdings and began to practise the 'new agriculture' recommended by agronomists and influenced by scientific thought.[5]

The new agricultural methods were first developed in Flanders and northern Italy, where urban and commercial expansion was particularly intense. In the sixteenth century they began to spread progressively to England, becoming particularly widespread in the United Kingdom and France by the eighteenth century. In place of the fallow system the new agriculture recommended the cultivation of forage crops. This meant that much more land could be cultivated regularly, it allowed stock-breeding to be increased considerably and had the effect of increasing the efficiency and productivity, and thus the earning power, of the peasant. Agriculture was then in a position to take on a function which was to be crucial to the history of Western society.[6]

As the new agriculture became more efficient, part of the agricultural labour force was released and could be channelled into new industries. Better paid, and more aware of the importance of his equipment, the agricultural worker became an attractive customer for industry, in which he in turn could invest his savings. Agriculture, with its increased production, provided newly developing industries with raw materials, and from the increase in stock-breeding, provided people with a richer and more plentiful food supply.

Now in a state of sustained growth, this progressive agricultural system was an important factor in the early stages of the industrial revolution, providing it with workers, raw materials, capital, and

[5] Discussed in 'Agriculture Nouvelle', Revue *Paysans*, no. 58, February–March, 1966.
[6] Its function is defined and analysed by Paul Bairoch in *Révolution Industrielle et Sous-développment*, SEDES (Société pour l'étude et le développement économique et social), Paris, 1963.

customers. Two industries, textile manufacturing and iron smelting, played a key role in the industrial revolution. Both are closely connected with agriculture, which is for the one a supplier of raw materials, and for the other a market for finished products. In addition, as it improved standards of nutrition, the growth of agriculture resulted in a great expansion of population. This was apparent from the 1750s in the United Kingdom and from the 1760s in France (that is after the period of agricultural expansion) and until it was arrested it hampered economic development.

Originally sustained by agricultural growth, industrial development soon became autonomous; moreover, progress in science and industrial technology did much to stimulate agricultural growth. Two of the main forces behind agricultural progress, chemical fertilizers in the nineteenth century and motorization and mechanization in the twentieth century, are the result of industrial progress. Carried along by the impetus of industrial expansion, agriculture in industrial societies tends itself to become industrialized, thus increasing man's control over his food resources.

What is the role of population expansion, the logical outcome of increased food production, in this historical process?

It is the terrifying demographic revolution of modern times which has led us to write this book. It started in western Europe around 1750. The standard of nutrition had improved as a result of progress in agriculture, standards of health and hygiene had improved as a result of progress in medicine, and in general the benefits of overall economic growth led to a continuous drop in the death rate. Using the new scientific methods at its disposal, society embarked on a relentless struggle against death. And, since the birth rate remained for a long time at the same level, the population began to rise. However, several decades after the drop in death rates, with the gradual rise in the cultural level and standard of living, another phenomenon began to appear in the European countries: an increasing tendency towards control of births, leading to a slow decline in the birth rate and consequently in the rate of growth of population.

The peoples of Europe gradually came to realize that they were being freed from famine and epidemic, two of the great curses of history by which population had been naturally controlled; and at this point they began themselves to take deliberate steps towards regulating world population.[7] Deliberate birth control became the population regulator of the modern world. The rate of population growth, which had been less than 0.2 per cent per year in Europe at the beginning of the eighteenth century, increased fivefold in the course of several decades, until in some countries it was at times about 1 per cent; it then began to decrease under the influence of the compensatory mechanism of birth control.

Thus, in agrarian society, before industrial development, the very low rate of population growth is due to the narrow margin between a high death rate and a high birth rate; on the other hand, in an industrial society, the widening gap between a low birth rate and a very low death rate leads to an accelerated rate of population growth.

3. THE THIRD WORLD: THE GREATEST POPULATION EXPLOSION OF ALL TIME

The industrial revolution has had only a limited effect on the countries of the Third World. The benefits of modern medicine – hygiene and low-cost modern methods of preventing epidemics – have been widely introduced into these countries without any significant steps being taken to promote corresponding economic or cultural development. In recent years, 150 years later than in Europe, the death rate of the countries of the Third World has dropped sharply, and no offsetting mechanism has yet been introduced to counteract its effects. These countries now have what Carlo Cipolla calls an 'industrial death rate'[8] and an 'agricultural birth rate', a combination which has caused the most colossal population explosion of world history.

Until the eighteenth century, the world population growth rate was considerably below 1 per cent per annum; this meant roughly that the population would double in size in about a thousand years.

[7] In the nineteenth century, emigration to the New World was another, by no means negligible, factor by which population was adjusted to food resources.
[8] It took a century for the death rate in England to drop by 50 per cent; in Ceylon it is more like eight years.

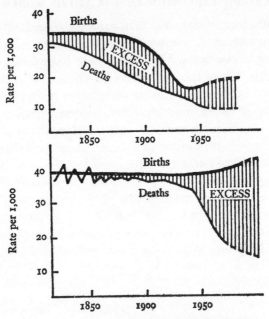

PLAN OF DEMOGRAPHIC GROWTH

in developed countries (above)
and in underdeveloped countries (below)

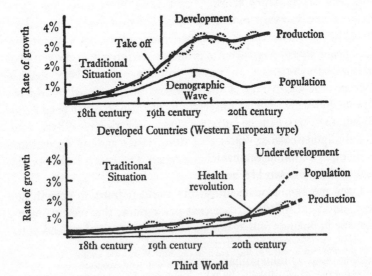

Developed Countries (Western European type)

Third World

The rate increased slowly during the eighteenth century, and then the moderate rate of expansion in the European countries brought the world increase from 0.5 per cent in 1800 to 0.6 per cent in 1900. It has increased rapidly in the twentieth century, reaching in 1965 a previously unattained level of 2 per cent (which would mean doubling in thirty-five years), as a result of the sharp rise in the population of all the Third World countries.

Thus we see not only a significant, steady increase in the size of the population of the world, but a constant acceleration in the rate of growth. In spite of only moderate expansion in industrialized countries the population growth in the world as a whole is racing ahead, like an engine with a broken regulator.

On the whole, the industrialized countries have a steady rate of population growth of less than 1 per cent per year: 0.7 per cent in France and the other Common Market countries – which would mean that the population would double in a hundred years – and 0.4 per cent in the other Western European countries. The United States and Canada are exceptional with a rate of 1.8 per cent, as is the USSR. Consequently, the industrialized countries have no difficulty in maintaining a growth rate in their economy, and in their food supplies in particular, which is higher than their rate of population increase; as a result their standard of living has improved steadily. The situation in the Third World countries is entirely different. Rates of population growth range from 2 per cent per year (doubling in thirty-five years) to 2.5 per cent (doubling in twenty-eight years), and even in some cases over 3.5 per cent (doubling in twenty years) in countries such as North Vietnam (3.6), the Philippines (3.7), Mexico (3.8), and Venezuela (as high as 4 per cent and doubling in fifteen years). And these rates are rising all the time.

The population of the Far Eastern countries, which in 1962 was about 1,600 million, has been increasing at an average rate of 2.3 per cent per year. This means 37 million more mouths to feed every year, about 12 million of them in India and perhaps 16 million in China, where the population growth may be starting to decline.

The Near Eastern and African Countries (excluding South Africa) have about 420 million inhabitants, increasing at a rate of about 2.5 per cent or 10.5 million people per year. The underfed population of Latin America[9] – 200 millions – beats all records with a growth rate of 2.7 per cent, or 5.5 million more consumers every year.

Thus, the hunger-stricken countries have an annual population increase of 50 million – equal to the whole population of France – when they cannot even feed their existing populations. At this rate, these countries, whose population is now 2,200 millions or two-thirds of the world total, will have about 5,000 million inhabitants or 80 per cent of the predicted population of the world in the year 2000. If their rate of expansion goes on accelerating as it has done for the past fifteen or twenty years, the number will be even greater. Experts are already forecasting an average population increase of about 2.7 per cent per year in the Third World.[10]

4. THE RESULT: A FOOD CRISIS

The population explosion would not be alarming if the production of consumer goods and above all of foodstuffs was expanding at a faster rate. Growth rates of production, however, are negligible when compared with the extraordinary leap forward in population size. Measures for the protection of health have been introduced from outside, unaccompanied by any profound economic changes.

The phenomenon of underdevelopment lies essentially in the fantastic gulf between a runaway population growth rate and a stagnant economy.[11] This pattern repeats itself in every country that has been only partially influenced by the modern industrial revolution. By sending our doctors and missionaries to these countries before our agronomists, we have enabled their children to survive epidemics but not to have enough food to live decent lives. We have allowed more people to live to a greater age but have not created enough employment for them. We do not contest the very praiseworthy humanitarian motives of such endeavours; we only point out their inadequacy.

[9] That is, Latin America except for the countries of the Rio de la Plata – Argentina, Uruguay and Paraguay – where the food situation is better.
[10] In a report by experts of the Development Assistance Committee of the OECD (Organization for Economic Cooperation and Development), July 1966 session.
[11] Such an essential aspect of underdevelopment that Yves Lacoste uses it as his definition of the term in, *Géographie du Sous-développement*, Presses Universitaires de France, 1965.

Using material collected by the FAO and by dieticians of various different countries, we can assess the world food situation region by region, comparing human requirements with available food resources (agricultural produce, fish, imported foodstuffs).

If we are to form an accurate picture of human requirements, we should not merely refer to calories, which only satisfy the body's energy needs – about 2,700 calories per day for an average adult. Not all foods have a nutritional value proportionate to their calorific value. Specific elements, such as proteins, mineral salts, and vitamins, are required for the maintenance and improvement of the organs, the muscle and bone structures, and the general functioning of the body. We should, therefore, assess not only the quantity of calories available, but also their quality, their nutritional content, and the balance between the different components.

Particular attention should be paid to protein content, especially animal protein content. If the tissues are to be improved, the human organism, like the animal, should build its own protein[12] from specified amino-acids in precise proportions. Consequently, the diet should contain this correct composition of amino-acids. The biological value of protein is determined by the proportion of amino-acids contained in it. If a protein does not contain amino-acids in the correct proportions, those in excess cannot be used and go to waste: whichever amino-acid is most deficient becomes the factor limiting protein use.[13] For example, if a foodstuff has a balanced protein content in every amino-acid but one, in which it is 50 per cent deficient, then its biological value is reduced by half.

Most essential acids are contained in all vegetable and animal foodstuffs but in very variable relative amounts. 'Supplementation' is used to rectify this imbalance; Jacquot[14] calls it the physiological illustration of the fable of the blind man who carries the crippled man on his shoulders. Supplementation is the rearrangement of the amino-acid content available in foodstuffs to form a balanced diet.

[12] The large complex molecules of proteins are made up of a series of elementary molecules of various amino-acids. The 'essential' amino-acids are those which are necessary for the make-up of tissues which the human body cannot synthesize or cannot synthesize fast enough.
[13] It is called the primary limiting factor and, by analogy, there are secondary and tertiary limiting factors.
[14] In 'Les facteurs d'efficacité alimentaires, les aliments', *Cours de Nutrition FAO*, ed. Leconte, Marseilles, 1958.

The value of animal foods – meats, dairy produce, eggs and fish – is that, due to their origin, they provide a concentrated supply of the proteins which complement staple foodstuffs such as cereals and starch.[15] Owing to their high lysine content they are usually used to supplement cereals. Animal protein content is, therefore, frequently used as an index of the quality of a diet[16]; daily intake is estimated at roughly 44 grammes in most developed countries but is as low as 9 grammes, one-fifth as much, in the Third World.

The figures given in analyses of the food situation of any country are very approximate averages. In all countries, particularly those of the Third World, foodstuffs, and more particularly protein-rich foodstuffs, are very unevenly distributed between social classes. An average ration of 2,600 calories per head may seem sufficient – but three out of ten of the inhabitants may consume 4,500 calories each, and the other seven only 1,800. Similarly, an inadequate average ration does not mean that a whole population is undernourished but that a large proportion of it is.

If, like the FAO, we base our analysis on the results of the few enquiries into consumption carried out in the Third World countries, taking account of variations in requirements according to sex, age and climate, we reach the following conclusions:

Undernourishment – nourishment which is inadequate in quantity: 300–500 million people, or about 1 in 8, normally suffer from undernourishment or hunger.

Malnutrition – nourishment which is defective in quality: about 1,600 million people, or 1 in 2, are regularly undernourished, which essentially means starved of protein.

This means that the world is now in the grip of a colossal famine. In developed countries it may affect only certain underprivileged classes (the old, the sub-proletariat), but it is a vast problem in the poor nations. This is why Professor Richet[17] calls it *Morbus Servorum*, the disease of the slaves. It should in fact be regarded as a disease,

[15] The function of the animal in human nutrition is not that it makes amino-acids but that it selects and concentrates the amino-acids present in the vegetable foods it has consumed and stores them in its tissues.

[16] Vegetable grains – soya beans, beans and peas – also provide high quality protein.

[17] Professor Richet and Antonin Mans, *La Famine*, Ecole pratique des Hautes Etudes, 6th section, Paris, 1965.

especially since famine in its modern form, less severe than previously when it could decimate a whole country in a few months, may be broadly defined as a chronic state of food deficiency which erodes the physical and mental capacities of its victims, ultimately causing premature death. Out of the annual total of 60 million deaths, 10 to 20 million are due to this relentless law. Even in modern times, one of the principal causes of death in the world is undernourishment.

The human body reacts to undernourishment by reducing its energy output and limiting its growth. When a man has insufficient energy, in the strict sense of the word, he withdraws from physical and intellectual effort and becomes a breeding-ground for disease. Deprived of the materials necessary for the building and replacement of the tissues, he can never attain normal physical or mental development.

Undernourished people are victims of lethargy, poor physical and intellectual development, general weakness, and low resistance to infectious disease. The consequences are obvious: a high rate of infant mortality, low expectation of life and general poor adaptation to work. In addition to these general results, deficiencies in various particular nutritional substances cause a large number of illnesses. Protein deficiency causes kwashiorkor, an illness which is all too common, particularly among children, in Africa, Latin America, and the Far East, where the diet has a high starch content. Its symptoms are muscular disintegration or retarded muscular development, and reduced physical growth; mental development is sometimes permanently impaired.

Vitamin deficiency affects those parts of the world where green vegetables, eggs, and dairy products are scarce or unobtainable. Lack of Vitamin A causes eye diseases, even total and incurable blindness, and skin diseases. When accompanied by lack of calcium, Vitamin D deficiency causes rickets, an illness which is still too common among children in these areas; it also produces malformation of bones in adults.

Without listing the whole range of diseases attributable either to undernourishment or to malnutrition, two basic points should be emphasized:

1. Chronic starvation prevents people from reaching their full mental or physical potential; it condemns them to premature senility and early death.

2. Chronic starvation causes irreparable harm to all organs of the human body[18]: even after being cured, a man who has once been starved will always suffer from after-effects such as debility, underweight, digestive and nervous upsets, cardio-vascular or mental disorders, tuberculosis, etc.

A starved or once starved man has all his human capacities impaired: starvation breeds men who are permanently diminished.

Many conclusions can be derived from these facts. Firstly, on a moral plane, our civilization is beginning to conquer space and has reached the moon, yet one man in two can never reach his full stature as a human being. Secondly, from the economic standpoint, starvation reduces human aptitude and capacity for work, and stunts not only the enterprise but the creative and productive capacities of its victims. This represents one of the most serious vicious circles of underdevelopment.

The term 'hunger-stricken' describes those countries where three-quarters of the population not only suffer from physical hunger and its numerous effects but also see their potentials frustrated and their future placed in jeopardy. In view of this situation, which shows that production growth is lagging behind population growth to an alarming degree, we should now examine the prospect for future improvement, paying particular attention to the hopes raised by the rapid agricultural progress noted in various countries in recent years. Can agricultural progress be extended throughout the world, and can food production catch up with, and eventually overtake, the growth of world population?

---

[18] According to Professor Richet (*op. cit.* p. 63 et seq.), some deficiencies do not have incurable effects.

CHAPTER TWO
The outlook for growth

I. TECHNICAL PROGRESS AND ECONOMIC DEVELOPMENT IN AGRICULTURE

Economic history can be regarded as an account of man's progress towards ascendancy over nature, a process by which he stabilized and increased the supply of goods needed for his survival and development. Continually increasing the efficiency of his production in all sectors of economic activity – and particularly in agriculture, the one operation vital for the survival of the species – man has been able to make constant improvements in his living conditions.

Agricultural progress, extremely slow for thousands of years, has gathered momentum in the last two hundred, fostered by the increasingly urgent food requirements of agrarian societies. It has become more and more closely connected with general economic and scientific developments, and is now founded on scientific investigations into the processes of agricultural production. For example, the use of animal manure and marl were once the only known methods of fertilization, which was regarded as a very simple process. Agricultural chemistry and plant biology, however, have proved that three main elements must be present in fertilizers – nitrogen, potassium, and phosphorus. This discovery, in the nineteenth century, showed that the renewal of fertility was not as simple as it appeared. With more recent advances in natural science and in plant physiology, fertilization has become an even more complex subject. Fertilization should establish a balance between a large number of different elements, including both major and minor nutrients, introduced in particular forms and at particular times.

It was the same with corn-growing, which was regarded as a

simple process until modern agronomy showed it to be highly complex and dependent on a large number of variables. In any given soil and region, various factors should be taken into account, such as the type of corn, the method and quality of ploughing, the method of sowing, the methods of fertilization, of pest control, irrigation, harvesting, storage, and so on.

Each of these new variables, which are now included in agricultural 'production functions', suggests new methods and operations. The quality of ploughing depends on the quality of ploughs and tools, the quality of the sowing depends on that of the seeders, and that of the harvest on the quality of the reaping-machines. These machines are far beyond the skills of the village blacksmith. They are industrial goods, developed after careful research with all the resources of industrial technology.

All motorized machines of this kind are directly dependent on the progress of mechanical industry; and the chemical industry provides agriculture with its fertilizers, weedkillers, fungicides, insecticides, and materials for building greenhouses and plastic hosepipes.

Thus, in industrialized countries, technical progress and the resulting increase in the division of labour penetrate also the agricultural sector. Operations which the agricultural worker once performed by himself, or with the help of an artisan, now need the cooperation of industry and commerce, and consequently they are now carried out more efficiently.

The agricultural workers obtain these new means of production in exchange for the additional goods they have produced. Up-to-date agriculture is also opened up to trade. In order to produce, it must obtain not only a great many industrial goods but also commercial services and the brainpower of research workers and technical and economic advisers.

Thus, modern agriculture cannot develop without the full support and cooperation of industry and commerce, research and education. Agricultural production is the result of a huge interconnected system of different operations. In industrial countries, as a result of increased productivity, the number of agricultural workers decreases and the number of para-agricultural workers in industry and commerce increases. In the course of its development, agriculture has lost its former autarchy and independence. It has built up a network of interdependent links with an ever-increasing number of new, specialized activities. How, then, in underdeveloped countries can we give precedence to industrialization at the expense of agriculture, or alternatively concentrate on agricultural development regardless of its implications? Industrial expansion can aim, as in China, at supplying the means of production necessary for modern agriculture and at processing agricultural produce. A dynamic inter-relationship is thus established between the two sectors.

In a country where the majority of the population works on the land, the development of agriculture not only represents an effective means of fighting famine, but can also be a cornerstone of comprehensive social and economic development.

2. AGRICULTURAL PROGRESS IN THE THIRD WORLD

The more each peasant produces, the better he can feed his family and the more he can supply to town-dwellers, in exchange for vital industrial goods and services. (On condition, of course, that the surplus is not appropriated by usurers and absentee landlords, as still happens all too often in Latin America and the Far East. We will come back to this point later.) Above all, the greater the value of the goods the peasant contributes to the wealth of the community, the more he can trade his goods, and so participate in general economic growth and improve his standard of living. The value-added[1] which he contributes to the general wealth represents not only the net productivity of his work, but also his source of income. Thus agricultural progress, so vital for the countries of the Third World, really means a gradual increase in the productivity of the peasant in Africa, Latin America, and Asia.

At the present time productivity varies considerably from country to country. The estimated average value-added of each worker in Europe, and even more so in America, is many times higher than that of the worker in tropical Africa. The Far East, excluding China, has a population 4.5 times the size of that of North America; it produces

---

[1] Value-added: the value of a product minus the value of the goods used to make it (intermediate goods and raw materials).

about the same quantity of cereal and vegetable produce and only 30 per cent of the animal produce. With 10 per cent more inhabitants, Africa produces less than one-sixth of the food harvested in the sub-continent of North America. These differences are a reflection of the enormous gap between the two areas in technical standards, productive capacity, and in quality of equipment and organization – the factors on which the efficiency of agricultural work is becoming ever more dependent. For example, in India, fifteen cows give the same amount of milk as one in North America, and seven hectares of ricefields in Laos produce only as much as one in Australia.[2]

In primitive systems of agriculture, as a result of technical unreliability, two factors of production assume supreme importance: these are human effort and the land itself. The whole process of agricultural development tends to be directed towards giving the peasant new means of production so that he can make better use of the land and the other natural resources. As these new factors increase in importance in relation to the soil, so the extent and division of cultivated land – its extension and its improvement – must no longer be regarded as the central question for agricultural expansion. The main objective of agricultural development is not simply to improve the use of the soil – this is only a means to an end; the object must be to increase the net agricultural production of the workers in any given society, that is, to increase the total value-added of the peasant[3] through the fullest use of the scarcest resources. Arable land is by no means always the scarcest commodity. On the contrary, technical expertise and modern means of production such as improved seed, fertilizer, insecticide, irrigation equipment, machines, and storage facilities, as well as improved land, are often in very short supply.

These facts should encourage agricultural policy-makers to investigate the best ways of employing the most capable and enlightened men, the most fertile land, the best-placed irrigation systems, the

[2] According to Narenda Singh, Budapest Congress of the World Federation of Scientific Workers, 1965.
[3] This means maximizing the difference between the value of manufactured agricultural goods and that of labour and agricultural production costs (taking account of the constraints imposed by relations with other variables and by the attempt to establish the overall optimum).

areas best provided with services, the few thousand tons of fertilizer or the few machines available. In other words, they should be attempting to concentrate their resources into places with the highest potential for growth, even if this requires a judicious policy of transfers (for example, by land taxes) to secure some equalization of incomes and food resources. In a country where equipment is in short supply, the one certain way to perpetuate poverty is to disperse public works instead of concentrating them.

There are now many modern methods of increasing the agricultural productivity of destitute areas.[4] Such methods, however, cannot be classified in any way which would establish priorities valid for all parts of the Third World. The various different methods are dependent on each other and their correct use will be different in each particular case.[5] For example, chemical fertilizer would be of little benefit without improved seed or if used in conjunction with bad agricultural methods or a poor irrigation system.

What are the principal ways of improving agricultural production?

Very generally, the first step would be to use better methods of cultivation: the preparation and upkeep of the soil are often inadequate and sowing is often carried out too late or in bad conditions. Ploughing, the removal of weeds and more systematic cultivation are all low cost improvements needing more efficient equipment. They are partly linked to the question of the establishment of permanent cultivation which is progressively organized, and which represents actual land capital. This change depends on using efficient techniques to preserve and enrich the fertility of the soil by crop rotation, fertilization, and measures against erosion.

The extremely important question of fertilization can be subdivided into two main parts:

1. Organic fertilization, which raises the connection between agriculture and stock-breeding, a major factor in the agricultural history of north-western Europe.

---

[4] On this subject, see Walter H. Pawley, *The Possibilities of Increasing World Food Production*, FAO, Rome, 1963 (No. 10 of Freedom from Hunger Campaign, Basic Studies), a study from which we have taken many of our examples.
[5] Not nearly enough research and systematic experimental work are being put into these methods at the present time.

2. Chemical fertilization, which holds great promise for under-developed countries.

Chemical fertilizers, the use of which has spread so quickly and effectively in the industrialized countries (mainly in the last fifty years), will undoubtedly be one of the main keys to the progress of agriculture in the Third World. These fertilizers are virtually unknown in most of the underdeveloped countries where the average grain yield per hectare varies between 2 and 12 quintals, whereas in the Low Countries, for instance, where nearly 450 kilogrammes of fertilizer are used per hectare, the average yield is well over 30 quintals (about 60 cwt.). The FAO considers that many countries could increase their production by 50 or even 100 per cent if they made more intensive use of organic and chemical fertilizers and introduced a rational crop rotation system.

But fertilization used in conjunction with proper cultivation methods can only be fully effective when plants with potentially high yields are grown. Improvements to cultivated plants by genetic selection of types and varieties are vital to agricultural progress and have been made extensively in most developed countries for the last century, and especially in the last twenty years. In the United States one of the greatest successes in this field was the invention of highly productive kinds of maize hybrids. In conjunction with satisfactory fertilization, this more than doubled maize production in the United States between the 1930s and 1960, even though land used was reduced by 13 per cent. Yugoslavia has made extensive use of discoveries in genetics for wheat as well as for maize growing. Between 1950 and 1960 the use of fertilizer tripled and the average wheat yield rose from 12 to 17 quintals per hectare. Again, careful attention to fertilizers in Japan led to an appreciable increase in the productivity of rice-growing. This should be an example to all the countries of the Far East, where average yields are sometimes only a quarter of Japan's. Even more important advances are expected in the future in plant improvement, notably those which would increase the production of chlorophyll.

Like domestic animals, however, cultivated plants are often attacked by fungal diseases or by insects; for instance, locusts are a common hazard. Chemical protection of cultivated plants and stored crops has made outstanding progress since the second world war, particularly with the invention of DDT, the use of which has doubled the yield of potatoes in the United States in the course of a few years. The destruction of plants and livestock by parasites now costs 7,000 million dollars each year; and the campaign against parasites alone is expected to result in an increase of about one-third in agricultural production during the next fifty years.

An important aid that has been used for thousands of years in the exploitation of poor lands is water control – drainage or protective measures in places where it is in excess, and dry-farming or irrigation where it is scarce. Water is the most important nutrient of all; without it, cultivation stops. The control of this key factor in agricultural production is generally given prime importance in places where it can radically alter the dimensions of an agricultural problem. The reclamation of new areas in arid zones depends on water. Supplementary watering by sprinkling is on the increase in developed countries, even where the climate is fairly moderate. Cruder forms of irrigation are spreading in the underdeveloped countries: by flood control on the Niger, by gravity in the Mediterranean Basin. Large dams have been built in China, India, Pakistan, the Maghreb, the UAR, Chile, and elsewhere. These expensive investments cannot be made economic, however, unless the agricultural workers' standards of efficiency are extremely high, even higher than they must be for using fertilizers; and, in addition, coherent development plans are needed. In so many places in the world, under-utilization or incorrect use of equipment have caused so many setbacks that extreme care should now be taken when formulating further projects, particularly those for soils with a high salt content. There is a vast range of unambitious projects – for example, earth dams[6] – which can be put into operation by groups of peasants, and these should be considered as a first step.

In some areas, greater intensity of agricultural production, due to new techniques and other factors on land already in use, could be accompanied by extending the area under cultivation through the reclamation of virgin land. At the present time, only 10 per cent of the

[6] Earth dam blocking a valley in a hilly area so as to make a reservoir of irrigation water.

earth's land area, or half a hectare per head of the population, is cultivated. Experts consider that it would be economically feasible to exploit about 20 per cent of the land which is now pastureland or forest; the remainder is regarded as completely unsuitable for agriculture because it is either too cold, too arid or too mountainous to provide an economic return.[7] The cultivated areas of the world could thus be almost tripled and this would offer substantial scope for increasing production. This statement must, however, be viewed with caution for several reasons:

1. Reserves of arable land are not generally found in the regions or countries where population pressure is greatest.

2. The cultivation of new land usually entails high costs of reclamation, as well as those of moving the existing population and introducing settlers.

3. When peasants extend the area of cultivated land, problems arise over peak work periods, whereas more intensive production tends to spread the work more evenly through the year.

Furthermore, the agricultural growth rates of the countries with large reserves of uncultivated land are not so very different – under similar conditions – from those of other countries. Nevertheless, for certain countries these reserves constitute a good safety valve which should be remembered when considering the future of agricultural production.

There is as much room for progress in stock-breeding as in cultivation, and this should provide much of the rich protein vital for better nutrition. However, in most of the Third World the weak genetic quality of the livestock, its poor diet, and, all too frequently, parasites, reduce its productive yield in meat, eggs, and milk to a very low level: for instance, 220 litres of milk per cow per year in India and 400 in Turkey, compared with 4,150 in the Low Countries and 4,330 in Israel.

Improvement in animals and their productivity is very closely connected with the promotion of agriculture. Although selective

[7] From a technical point of view, all land can be cultivated, but very often the cost of bringing it into cultivation is too high in relation to production potential.

breeding of livestock and animal health are vital in themselves, they would have little effect unless corresponding efforts were made to improve animal nutrition by protecting and fencing fields, and, above all, by growing fodder crops, root crops, and secondary cereals. Cultivated fodder crops, particularly vegetable crops, in rotation with human food crops or industrial crops, and the use of animal manure could then make an important contribution towards preserving the fertility of the soil. In many places, small-scale stock-breeding, requiring little initial investment, such as poultry, pig or goat breeding, could bring about a rapid improvement in the protein rations of a peasant population.

The question of improving the methods of production usually raises the problem of introducing new implements and mechaniza-tion. Mechanization has completely transformed the appearance of the European countryside, mainly since the second world war. Because of its cost, however, equipment has to be treated with great respect in poor countries. Usually, preference must be given to machines which can break a bottleneck, performing operations which one man is unable to carry out single-handed. Such machines are the plough, the hydraulic pump, and the insecticide spray.

In general, motorization should only be introduced after animal traction. Important first steps at reasonable cost can be accomplished with animal traction and it also helps to form a link between agricul-ture and stock-breeding, as has now been proved by various experi-ments in Africa. Nevertheless, in certain specific cases (irrigation, land reclamation, and some other processes) the motor could become an important factor in agricultural expansion.

In every case, great attention should be given to assessing economic viability in money terms – the long term relation between the re-turns and costs of any operation – and also the extent to which the projected innovation will transform the economic and social life of the community.

This immediately raises the question of the reaction of peasant groups to new ideas, the dissemination of the new concept of invest-ment, and the introduction of a completely new system of marketing to peasant communities.

3. PROBLEMS AND POSSIBILITIES FOR AGRICULTURAL PROGRESS

The expansion of agricultural production in the countries of the Third World depends as much on the peasant communities' capacity for change and reaction to new ideas as it does on the use of new methods or the reclamation of new land.

Thus calculations based on the amount of land which can in theory be cultivated and the size of the yields which are in principle possible are unrealistic. Peasants are hard-headed, and only accept technical progress slowly and when they are convinced that it is efficient and compatible with their financial means and their social life.

The dissemination of new ideas in traditional environments presents a major problem for agricultural development. The peasant societies of Africa, Asia and Latin America have been living in the same established rhythm for centuries. With their long experience of success and failure, they have created their own system of land cultivation, a crude system but one which is comparatively efficient and makes sense to people who have been familiar with disaster for thousands of years.

Closely connected to this economic fact is the question of social organization. In Africa, there are thousands of autonomous tribes that have not yet been fully integrated into the new national states; in parts of Latin America and the Far East the people have been under the sway of rigid feudal systems for centuries; such societies are often petrified or frozen in their archaic social structures. Traditionalism is a great hindrance to the propagation of new ideas, as much for psychological reasons as for social ones.

As the concept of innovation implies that generally accepted ideas should be questioned, peasant societies often come to see it as symbolizing the force of anti-tradition. To the peasant, tradition represents security, and innovation often seems to constitute a direct attack on his way of life or a complete break with it, therefore conjuring up unforeseeable dangers in his mind. An individual or a group may be acting in self-defence when resisting new ideas. Thus, when a technical innovation is introduced into a traditional rural environment, it often causes difficult problems. This becomes even more complicated when a change in methods provokes a series of chain reactions affecting not only systems of production but also social life.

With ploughing and fertilization, a strip of land worked on a yearly basis may become a properly, permanently cultivated field. At first glance, this operation seems comparatively simple. In fact, its social implications are enormous. Throwing suspicion on the whole technical system, it upsets the organization and pattern of work, thereby the times of work and leisure, and so the whole structure of habits and customs.

Moreover, in some traditional societies, particularly in Africa, social life really means community life. The individual is completely involved in the group and feels at one with it. The concept of individuality refers more to the group as a whole than to a single person – the basic reason for the social conformity that is often displayed on the arrival of an innovator.

It is, therefore, vital that any serious attempt at agricultural promotion should include education: people must be taught to accept new ideas. Consequently, it is generally important to avoid partial interventions which overlook the range of important but often neglected social effects brought about by a technical change.

In fact, many consequences may follow from bringing improved methods and thereby additional money income without teaching the peasants through some simple economic or civic training how to make sensible use of their extra revenue. So many projects in peasant societies fail to promote economic development; income is dissipated on ill-considered purchases of consumer goods (alcoholic drink, garments and transistors) at the expense of vital investment goods such as tools, barrows and fertilizers. Such incentives should by no means be eliminated altogether, as they can certainly be used to encourage further effort, but they should be restricted and the way in which they are used should be supervised.

Education in new ideas should overlap with technical education, which is so often a failure. It needs a capable and devoted staff who can discover which young peasant leaders would be able to stimulate the advancement of traditional rural societies.

But in many places, particularly in Latin America and the Far

East, social structures are the greatest hindrance to economic progress, since the peasant knows that his additional effort will be of little benefit tó him. In such circumstances, the dissemination of improved methods can only be worthwhile if it is preceded by far-reaching reforms in the juridical and institutional framework, seeking to make fairly basic changes in the social position of the peasant-producer.

Thus a policy of agrarian reform seems an indispensable preliminary wherever lands are in the possession of a small class of society, privileged as regards property but backward from a technical and social point of view. Such a policy could certainly be justified on social grounds alone, since the vast mass of landless peasants frequently live in deplorable conditions. It can be justified equally well on economic grounds since, in many cases, land monopolists or oligopolists sterilize or under-exploit a particular factor of production whose maximum use may be a fundamental necessity for economic development. Land distribution and the social framework resulting from it must then be radically changed. China, Cuba, Chile, and the peasants of Colombia can be used as examples to prove that agrarian reform can have political overtones and broad economic implications.

Such policies, however, do not always suit the short-term interests of the ruling classes and the great landowners. This is why Galbraith, the American economist, writes: 'It takes revolution, not reform, to dislodge a non-functional class from its position of power. Land will never be redistributed and the power of the army will never be reduced by decree, particularly when it is the landowners or the army who are in power. . . .'[8]

Technical and economic reform can only be successful when the general agricultural structure can accommodate the technical system; when it can allow its members to develop their creative powers

[8] Quoted in *Courrier de la République*, no. 35. A former adviser to President Kennedy, Galbraith is a professor at Harvard University. He is restating Karl Marx's analysis of the evolution of social structures. 'At a certain stage of their development, the material productive forces of society came in conflict with the existing relations of production, or – what is but a legal expression for the same thing – with the property relations within which they have been at work hitherto. From forms of development of the productive forces these relations turn into their fetters. Then begins an epoch of social revolution.' (Karl Marx, Preface to the *Critique of Political Economy*.)

freely and to benefit from their capacities for work and investment; and where these three propensities, basic for development policies, are given active encouragement.

Therefore, even when supported by agrarian reform, agricultural enterprises must form part of a vast trade network, dealing in ideas, goods and services, and encouraging communication between the most dynamic elements of the nation and the peasant communities, now often isolated village autarchies. This trade network should create a new civic and technical structure within the peasant community and it should provide the necessary new factors of production, such as seed, fertilizer, and tools, as well as a number of services. The peasants in their turn should keep it informed of their wants and needs; if it is to be successful the network should see that the agricultural goods produced by the new techniques are sold at a fair price.

Thus we must aim at forming a co-ordinated system of interconnected activities. Only by an integrated system of services can the peasants be assured of a new form of security to replace the traditional one. If it is to fulfil its role as a national service for agricultural development and peasant advancement, this network must be very flexible in its organization. It must be sponsored by energetic and responsible men who are not hampered by administrative restrictions and who have a direct interest in the economic result of their work. Bureaucracy is an obstacle which should be avoided at all costs. The most receptive of the peasants could soon become the organizers of basic development work. Grouped into peasant associations, they would be involved in the local management of National Development Organizations, forming the preliminary basis for a co operative system.

Agricultural development policy is thus a complicated subject. But partial measures tend to fail when peasants who have been taught new methods do not know what to do with their produce, are bewildered or discouraged by fluctuations in prices, or else, instead of contributing to capital accumulation, spend thoughtlessly and retard their own economic development.

An agricultural policy of this kind presupposes the training of organizers who are capable and aware of their responsibilities and who know how technical methods should be used: it is thus inseparable from education. In many countries, educational policies should be completely revised in the light of the necessities of development.

4. A COMPARISON OF AGRICULTURAL GROWTH RATES IN DIFFERENT COUNTRIES: CONSEQUENCES FOR THE THIRD WORLD

An analysis of the statistics published by the FAO of the total agricultural product[9] of different countries over the past twenty years shows that growth rates vary enormously from one country to another.

Even more important than this disparity at the present time, however, is the future trend of the same growth rates. In the light of the explosion in the population growth rate in the Third World, the growth of agricultural production, particularly food production, takes on overriding importance. As it is, in some countries other more remunerative forms of production are growing much faster than food production.

The history of agricultural production in France, as revealed by J.-C. Toutain, is particularly relevant here: the period since the agricultural revolution of the eighteenth century (see Chapter I, section 2) is divided into four separate stages, each characterized by increasing rates of growth. With the dissemination of the 'new agriculture', the seventy-five years after 1750 was a period of 'take-off' for the agricultural economy of France, at the very modest growth rate of about 0.6 per cent per year.

A new period then started, lasting for about a century and ending in 1914, with a slightly higher sustained average growth rate of about 0.9 per cent per year. This expansion was the result of the steadily increasing popularity of the 'new agriculture', supported at the end of the nineteenth century by the invention and diffusion of other means such as chemical fertilizers, vaccination, selective breeding of domestic animals, attention to animal nutrition, and the reclamation

[9] Total value of production in the agricultural sector, after the cost of intermediate goods – in particular seed and animal food – has been deducted.

and cultivation of fallow lands. Due to better communications and agricultural education, these new ideas spread faster than the earlier ones. The expansion and modernization of French agriculture, however, were to be held back until after 1945 by a protectionist agricultural policy and a complete failure to understand the idea behind the rural exodus for which the farmers' union leaders of the time were as responsible as the successive ministers of agriculture.

In the twentieth century the French agricultural economy suffered two major setbacks with the two world wars and some of its productive capacity was destroyed. By contrast, the two post-war periods, times of reconstruction, hardship, and rising prices, favourable conditions for mobility, are characterized by a revival of economic growth. In the inter-war period, France had an average agricultural growth rate of about 1.3 per cent,[10] while the last fifteen years have been a time of much faster expansion, with a growth rate of about 3 per cent per year.[11]

As this most recent period is unlike any other, interpretations should only be made with great caution. The present conditions for agricultural expansion are also completely different from those of any other period. The trend towards the industrialization of agriculture, due to more and more complete control over the conditions of production, means that it is possible, indeed necessary, to plan agricultural production in accordance with the needs of the consumer market where profitability is greatest. In other words, we are dealing with a system of production that is becoming more and more like industrial production in that its total output, composition and quality can be controlled.

Since demand for agricultural produce, however, has a low income-elasticity, production should grow at a slower rate than incomes. It is, therefore, more appropriate to define an economically advanced agricultural system in terms of increases in productivity rather than increases in production.

This definition is particularly apposite in the case of American agriculture. Because of the rapid growth in productivity the government introduced measures to restrict production and prevent

[10] With a period of growth between 1919 and 1930 and then a period of stagnation after the great crash.
[11] Even more since 1959.

excessive accumulation of surpluses (see Chapter V, section 4), so the rate of increase of agricultural production in the United States is fairly low. Its historical development is particularly interesting.

The second half of the nineteenth century[12] saw an extremely rapid expansion rate of about 2.7 per cent per year; this was the time of high immigration and territorial expansion by enterprising settlers who brought the technical knowledge and experience of Europe with them. This time of conquest and rapid expansion lasted until the beginning of the twentieth century; then the growth rate settled down at about 0.75 per cent until the 1929 crisis. Later, with the war economy, followed by the Marshall Plan, a time of rapid agricultural modernization, and a new phase of population increase, the average growth rate in the United States was raised to a regular 2 per cent per year, at which, in spite of restrictive measures, it has remained since 1937. The rate is slightly higher for food products alone.[13]

In this period since 1937, however, under the stimulus of rapid modernization, the productivity of American agriculture has grown at the much higher rate of about 5 per cent per year; and that of France is growing at the unusually fast rate of 7 per cent.

The pattern of France and the United States of America repeats itself with variations in most of the Western industrialized countries; on the whole, the agricultural growth rates of western European countries fall somewhere between these two.

The agriculture of Denmark and the Low Countries can be regarded as models of good organization and comparative modernity. The high level of technical skill of their agricultural workers compensates for their small land resources. The agricultural growth rates of these countries, both exporters of food produce to long-established markets, have remained level for the past fifteen years at 2.4 per cent in Denmark and 1.7 per cent in the Low Countries.

In both the United Kingdom and West Germany agriculture can develop with no risk of overproduction.[14] In the former, the first

---

[12] Unfortunately, no assessment can be made prior to this date from available statistics.
[13] So this rate is slightly higher than the present rate of population growth. The stagnation of agricultural production following the great depression gave way to a rapid recovery after 1940.
[14] The United Kingdom imports about 50 per cent of her foodstuffs.

country to become industrialized, the agricultural growth rate is about 3 per cent per year, while in the latter it has been about 2.5 per cent per year for the last twelve years.[15] A general view of the industrialized countries of north-western Europe shows that their agriculture has been growing at the average annual rate of about 2.5 per cent for the last twelve years.

A study of the industrialized socialist countries shows that in spite of frequently heavy demands for food products, none has been able to sustain a growth rate significantly higher than that of the Western countries. For Eastern Europe and the USSR taken together, there was a growth rate of a little more than 3 per cent per year for the ten years from 1950 to 1960, though in 1959 it began to slow down.

Yugoslavia, whose agricultural policy has been to concentrate its best resources into the great self-managed agro-industrial enterprises of the Danube plain, has been able to establish a rapidly expanding potential for modern agricultural production over part of the country. The growth of the final agricultural product was at an irregular but fairly high rate until the last few years, when it has slowed down.

Since about 1950, Israel has been beating all records for agricultural growth with a sustained rate of growth of about 10 per cent. Food production alone has a growth rate of over 5 per cent per head. Moreover, it should be emphasized that this unusually high rate of growth is the direct result of increasing the area of irrigated land by about 9.6 per cent per year. It will, of course, slow down considerably when the possibilities offered by this key to progress have been exhausted. It should also be remembered that agricultural expansion in Israel is connected to an unusually high level of investment and to the rather exceptional circumstances of a nation with the advantages of imported capital and a high level of technical knowledge among its agricultural workers.

From this brief analysis of the agricultural growth of the most economically advanced countries, it becomes clear that the poor countries have only limited prospects for expansion. These prospects are limited still further: the countries we have been studying

[15] In the United Kingdom, the rate has been accelerating since 1960.

have all the advantages of a long agricultural tradition, good investment possibilities, and a well-established technical and commercial
framework for their agriculture, quite apart from generally favourable natural conditions and social structures.

We must, therefore, be realistic about forecasts for the Third
World. In the light of the fact that growth rates of agricultural
production of over 3 per cent sustained over a long period are really
exceptional in most of the industrialized countries except in unusual
circumstances, the Third World cannot be expected to reach such
high rates for many years to come. No doubt these countries have
great scope for progress but they still have all their equipment to
make and, above all, most of them must convert their agrarian
systems into systems which can develop efficiently and their traditional peasants into modern agricultural workers.

This conclusion suggests that we should now pay serious attention
to the outlook for non-agricultural food production.

CHAPTER THREE
Non-agricultural foodstuffs. The answer of the future?

The countries of the Third World have unusually high population growth rates and limited prospects for agricultural expansion, particularly in food production. It is, therefore, essential to establish whether other forms of production could provide their starving populations with the food they now lack.

Ever since the beginning of human life man has been a fisherman, exploiting rivers, lakes, and seas. More recently, with advances in biochemistry and microbiology, new food resources have been discovered, of which the most important are yeasts and various synthetic products.

I. UNDEREXPLOITED FOOD RESOURCES IN THE SEA AND INLAND WATERS

Although oceans and seas cover about three-quarters of the world's surface – 240 million square kilometres – less than 1 per cent of our food supply and only 10 per cent of our animal protein are derived from them at the present time. In fact, they contain very varied, protein-rich flora and fauna: every year an enormous quantity of vegetable matter, about 500,000 million tons,[1] is produced in the sea by the same process, photosynthesis, and at the same rate per hectare as on land. This matter is consumed by fish, molluscs, and other small herbivorous sea animals which are eaten, in their turn, by fish and carnivorous shellfish, following the same cycle as land animals. The total tonnage of fish, shellfish, and molluscs

[1] According to an estimate made by Graham and Edwards, in *The World Biomass of Marine Fishes*, Paper no. R/1.1, FAO, Conference on Fish and Nutrition, 1961.

available in the sea every year might be between 1,000 million and 100,000 million.[2]

At present only a minute part of this biological material is exploited – less than 3 per cent. Only one-tenth of the total surface of the sea is now used for fishing, and of this about 95 per cent is in the northern hemisphere near to coasts: only certain kinds of fish, molluscs, and shellfish are exploited systematically. The harvesting and use of seaweed, and more recently of plankton,[3] is only carried on in certain parts of Asia.

Fifteen per cent of the total production of fish is derived from freshwater fishing. A large proportion of this amount comes from the paddy fields of the Far East and South East Asia.

A study of world fish production since the second world war shows that it has increased fairly rapidly: with an average annual growth rate of 6.3 per cent (6.7 per cent for sea fish alone) sustained over the past fifteen years, it doubles every twelve years. In 1965, it reached almost 55 million tons, 80 per cent of which was sea fish. The most important types are herrings, sardines, and anchovies: the catches of these are increasing fast, comprising more than 45 per cent of the present tonnage figures, though money values are low, especially for herrings.

The ocean has been little exploited until now because the rich off-shore regions provided adequate resources. Furthermore, the vast shoals of deep-sea fish can only be used if the fish can be preserved for fairly long periods of time and if there are boats large enough to make the journeys worthwhile. Salting, the traditional way of preserving fish, was only really suitable for types with low fat content, such as cod.

Deep-freezing has done much to solve this problem recently, since it can be used to preserve other kinds of fish. In the last twelve years or so this process has played an increasingly important part in the world food economy. Maritime resources can be more systematically, therefore more intensively and rationally, exploited now that big ships are equipped with deep-freezers and can make long expeditions. Progress in fishing techniques and fish processing has led to

[2] Graham and Edwards, *op. cit.*
[3] Plankton: collection of micro-organisms and small algae living in the sea.

the development of the drag-net trawler[4] with a deep-freezer and also of the factory-ship, which has been in use since the 1950s. Able to stay at sea for several months at a time, they have both sonar equipment for locating shoals of fish and facilities for processing, deep-freezing, and storing the catches at a temperature of −20 °C to −30° C. The factory-ship even fillets the products ready for consumption.

The Soviet Union was one of the first countries to use factory-ships and the growth of its fish production has been particularly rapid in the last ten years – rising by about 7 per cent per year. It was also the first country to send out into the distant seas around Africa complete, self-sufficient fishing fleets, including a factory-ship, deep-freeze trawlers, and refrigerated transport ships into which the factory-ship can discharge its cargo at regular intervals. This method has been copied by several European countries which now have similar fleets.

Thus, in the course of the last twenty or thirty years, technical progress has made traditional fishing methods outmoded. As much in the location of fish, as in the speed and equipment of the trawlers and the treatment, preservation, and distribution of the fish, we are witnessing the industrialization of sea fishing and fish processing.

Fishermen, however, like agricultural workers, can improve their productivity without immediate industrialization. Considerable progress could be made by means of a number of simple methods requiring less investment outlay. First among these we should mention the motorization of boats, enabling fishermen to expand their field of operations, and so to exploit new areas and increase the time which they can devote to actual fishing. Motorization, the improvement of nets, and the substitution of nylon nets for traditional ones are already being organized, often on the advice of the FAO, by certain countries, such as Chile, Malaysia, Jamaica, India, and Senegal. These improvements increase the daily catches and so increase the productivity of the fishermen, which, in Ceylon, for example, has risen tenfold. These methods open up good prospects for progress and could be followed by many countries.

---

[4] The process of 'drag-net fishing', with the trawl stretched behind the boat instead of beside it, is an important technical improvement.

But one question must still be answered: if sea fishing increases, will supplies become exhausted? A systematic study of this problem would involve drawing up a catalogue of maritime resources, and unfortunately this has never been done. There is therefore need for caution. It is reasonable to imagine that the volume of annual catches could be doubled even from known resources on condition that strict rules were drawn up to ensure that reserves were not exhausted and that the sea was exploited in a rational way. Immense areas of the sea have not yet been explored, particularly around many of the Third World countries, and these probably hold vast resources.

In other words, the desirable expansion is being delayed not so much because supplies are short but because of other problems, similar to those encountered in agricultural development: traditional habits must be altered substantially and fishermen must be trained. Comparatively large sums should be invested in establishing advisory centres, equipping launches, and standardizing methods of using produce. Low-cost methods which are acceptable to the consumer should be devised for preserving and processing. Finally, networks for the transportation and distribution of goods should be established and, sometimes, consumer habits need to be altered.

Three developing countries, Peru, China and Chile, at present have the world's highest growth rates for sea fishing. Peru, the major fishing country of the world, with a catch of over 9 million tons in 1964, has had a growth rate greater than 20 per cent per year for more than ten years. This is largely due to the improvements made by private firms, with strong American participation; they have a modern fish-processing industry, geared to exports, but problems are arising over the unsystematic use of hitherto untapped fishing areas with good supplies of anchovies.[5]

As regards fish and nutrition, particularly interesting new opportunities have been opened up by the possibility of developing fish flour, especially deodorized flour. This has two advantages: it provides a use for kinds of fish and parts of fish – including bones, fins and scales – which are not acceptable in their natural state, and can substantially reduce losses through deterioration during transport. It can be treated, stored, and preserved very easily and is compara-

[5] Production in 1965 was lower than it was in 1964.

tively cheap, being virtually a by-product. It consists almost exclusively – about 65 per cent – of protein,[6] rich in essential calcium, phosphorus, and vitamins, particularly vitamin B. This should single it out as a choice foodstuff in the fight against hunger. Dieticians consider that fish flour could provide at least 10 to 15 per cent of our protein ration with no difficulty. Due to its protein content, fish flour is an almost ideal complement for cereal foods, which constitute the staple diet of a large number of undernourished peoples. This has been proved by a number of tests showing the excellent effect of this substance on health, particularly children's, who have a very high tolerance for it.[7] Deodorized and made tasteless by the extraction of odorous fats, fish flour, really a concentrate of proteins, vitamins and mineral salts, can be mixed with any traditional dish, biscuits and bread for example, without upsetting eating habits – an important factor when considering its general acceptability.

A powerful argument against fish meal[8] is that it often has a strong smell and tastes of raw flour. Apart from the fact that some people like this taste and eat raw flour anyway,[9] research into the difficult problem of deodorization is already well under way, particularly at the University of Maryland in the United States. But, as various research institutes pointed out at the Congress 'Fish in Nutrition' (Washington, 1961), work on deodorization frequently has had to be broken off through lack of interest on the part of possible buyers. Only the pigs and poultry of developed countries are given this first-class protein, not starving people.

This highly nutritive foodstuff is now manufactured on various trawlers and factory-ships (appreciably increasing their productivity) and in the dock factories of Peru (the world's largest producer, with 40 per cent of total world production), Japan, the United States, South Africa, Norway, the USSR, Chile, and Iceland. It is used almost exclusively without deodorization in the most developed

[6] Especially lysine and methionine. In fact the ingredients of fish flours vary according to species and according to whether the flour is made of the whole fish or of by-products.
[7] See in particular the collected essays produced by Professor Georg Borgstrom, the American specialist on fish nutrition: *Fish as food*, 4 volumes, Academic Press, New York and London, 1962–1965.
[8] In English, we distinguish between fish meal for animal consumption, and fish flour for human consumption. This distinction does not exist in French.
[9] See in particular 'Note sur quelques farines de poissons tropicaux', by Aldrin, in *Revue des Travaux de l'Institut des Pêches maritimes*, Paris, Dec., 1965.

countries – the United States, West Germany, the United Kingdom, and the Low Countries – for feeding animals.

Thus, all the fish meal produced in Peru, where the average daily consumption of animal protein is 12 grammes per head, is now exported to Europe, the United States, and Japan. If it were consumed in the underdeveloped countries of South America, it would almost double the people's ration of animal protein.

A great effort should be made to make this valuable foodstuff available to the undernourished and to expand its production. It should become one of the main weapons in the fight against malnutrition. Research should be carried out into methods of deodorizing, storing, and using fish meal for human consumption. We should point out that if the annual production of fish meal were tripled and brought up to 9 million tons – as compared with 3 million in 1964 – and used for human nutrition, it would satisfy the protein requirements of 300 million people each year; this would go a long way towards solving the problem of protein deficiency.

This would not be an unreasonable target for the very near future, given that a trend towards rapid expansion has been established. It is already being held back, however, by the large requirements of animal-food manufacturers, who alone constitute a profitable market. As we shall see in section 3 of this chapter, demand may fall as a result of developments in nutritional techniques, and difficulties in selling the product may arise.

Apart from sea fishing, freshwater fishing (a high proportion of which takes place in the paddy fields of South East Asia) could also be substantially increased if natural resources were used more rationally. The Soviet Union is advancing rapidly in this direction.

But, in so far as it is desirable to increase aquatic food supplies, we must abandon the simple 'gathering economy' of fishing – at the moment we collect the fish provided by nature – and replace it, as in the case of agricultural products, with the actual production of sea animals and plants. 'Aquiculture', analogous to agriculture, should be developing rapidly; this is particularly true of fish-breeding, comparable to stock-breeding and with the same limitations and the same possibilities for genetic, nutritional, and health improvements. Fish-breeding could be developed in many countries, in either natural or artificial water reserves. It could then gradually spread to lagoons and coastal waters and eventually perhaps to the great maritime fishing areas, as has been done in Japan, the pioneer of marine fish culture. There, bays have been closed for this purpose and young fish deposited in the ocean.[10]

Fish culture, an important traditional occupation in the Far East, is already well advanced in certain other countries. Israel certainly holds the record for productivity: 5,000 hectares of water reserves are specially laid out in fish farms where the average yield is over 2 tons of fish per hectare, sometimes reaching as much as 3.5 tons, comprising over 56 per cent of the annual fish production. These yields are obtained by the high level of technical skill used in selecting the fish (particularly carp), the fertilization of water, supplementary feeding, and mechanization. Israeli experts estimate that of every 2 tons produced, 400 kilogrammes can be attributed to natural nutrition, 400 to fertilization, and 1,200 to supplementary artificial nutrition. The Soviet Union is also aiming at a substantial increase in fish culture, in collectives where work productivity is very much higher than in their agricultural counterparts.

There is much room for expansion in mollusc and shellfish production, mainly in coastal areas.[11] Furthermore, the natural reserves of these small animals have so far been little exploited and there is great scope for development.

Finally, we should mention various maritime and freshwater plants: these are edible *algae*, which are already used in South East Asia for human consumption and for feeding pigs. The Japanese consume a number of different kinds, about 400,000 tons per year altogether. Some are merely harvested (270,000 tons in 1960) while others are actually cultivated by very complicated processes employing 70,000 workers.[12] Also in Japan, Professor Hiroshi Tamija has studied and perfected methods of using and cultivating *chlorella* for human consumption.

[10] See Professor Strickland's paper to the International Oceanographic Congress in Mowcow, July, 1966.
[11] Shrimp breeding is also an interesting possibility for some areas, as is shown by Japan's example.
[12] These algae are Amanori (*Porphyra*) and Aonori (*Monostroma* and *Enteromorpha*).

Chlorella is a unicellular green alga with a very fast rate of reproduction. It is particularly nutritious because it has a high content of amino-acids and vitamins and is easily assimilated by the human body. It is still, however, comparatively expensive to produce and its green colour, spreading to any foodstuff mixed with it, definitely counts against it, so strong are consumption habits.

It is definitely fish, sea or freshwater, natural or cultivated, rather than any other water product, which is the most important foodstuff. The volume of water products consumed annually could be expanded appreciably through the increased eating of fish. If particular efforts were made, as much in publicizing modern methods of fishing and production as in providing fishermen and producers with equipment, the present high rate of growth could be maintained or even increased. In this case, world production could double in the next ten years or so. With the population increasing by about 20 per cent in the same time, water products could increase average *per capita* resources of this kind by about two-thirds. With more widespread use of fish flour for human consumption, this increase would be even greater. It is particularly important that production should be more evenly distributed between the different parts of the world.

But if maritime resources are to be exploited systematically and are to rectify dietary deficiencies, aspects of world economy and of international trade must be reconsidered. The same will probably be true for another new foodstuff which seems a hope for the future. This is yeast.

2. NEW FOODSTUFFS: YEASTS

Yeasts, microscopic fungi, have been used since time immemorial as leaven for bread and as the fermenting agent in various drinks: mead, wine, beer, and brandy. By aerobic reproduction in sugar solutions, yeasts ferment and convert these sugars into alcohol. What is now new is the use of yeast not as a means of making other products, but as a product in itself, as a foodstuff. Dieticians have been examining this idea for about fifty years.

When certain kinds of yeast, particularly the kind used in beer, come into contact with air, they multiply extremely fast on the sugary liquids which are by-products of sugar refineries, beet distilleries, and pulp and paper factories. Now, reproducing in this way from sugar and nitrogen, the yeasts make their own living culture, which has turned out to have a very high protein content and to be rich in essential vitamins, particularly the B group vitamins. The resulting nutritive value is such that yeasts should be regarded as primary foodstuffs.[13] The League of Nations was certainly right when, in 1938, it recommended the distribution of yeasts to the undernourished.

After drying and appropriate treatment, yeast takes the form of a powder or of little tasteless chips. Like fish flour these can be consumed with traditional foodstuffs, such as soups, sauces, cakes, bread, and biscuits, appreciably increasing their protein and vitamin content.

Yeast was not used as a foodstuff until the first world war in Germany, when it was often added to broths or used in powder form. Because of its nutritive value and low cost, production was continued after the first world war and even more after the Second, for feeding animals. The use of yeasts for animal consumption has even increased since the last war, with the utilization of new kinds (Torula, for example) which are easier to grow and can be produced from waste products – such as those from wine distilleries, which are purified at the same time as they grow.

Thus, though yeasts could make some contribution to solving human protein starvation, they are, like fish meal, now used almost exclusively for feeding the livestock of rich countries. The Eastern bloc countries, however, in particular the Soviet Union, are beginning to take a serious interest in yeasts for human consumption.

Many underdeveloped countries could produce large quantities of yeast in different substrates. This would be particularly easy for sugar-producing and fruit-producing countries – Cuba has been taking an interest in it. The growth of yeast on cellulose – chips of wood or reeds – which has first been broken down by chemical treatment is much more complicated and costly and needs sulphuric acid; but the USSR is building a factory for this purpose.

[13] Note here the essential difference, in spite of their common origin, between yeast used for food and yeast used in medicine. The latter is a suspension of living micro-organisms used for medicinal purposes, while the former are dead cells which, after drying, have ruptured their cell-walls without any alteration in their chemical composition.

Due credit should be given to the recent discovery by the French biochemist Alfred Champagnat[14] who has found a new substrate for yeast, entirely altering the dimensions of the problem and opening up completely new possibilities for yeast production. In 1958 Champagnat discovered that, of the by-products from oil refineries, heavy oils, on account of their paraffin content, provide a particularly good medium for growing yeasts identical to those produced from sugar by-products. Aware of the importance of his discovery, he has been concentrating his attention ever since on perfecting a process for the industrial production of petroleum yeasts and large resources have been put at his disposal by his company. These yeasts grow and multiply at a remarkable speed. Apart from the oxygen in the atmosphere they also need ammonia to provide them with the nitrogen indispensable to their growth. These yeasts can, therefore, be grown on heavy diesel oil in a ventilated fermentation room with a controlled ammonia content in the atmosphere.

This oil-based culture, a kind of cultivation with no soil (though yeasts are vegetable), occurs in an entirely artificial medium. All the properties of the medium are in effect controlled and directed towards the biosynthesis of immediately useful protein and vitamins. The so-called nitrogenous fertilizers, assimilated by the yeasts with no intervening stages, have an operative yield of about 100 per cent – far greater than that of so-called natural fertilizers. The yeasts' speed of reproduction is several thousand times higher than that of livestock.

The yeasts produced in this way must be separated from their medium, a delicate operation which has taken a long time to perfect, since no trace of petrol must remain in the final product. After drying they appear as a protein-vitamin concentrate in chip or powder form containing about 50 per cent protein, and are odourless, tasteless and digestible; they can be stored in sacks like flour. This concentrate is particularly useful for the supplementation of cereals,[15] since it has a high content of the proteins lysine and threonine. Different kinds of yeast could perhaps be adapted to each different cereal. When added to flour, vegetable oil and sugar the

[14] Now the director of the Société International de Recherches BP, which is concentrating exclusively on yeasts.
[15] R. Jacquot, *op. cit.*

concentrates can be made into biscuits containing up to 40 per cent concentrated protein. They could equally well be added to pastes and, indeed, to a whole variety of dishes in every part of the world. With special treatment, the yeast protein could be used to make soup concentrates and soluble powders, which would be particularly acceptable as they have a strong meat taste or the taste of Far Eastern *nuoc-man*. Most important, the price of this concentrate (about one franc per kilo, ex-factory) is very attractive and competitive compared with traditional sources of protein.

After only a few years of research, the present yield of petrol yeasts is about 2 tons – that is, 1 ton of pure protein – for every 60 tons of crude petroleum containing paraffin. On the basis of oil production figures for 1966, all the oil-refining companies of the world together could produce about 40 million tons of the concentrate or 20 million tons of pure protein – as much as is now produced by the combined output of stockfarming and fishing. If this amount of petrol yeast was distributed among the undernourished peoples of the world, it could provide about 25 grammes of pure protein per person per day, which would make a considerable inroad on protein starvation.

But we must not indulge in fantasies. While research work is far advanced, having already reached the semi-industrial stage, the research workers want to ensure that there are strict controls against toxic elements and to offer a product which is absolutely safe for human consumption; by 1966 they have not yet succeeded in doing so.

Furthermore, even when all the research work has been finished and dieticians and doctors have declared the product safe, production must be made economic for the refineries. This can only be done through long-term contracts between governments and petrol companies, which would assure the profitability of the producers' investments and which could be guaranteed by an international organization. Arrangements would have to be made for the transportation of the yeast concentrates and the subsequent processing and distribution of the products.

In other words, it will be many years before petrol proteins begin to play a role of any significance in human nutrition – several years to make a beginning and another ten to fifteen to distribute on a world-wide scale.[16]

Petrol yeasts do nevertheless have three great advantages:

1. Since the potential manufacturers are few in number and have a high level of technical knowledge and high investment capacities, the process will probably be widely publicized as soon as it is found to be valuable and economic.

2. The product has a high nutritive quality, takes up little space, and can be stored easily and used without altering eating habits.

3. Its price is a great advantage: estimated at 40 US cents per kilo after transport and distribution, 40 million tons after distribution would cost 16 thousand million dollars, or 2.4 per cent of the national income of the United States.

The Soviet Union is apparently giving careful attention to this question and has already set up some important research centres. The FAO, the World Health Organization, and UNICEF should make a joint effort to test the value of this new foodstuff. If results are positive, steps should be taken to enable the hopes it has raised to be fulfilled.

3. NEW WEAPONS IN THE FIGHT AGAINST MALNUTRITION: SYNTHETIC CHEMICAL FOODSTUFFS

Like agricultural produce, water foods and yeasts are living organisms. Side by side with these biological foodstuffs, the chemical industry has developed a completely new category of foodstuffs: synthetic products.

The food situation being what it is, the most careful interest and attention should be given to the possibility of manufacturing low-cost synthetic proteins.[17]

[16] A speed bearing no relation to the extremely slow spread of progress in stock-breeding which would be needed to produce the same quantity of first-class protein.
[17] In the present state of knowledge, carbohydrates cannot yet be synthesized, but can be 'saccharized'; that is, carbohydrates which cannot normally be assimilated, such as cellulose (reeds and chips of wood) can be transformed into edible sugars. These can also be used as sugar substrate for the growth of yeasts. Various processes for synthesizing fats have also been perfected.

As with fish meal and yeasts, however, the position is paradoxical. In spite of the drastic protein deficiencies of half the human race, it is just not profitable to satisfy these crying human needs, and research and its initial industrial application have predominantly aimed at improving the quality and lowering the cost of foodstuffs for animals that supply the food of the industrial countries. The research is at such a basic level, however, that it is not only applicable to animal nutrition.

Applying the theory of supplementation (see Chapter I, section 4), researchers came up with the following question: instead of increasing the general content of protein in food rations until the scarcest elements are present in sufficient quantity, thereby wasting other surplus chemicals in the process, would it not be possible simply to manufacture pure proteins? Experiments were carried out and the answer turned out to be yes. This has brought about the practice of narrow supplementation. Methionine, the first synthetic protein to be manufactured, has already built up a wide market. In 1964, in the world as a whole, about 6,000 tons of methionine (half of which was produced in France[18]) were put into mixed foodstuffs given to pigs and poultry. Its use allowed some of the flours hitherto used to provide proteins (fish or meat meal, yeasts) to be replaced by soya cakes at half the price, or by cereals. With 12 grammes of methionine, a chicken can be fed on a kilo of soya cake instead of a kilo of fish meal which, at the 1965 price of $2.10 per kilo of methionine – reduces the cost by one-third.

Furthermore, with advances in our knowledge of animal nutrition, and technological progress in industrial biochemistry (especially the chemistry of lysine) rich flours and oilcakes[19] need no longer be included in the fodder of grown pigs. The first diets based on cereals and the synthetic proteins that supplement cereals[20] are being tested on fully grown pigs, whose digestive and alimentary systems are comparatively close to those of human beings.

[18] *A Commentary*, by the Société de Chimie Organique et biologique.
[19] For a general survey of this subject, see: André Brette, 'Les acides amines de synthèse', *Revue de l'Elevage*, special number 38, Paris, 1965.
[20] Naturally with the appropriate amount of mineral salts and vitamins, also made by synthesis.

This research, which is already leading to the industrialization of animal nutrition, raises two important points about human nutrition:

1. In animal nutrition the use of synthetic proteins is beginning to offer serious competition to flours; for 12,000 tons of methionine could leave 1 million tons of fish meal free for other uses, and this quantity would cover the protein requirements of a country with 150 million inhabitants. Does this mean that the manufacture of yeasts and fish meal will be abandoned, their expansion halted, and their uses curtailed? Or will we succeed in making use of their capacity to expand production for the full benefit of mankind?

2. Together with this indirect effect, could not the industrial production of synthetic proteins be used directly for human nutrition and even radically transform the whole problem?

If man has relied on animals until now for part of his nutrition it is because, apart from considerations of taste, vegetables do not contain sufficient quantities of the necessary protein. This is simply because vegetable protein is seriously deficient in one or two necessary amino-acids. For example, deficiency in lysine alone almost halves the biological value of cereals. Thus, the distinction between so-called first-class proteins and the others is essentially the result of lack of lysine in the latter.[21]

Supplemented with about a gramme of lysine and half a gramme of methionine for every hundred grammes, the full biological value of corn can be restored. This gramme and a half, worth less than half a US cent, can save about 25 grammes of meat.

When completely new perspectives are being opened up in animal nutrition, it is to be hoped that ways of applying them to human nutrition will be carefully studied and that results will follow quickly. It is encouraging that the US Secretary of Agriculture is working on plans for supplementing the shipments of wheat for India with

[21] Owing to lysine and methionine deficiencies, the 10 grammes of protein contained in about 100 grammes of corn have the biological value of only 5 grammes.

lysine, and a firm of supermarkets in Washington is already selling bread with this element added.[22]

In conclusion, we return to agriculture to mention a new and successful line of research which will perhaps one day come to compete with the processes we have been discussing. It involves making a complete change in the composition of vegetable protein, particularly in cereals, by selection and genetic improvement, in order to make it comparable with animal protein. One kind of maize, Opaque-2, was selected for this process in the United States and it is already giving encouraging results.[23] The animal, a costly source of food, could one day no longer be required as a supplier of first-class protein. Since, as we know, cereals provide more than half the protein ration of the poor countries at the present time, such possibilities clearly raise hopes for a revolution in nutrition.

Thus new methods and prospects are appearing in the realm of human nutrition, hitherto almost exclusively tied to agriculture. A great deal of research, however, will have to be done before they can be put into operation; new habits must be formed, money must be invested and, most important of all, new relationships must be built up between countries.

These points must be borne in mind if we are to form a realistic picture of the future development of the food situation in the Third World.

[22] See Archibald T. McPherson, 'Synthetic foods can help close the world food gap', a paper presented to a special seminar on agricultural marketing organized by the Washington section of the American Marketing Association on May 3rd, 1966.
   The publicity produced for the launching of this new product says that: 'as nature forgot to put in enough lysine, corn protein cannot be fully used for the improvement of bodily tissues'. It omits to mention that cereal is not the only food resource of the average American. The author regrets that supplemented bread is made and sold in the United States instead of India.
[23] The lysine content of this maize hybrid is 70 per cent higher than that of other known varieties; its nutritional value is higher by the same proportion.

CHAPTER FOUR

The dangers before us

I. SEVERE FAMINE IF THE PRESENT TRENDS CONTINUE

Even more serious than the food situation in different parts of the world at the present time are the prospects for the future. The future situation will be the inevitable result of the two trends we have just outlined – that of the food needs of an increasing population on the one hand, and that of methods of food production determining supply on the other. Food production *per capita* will be the outcome of these two trends.

If in spite of an expanding population the world already had an adequate food supply, the growth of food resources would only have to keep pace with that of population for production per head to remain constant and sufficient. In our world, however, there is both undernourishment and a rapidly increasing population. We must, therefore, both make up the existing deficit and also keep pace with the demographic trend. Food production will have to grow at an appreciably faster rate than population.

On a world scale, there is no sign of this happening at the present time. Since 1958, which was a particularly good year in many countries, agricultural production, and especially food production, has barely kept up with population increase: average world production per head has been dangerously close to a standstill since 1959 and has even begun to fall off significantly since 1963. During 1964, world population grew twice as fast (2 per cent) as food resources (1 per cent).[1] This means that the world food situation is deteriorating to an alarming degree.

[1] Whereas agricultural production grew appreciably faster than general food production, at the rate of 1.5 per cent per year.

Moreover, this world picture can be broken down to show an enormous disparity between the situation in the industrialized countries and that in the Third World. In the thirty-three developed or semi-developed countries where the standard of nutrition is good – an average daily intake of 3,000 calories and 44 grammes of animal protein per head – *per capita* agricultural production is increasing slowly but steadily. In the ninety underdeveloped countries, on the other hand, where the standard of nutrition is low – 2,150 calories and 9 grammes of animal protein per day – there has been a slow decline in *per capita* agricultural production ever since 1959, in spite

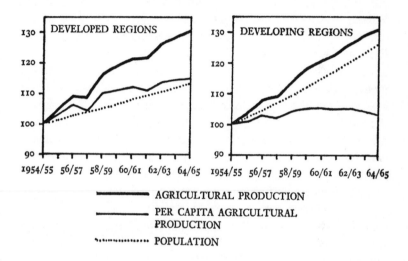

AGRICULTURAL PRODUCTION
PER CAPITA AGRICULTURAL PRODUCTION
POPULATION

of an increase in total real agricultural production. The average rate of agricultural expansion in the Third World – barely 2 per cent per year – and above all the expansion of food resources can no longer keep pace with the rate of population increase of about 2.5 per cent. But the situation varies considerably within this group of countries.

During the years 1956–66, *per capita* agricultural production has been falling in Chile, Cuba, Colombia, Peru, and Uruguay; it has improved slightly in Brazil, Guatemala, Venezuela, and Mexico. In Latin America, therefore, where the population growth rate is higher than in any other large area of the world, the food situation, already poor, is generally deteriorating.[2] But the situation in the Far East and Africa is even more desperate.

In the Far East, where the average standard of nutrition is even lower than it was before 1939, only North and South Korea, Formosa, Malaysia, and, most of all, Japan and Thailand, have succeeded in increasing their production at a significantly faster rate than their population.

In Africa, the growth of food resources is lagging behind the rapid population increase, which at 2.6 per cent is almost as high as that of Latin America. Production per head has been falling steadily for the past ten years, particularly in North West Africa. South of the Sahara, the trend is not so bad; it is, however, falling off in the Central African Republic, in Dahomey, and in large parts of Nigeria.

In the Near East, although food production is increasing at a moderately satisfactory rate, it has not been keeping pace with the sustained population growth of 2.5 per cent per year. This means that the food situation in this part of the world has been deteriorating continuously for several years. Of course, the climate in this area is very unreliable; Iraq, Jordan, Lebanon, and Syria had four consecutive years of drought from 1958 to 1962. Israel is the only exception, on account of the extent of her irrigation work.

Thus a real food crisis, particularly serious for countries where the standard of nutrition is in any case low, has been developing for several years in an increasing number of countries. This crisis is the precursor of famine. 'Some people thought that this crisis was a long-term danger; they will have to revise their opinion and realize that the crisis is here',[3] an economic adviser to the American government was forced to admit in a speech in February, 1966. Dr Sen, director general of the FAO, has pronounced that the general situation is 'truly alarming'.[4]

It is, of course, foolish to make calculations based on recent

[2] *Per capita* food production has been falling steadily since 1959; in 1964 it was probably 8 per cent lower than in 1954. In Chile, for example, the average growth rate for food production for the last twenty-five years is 2 per cent and for population 2.25 per cent.
[3] See Lester Brown, *World Population, Food Problems, and the Future of Man*, United States Department of Agriculture, Washington, February 1966.
[4] 'Nutrition, population and the rights of man', speech given to the World Congress on Population, Belgrade, 1965.

developments since many unpredictable factors may arise. But even if it means making mistakes, we must try to make some forecasts of the impending dangers, for public opinion seriously underestimates them.

If nothing is done and present trends continue, there is a serious danger that famine, which had already taken hold in India by 1966, will spread over most of the Third World. After India, the most vulnerable areas are East Pakistan, Java, Egypt (where there is starvation already), the Maghreb, the Middle East, the Sahel of the western Sahara (where harvests are scanty), and the Andes from Chile to Mexico; and after that the Caribbean, the Sertão in Brazil, and perhaps even Anatolia in Turkey. The situation in China has been dangerous, as it has been in Vietnam, but it is now being regulated, after immense efforts, by population control.

As things are now, it is difficult to see what could be done to modify the present trends either in population growth or in food production.

As a result of population growth, children under 15 make up 40 per cent of the population of the Third World countries. When these generations, each age-group larger than the previous one, are old enough to have families themselves, the rate of population growth will remain high, even if the size of families decreases. Methods of controlling population growth will eventually bring results, but these cannot be immediate. On the other hand, progress in medicine and new discoveries in the treatment of disease – particularly now that a successful campaign against bilharzia is possible – are spreading much faster than agricultural advances; and this will actually increase the rate of population expansion.

As for food production, in spite of the new prospects which have arisen it must be recognized that in most countries no adequate steps are being taken to promote rapid expansion and less unequal distribution. In particular, the new non-agricultural products cannot be expected to play a significant role for many years to come. Even at the present time, as we have seen, there is a large gap between actual and adequate standards of nutrition in the Third World. Forecasts for the future show that the gap between human food requirements and supplies will widen further.

The disequilibrium between the ever more rapidly growing population of the world and its inadequate food resources will, therefore, continue, though varying in degree between regions and social classes. It will reveal itself through chronic undernourishment and its consequences, disease and premature death, and then by the spread of famine.

2. DELIBERATE STEPS TO RECTIFY THE SITUATION

Aware of the gravity of the situation, the FAO has set up production targets, region by region, for the undernourished countries.[5] These are minimal targets that must be reached if we are to face the population explosion and also improve the food situation in the Third World.

The short term target set for 1975 is a 50 per cent increase in the daily animal protein ration of the Third World countries. If nutritive foodstuffs were distributed according to bodily requirements, this increase would just satisfy the most vulnerable classes of people[6]: infants, children, pregnant and nursing mothers, the ill, and the infirm. But world production will have to increase by more than 50 per cent in the next ten years if this modest aim is to be achieved. It would need a rate of growth of more than 4 per cent per year, reaching almost 5 per cent for animal produce, and over 6 per cent for vegetables.

The long-term targets, up to the year 2000, should allow another 50 per cent improvement in the animal protein rations of the Third World. This target should reasonably satisfy the vulnerable classes of people, and would go some of the way towards meeting the demands of other sections of the population. But if this target is to be reached, world food resources must triple between now and the year 2000, with particular emphasis on animal and vegetable produce. The materials needed by the Third World alone would, therefore, have to quadruple. This would demand an average growth rate for food production, sustained for 35 years, of 3.2 per cent for the whole world and 4 per cent for the Third World.

[5] *Third World Food Survey, No. 11.* of Freedom from Hunger Campaign, Basic Studies, FAO, Rome, 1963.
[6] Problems would also arise over the degree of priority to be given to each group.

This rate of expansion would have to be especially high in certain parts of the world, notably the Far East, where food supplies now only cover 60 per cent of human requirements as specified in the long-term target. As we have seen, in present conditions it has been extremely difficult to sustain an agricultural growth rate of 3 per cent for long periods, even in industrialized countries.

And yet the FAO's targets are by no means unreasonable. In the age of nuclear power and the space race, it should not be hopelessly ambitious to take the year 2000 as the deadline by which every human being is ensured of a more or less adequate daily diet. If the situation is to be rectified, however, by the FAO's target date of 2000, then recent trends must be radically altered. It will be necessary to take fundamental action on both fronts of the problem at once – on food production and on population growth – otherwise the year 2000 will be the date at which some of the gloomier prophecies for the year 1000 are in fact fulfilled.

If we express the problem in the most rigorous possible terms and on the evidence of our most recent knowledge, this should help to bring about a solution and to eliminate the contradiction inherent in objectives that are desirable in human terms but at the same time difficult to achieve in economic terms.

3. THE NUTRITIONAL PROBLEM IN NEW TERMS

Now that we find ourselves face to face with the problem of widespread malnutrition, we must alter the general direction of research into human nutrition; with striking exceptions, research until now has been concentrated on the problems of the industrialized countries. These countries may be able to afford the luxury of an expensive, sophisticated diet at the price of immense wastage, but the other two-thirds of the world cannot.

International institutions should either give systematic encouragement to, or else themselves undertake, research projects and experiments into the forms of diet appropriate to the particular conditions of the poor countries. In these countries the main objective is not to have the best possible diet regardless of cost, but to obtain at the lowest possible cost a daily food ration containing all the elements necessary for normal physical and mental development.

The methods perfected in the industrialized countries for feeding domestic animals – and they are better fed than many people – could perhaps be taken more or less as a model. Specialists in animal nutrition are investigating each form and stage of development to find out which diet will satisfy all the needs of growth, upkeep and reproduction at the lowest economic cost. With this aim in view they have specified the minimum necessary quantities of calories, proteins, vitamins, and mineral salts, and are using modern methods of economic calculation.

For human nutrition we must also abandon obsolete ideas, particularly the distinction between plant proteins and animal proteins. A great deal of attention is still paid to this distinction when making statistical estimates about the quality of diets at the present time. But it does not allow the nutritional problem to be posed in the sort of operational forms that are essential if the battle against hunger is to be won.

Unfortunately our ability to express the food needs of both children and adults in terms of basic substances is less advanced than our knowledge of the composition of these basic foodstuffs. It should be recognized that it is more difficult to do this for people than for animals, for the latter can more easily be used for experiments; we shall never be able to reach such precise conclusions about human beings, since human physiology and living conditions are so varied in contrast with the gradual standardization of those of animals.

Even at the cost of a certain amount of inaccuracy, however, we must systematically consider and experiment with all the possible ways of providing human beings with a correctly balanced minimum quantity of the protein they need; and we must try to establish the best possible economic conditions for doing so. It is now known that there are many different ways of doing this. In particular, by means of balanced supplementation, cereals or, even more easily, vegetables (peas, beans and soya beans),[7] can be given the same in protein value as animal foods.

[7] Africa, in particular, produces good vegetables, principally the Soudan bean or Niebe in dry areas and the Kissi pea in humid areas.

As synthetic vitamins and mineral salts can also be produced by industrial chemistry, two new possibilities arise over and above the traditional answers: first of all there is supplementation of foods or of their ingredients (cereal flour in particular) with tasteless synthetic products; and secondly, we must consider the possibility of manufacturing concentrated complementary foodstuffs to supplement deficiencies in the protein, vitamin, and mineral content of traditional local diets.[8] The latter would be a good way to safeguard the health of the most vulnerable sections of the population.

Careful thought should be given to methods of introducing such supplementary foodstuffs to the population in a way that would make them acceptable. Initially, the best system would be to distribute them in schools and dispensaries. Such considerations are important for, as Professor Trémollières has pointed out, a foodstuff should have not only nutritional value; it must also satisfy certain psychological needs and tastes as well as playing a symbolic role based on traditions and culture.

There is already a good example of an achievement of this kind in *Incaparina*, manufactured by the Institute of Nutrition in Guatemala.[9] A mixture of maize flours, cottonseed, soya beans, yeasts, vitamins, and mineral salts, its protein content and nutritive value are similar to milk. It is very cheap[10] and has been used widely in South America – 3 million tons in 1965 – at the suggestion of international institutions. ORANA[11] in Dakar and the Institute of Mysore in India are working along similar lines.

From these general trends and examples it can be seen that actual nutritional policies must be formulated country by country, or preferably, by large geographical areas; by such policies must innovations be made and newly discovered resources used.

[8] Modern stock-breeders who follow zoologists' advice have been supplementing the basic foods made of farm products for some time.
[9] Institute of Nutrition of Central America and Panama, INCAP, from which the product takes its name. See 'Incaparina, the low cost protein rich food product', by R. L. Shaw, in the report given by the study group on proteins, FAO–OMS–UNICEF in April, 1966.
[10] In Colombia in 1965 it cost 22 US cents per kg. of flour. After water and sugar have been added and after boiling, this makes 40 glasses of a drink which has the same nutritional value as a glass of milk. Cost about 3/3d (40 US cents).
[11] Office de Recherche sur l'Alimentation et la Nutrition en Afrique, directed by Dr Dupin. It has produced, in particular, 'Flour 21' (21 per cent protein), a mixture of millet flour (75 per cent) and ground-nut flour (the dry waste product from oil-works).

We then come up against a fundamental problem: that of establishing a close connection between the food problem, the agricultural development policy, and the policy for general economic growth.

Improvements in nutrition should be among the objectives of economic and social development policies. This seems obvious; but all too frequently, the purpose of growth – which can only be greater happiness for all men – is forgotten. Need we add that frequently a better diet is a necessary precondition for the employment of men weakened by malnutrition?

If progress in nutrition is still largely dependent on the expansion of agricultural production, it is also dependent on a bold policy of innovations in other sectors. This should be remembered when formulating policies of industrialization, as well as the fact that industry should provide the goods necessary for the expansion of agriculture – tools, fertilizers, insecticides and so on – and so for the growth of food production. Supported by research and experiment, and organized by teams of expert agronomists, doctors, dieticians, and economists, nutritional policies could thus become a cornerstone of development policies. One thing cannot be emphasized too strongly: the war against hunger and malnutrition can be waged successfully only if it is treated as one component part of an active policy for overall economic development.

The formulation of new and rational policies of nutrition would bring about a better use of existing food resources, but, in the light of the present situation and of the outlook for the future, enormous efforts will still have to be made to expand food production.

4. A CHALLENGE FOR OUR TIME: TRIPLING FOOD PRODUCTION BEFORE THE END OF THE CENTURY

If our generation is to take up the challenge of history, its primary task should be to triple food production between now and the year 2000. To do this, all possible means should be used at the same time: the acceleration of the agricultural development of each nation or group of nations in the Third World, the expansion or exploitation of all non-agricultural foodstuffs, and the reorganization of international trade.

The acceleration of agricultural development is a fundamental goal for all nations of the Third World (see Part IV). They should exploit all their resources within a general pattern of medium- and long-term development plans, define a coherent overall scheme of objectives, methods, and deadlines, and at the same time investigate the best way to use scarce resources. Planning facilitates the most economic use of available means of production and accelerates growth. (In this respect, the FAO's project to draw up a world indicative plan for agricultural development[12] should be given careful attention.)

Protein requirements – the most urgent of all food requirements – are such that they could scarcely be met by the expansion of stock-breeding alone. It would not be going too far to mobilize all available first-class protein resources in the attempt to eliminate protein starvation. The promotion of fishing and the development of fish flour for human consumption, the manufacture of yeasts on an ever-increasing scale and of synthetic protein in edible form are all promising methods. Absolute priority should be given to research in these fields, either sponsored or carried out by big international organizations.

It might seem that international trade could do much to narrow the gap between the nutritional standards of different countries. Traditionally, however, it is the industrialized countries, like the United Kingdom and Germany, which have always been the major importers of food products, in exchange for which they sell manufactured goods. Soviet Russia – whose agricultural problems will be examined later – has now joined this group of countries, becoming the world's largest wheat importer, with imports of 11 million tons in 1964.

In the past few years, however, faced with a more and more difficult food situation, a growing number of Third World countries also have started to buy cereals on the international market.[13] The largest buyers are India and China, which now import between

[12] See the memorandum of the Director General of the FAO, October 14, 1965.
[13] The structure of commercial trade in food products, in cereals in particular, has changed radically in the course of the past twenty-five years: North America and Oceania are the only continents where exports exceed imports to an appreciable degree whereas before 1939 Western Europe was the only net importer.

5 million and 6 million tons per year; Brazil, Egypt, Pakistan, the Congo, Morocco, and Chile are all following them. In order to do this they are forced to cut down on their purchases of capital equipment, thereby impairing their prospects for future development. Furthermore, the real cost of imports to these countries becomes higher and higher while the prices of the primary products they export – minerals, cotton, coffee, cocoa, palm oil – are constantly falling (see Chapter XII, section 7). Consequently it is only when faced with absolute necessity that a growing number of Third World countries are resigning themselves to importing food; and this is a particularly disturbing sign. Stocks of cereals in exporting countries of the West (the most important being the United States and Canada) have been decreasing steadily since 1957.

Until now short-term profitable opportunities have almost exclusively determined the pattern of international trade. This pattern has been distorted by the grossly unequal strength of different countries and by the forms of economic domination which this produces. Yet in the fight against hunger and underdevelopment the entire productive capacity available in the world must be used for the benefit of mankind; at the present time this is prevented by the structure of international trade (see also Chapter V). But if international trade is to play its part in mobilizing productive resources (and it is becoming increasingly clear that it must), then its whole structure needs to undergo a radical revision.

5. ARRESTING POPULATION GROWTH BY BIRTH CONTROL

All possible steps should be taken to bring about a regular increase in the quantity and quality of food resources. At the same time, however, men should take conscious and deliberate steps to control their own numbers. In place of the hazards of nature they should establish clearly understood controls. In an age of enlightenment and scientific analysis this should surely be the general purpose of human action.

In seeking a solution to population problems, rejecting, of course, the possibility of an increase in the mortality rate, we must turn to the question of the birth rate. Over the past two centuries all industrial societies have succeeded in replacing the crude and ugly 'natural regulators' of population – famine, epidemic and war – by other methods of regulation, based on freedom of choice and responsibility. Industrial societies now have a comparative measure of control over the increase of their population, although admittedly the rate of growth is still ten times as great as it was in pre-industrial times.

The elimination of some of the natural regulators by life-saving advances in medicine has, as we all know, caused an expansion of population in the Third World that is in no way linked to economic growth. It is, therefore, vital that new means of regulation should be introduced into these countries, not merely for economic reasons, but also for the sake of simple human dignity. To give men and women the chance not to be overburdened by families which they do not want and cannot feed surely amounts to giving them the chance of developing as people. The issue here is not simply one of limiting the total number of births, but also of ensuring that it is not only the men and women of the richest countries or social classes who are given the luxury of being responsible fathers and mothers. We are faced by a desperate choice: either the human race increases in number, and larger and larger sections of it live in physical hardship and deteriorating conditions, or else the human race controls its size and improves its living conditions.

It seems vital that the steps taken to check uncontrolled population growth, even in the less densely populated countries, should be immediate, for the dissemination of knowledge on this subject will be slow, after man's resignation for thousands of years to the course of nature, and in the face of a vast legacy of prejudices and myths. Besides, different countries will need different methods, selected according to codes of morality, cultural levels, and financial means. More research is needed here, and it is surprising that all the serious work on this highly important issue has been carried out only recently.

As a final point, birth control should preferably be introduced gradually, since abrupt variations in the population curve are better avoided. Meanwhile, some of the Third World countries have already decided to adopt family-planning policies and their experiments could serve as examples for others.

Birth control should not, however, become a convenient alibi for supporters of the *status quo*. It is far from being a panacea or miraculous remedy for every problem. A policy of birth control will not exempt any country from making a tremendous effort to accelerate economic growth. It can only be regarded as one facet of the general programme for economic and social progress and should not distract thinking and responsible people in every country of the world from the objective which, sooner or later, will have to be faced: united action for the improvement of the lot of the poorest of the world's people.

Will the industrialized countries continue to take advantage of their advanced position, mainly the result of the work of preceding generations? Will the vast majority of the riches of the world continue to be monopolized for the benefit of a minority whose relative wealth is constantly increasing? Should not this wealth promote greater responsibility for the common good? Should not the heritage of progress be put to the service of mankind in general?

Before even thinking of conquering space or of building deadly weapons, should the rich countries not put a small part of their enormous wealth at the service of the only just war, man's war against his traditional enemies – famine, pestilence and, now, overpopulation?

Before tracing the broad outlines of what could be a vast coordinated world programme for fighting hunger, we must enlarge the preceding analysis and try to define the characteristics of the present situation and of the future outlook for agriculture and nutrition in each of the three major groups of countries:

1. The Western industrial countries, where the potential for agricultural production is highest at the present time but cannot be exploited to the full through lack of markets.

2. The Socialist countries, some already industrialized (USSR, Czechoslovakia, for example) and others in the process of development (China, Cuba, for example), which have been more successful in industrial than in agricultural development; this has largely been the result of dogmatism and of exploiting and (though this is not the case in China) despising their peasant populations.

3. The countries of the Third World, which are grappling with a situation unknown in pre-industrial Europe – with the manifold difficulties of underdevelopment, including shortage of organization and capital, the after-effects of colonialism, and, above all, the population explosion. These difficulties are aggravated by other factors – in South America by the *latifundia*,[15] in Africa by a semi-parasitic bourgeoisie in public and political life, and in India, the Middle East, and the Maghreb by share-cropping and usury.

[15] Large estates.

PART TWO The Dilemma for Western
Agriculture – Overproduction or Malthusianism?

CHAPTER FIVE

Lack of outlets for the agricultural produce of Western Europe, North America and Australia

I. AGRICULTURE IN TRANSITION

Until the industrial revolution agriculture constituted not merely the basis but the very substance of economic life in the west. This means that agricultural problems must be posed in completely different terms from those of other sectors.

Technical progress, which brought about the vast industrial revolution, had an equally important, though slower and much less studied, effect on agriculture. Set in motion in the sixteenth century in the United Kingdom and other parts of Europe, in full swing in the eighteenth century in England and then in France, the agricultural revolution has been accelerating sharply in the twentieth century, particularly in the last twenty years. It has caused an unparalleled increase in the productivity of agricultural workers and the productive potential of the agricultural sector.

As a consequence of increased agricultural productivity and of the expansion of employment in industry, commerce, and various service industries which attract rural labour, agriculture now achieves greater output with far fewer workers. In the United States the amount of agricultural labour needed to produce enough food for three people in 1800 can produce enough for at least twenty-five in 1966. Therefore, the active agricultural labour force and the importance of agriculture in the economy as a whole have decreased and will have to go on decreasing.

Agricultural workers made up three-quarters of the working population of the United States in 1800, but they now account for only 7 per cent of it. Only 5 million people now work on the land compared with about 12 million in 1910, and operations are now mechanized. The rural exodus can thus be seen to have affected millions and millions of agricultural workers in the industrialized countries: finding that there was no more room for them on the land, they were attracted to industry.

We are now witnessing the transition from the traditional methods of agriculture, directly descended from the former peasant civilization, to a modern agriculture making use of industrial methods of production – agriculture without peasants[1]; we may expect this trend to continue for the next ten years. This basic transformation was at first only a very slow process of evolution, unrecognized by agricultural workers, their representatives, and politicians. It has now suddenly accelerated, and, stimulated by technical progress and the use of modern techniques by the farmers themselves, it is at a point of rapid transition.

2. NECESSARY STRUCTURAL REFORMS: THE FAMILY FARM

Western agriculture is still essentially founded on the family, which, even now, constitutes the basic unit of the agricultural economy.

Until recently this system fitted logically into its historical context. The known methods were really only suitable for traditional production, relying largely on experience, skill, and commonsense. With these qualities the peasant could counterbalance the inadequacy of his technical precision, making day-to-day, empirical, individual decisions.

But with the advance of agronomy, the processes of production can be understood in detail and the peasant can find out how to deal with certain situations in advance, such as a threat of frost, the outbreak of an epidemic, and so on. Technology gradually replaces commonsense and experience. The peasant should constantly be learning outside his farm. Furthermore, technology puts machines and more and more expensive processes at the disposal of the farm

[1] By analogy with the work: *Une France sans paysans*, by M. Gervais, C. Servolin, and G. Weil (coll. 'Société', ed. du Seuil, Paris, 1965), which outlines the problem very clearly.

worker; if these are to be made economically viable, units of production must be larger. Small holdings have become anachronistic
and should be concentrated into larger units.

At the same time, some of the traditional functions of agriculture
have been taken over by the new specialized concerns which have
grown up around it: the manufacture of tools and of fertilizers has
long ceased to come within the province of the agricultural worker
and is now an industrial function. Recently the manufacture of
fodder for livestock has begun to be transferred from the farm and
now forms a flourishing industry of its own. The processing of raw
agricultural produce into more and more elaborate consumer goods
has also become an industrial matter, constantly increasing in
importance. For every dollar spent on food by the American
consumer, more than two-thirds now goes to industrialists and
traders.

Farming has not been unaffected by the development of a powerful industrial and commercial sector attached to it. In the attempt to
secure both outlets and supplies, stable and reliable in both quantity
and quality, industrialists have been trying to make contracts with
strict technical stipulations for purchases from and deliveries to the
farmer. In this way, they bring about an economic and contractual
linkage between farms and industrial and commercial firms, a process similar to vertical integration in industry. In every advanced
branch of agriculture contracts of this kind are becoming more and
more common, particularly in the United States. Ninety per cent of
poultry farming has been integrated in this sense; vegetable production for canning or deep-freezing is three-quarters or sometimes
fully integrated.

The agricultural worker in these branches has become a factory
outworker, with restricted independence. Since he has to negotiate
with firms virtually single-handed, the ensuing contracts are not
always favourable to his interests. Farmers are now trying to
group themselves together in order to increase their bargaining
power. They are also forming cooperatives in an attempt to acquire
the gains from industrial and commercial transactions, which are
generally more profitable than agriculture. Except in northern
countries, however, agricultural cooperatives have seldom been

able to make very much headway. In any case, the value of the traditional family farm is being called into question by technical and economic development.[2]

The agriculture of tomorrow will be in contact with the outside world, which introduces it to new techniques and ideas, provides new means of production based on a rational division of labour, and buys a larger and larger proportion of its output; it will be fully integrated into the economic system. It will have to specialize, and produce properly processed, standardized goods on a large scale. Industrial methods are already appearing in some branches of agriculture; some farms, for example, have twenty or thirty thousand laying hens or several hundred dairy cows, with automatic feeding methods. Such is the irreversible movement towards the industrialization of agriculture. We must now look at it closely so as to decide what further steps should be taken.

In Western Europe, as a result of thousands of years of peasant atavism, agricultural workers have become attached to their status as private independent workers. This presents many problems, and so does the myth that has grown up around rural life: it holds that the most worthy social values stem from peasant agriculture, that the private, family farm is their most reliable safeguard at the same time as being a solid bastion of free enterprise. In all Western countries, the peasant population has indeed always been valued as a solid electoral counterweight to the urban workers.

As agriculture becomes industrialized, holdings of the traditional size in most places become too limiting. The former agrarian structures are completely unable to meet the demands of machinery, equipment, and mass production. Technical progress in farming advances faster than an organizational structure which depends for most forms of production on the area of land available. The land question places a heavy restriction on agricultural development in most Western countries. The rural exodus, the cause of so many social problems, is too slow for the remaining farm holdings to be able to expand into large modern units or for agricultural workers

[2] The American economist, G. Johnson, also states that 'there are many reasons for wondering whether the family holding can still survive in Western economies in a rapid state of change and modernization.' (International Economic Association Conference, Rome, September, 1965.)

to be assured of an income equal to that of other workers of similar status.

Some areas are of course exceptional – in the United States, for example, or the France of the Paris Basin. In the United States, the peasant has been replaced by the agricultural entrepreneur: he manages big mechanized farms which are well integrated into the modern economy. In France the Nouvelle Entreprise Agricole (NEA) is an example of a dynamic form of modern agricultural capitalism.

Bernard Poulain's NEA[3] is industrialized, well organized into specialist departments, and has close contacts with the outside world to which it can offer large quantities of standardized produce. It attempts to give its employees the status of skilled workers and 'give them both a satisfactory standard of living and a satisfactory way of life'.

But it is the status of the salaried worker, though in fact it has improved, that the young French agricultural workers of the CNJA[4] object to. 'Cooperative agriculture' is their battlecry against the absorption of the peasants into the proletariat.[5] Campaigning for the association of small, unviable farms into units of useful industrial and commercial size, they want to keep overall responsibility within the group. But their movement is making little progress.

On the whole, and in north western Europe in particular, most agricultural units are still too small; this means that workers and capital are not used to maximum advantage, that income among agricultural workers is low, that liaison between production and demand is poor, and that agricultural prices tend to fluctuate and fall. For while production tends to follow a similar path of growth, domestic demand for foodstuffs grows less fast than demand for manufactured goods.

In response to these general patterns, the heritage of our peasant history, governments have intervened in the agricultural economy

---

[3] He gives an account of the theory behind the NEA in no. 166 of *Jeunes Patrons* (June–July, 1963).
[4] Centre National des Jeunes Agriculteurs.
[5] See: Michel Debatisse, *La Révolution silencieuse, le combat des paysans*, ed. Denoël, Paris, 1963.

to prevent decreases in peasant income: in several countries they support and guarantee agricultural prices. Prices then also become what Raymond Barre calls 'political prices', fixed by bitter negotiation between the government and the farmers' unions.

Though useful for stabilizing peasant incomes and the prices of the goods, price supports sometimes have the disadvantage of distracting attention from the real problem – the modernization of the work system and the structural change of agriculture; these are the only measures that can bring about a real improvement in peasant conditions[6] and must be included in any general policy for modernizing agriculture.

3. AGRICULTURE IN NEED OF MARKETS

In spite of numerous hindrances to modernization the productive capacity of Western agriculture has increased appreciably in the last twenty or thirty years in response to price support. In several countries, France among them, it has increased so much that agricultural production can easily exceed national demand.

Here we should distinguish between different countries. Apart from the less industrialized Western countries – Spain, Greece, and Portugal – the others can be divided into three categories.

Some countries have for a long time been specializing in exporting rather elaborate food products, mainly animal, amounting to well over half of their exports. These are, in order of importance, Australia, Argentina, Denmark, and New Zealand (where the sale of agricultural products makes up 96 per cent of exports), Ireland, and Iceland.[7] The Low Countries, even though agricultural products make up less than a third of their exports, should also be included, since, like the other countries, Holland has long-standing markets for specific products in European countries. In the same way, Australia and New Zealand provide the United Kingdom with

[6] Under the stimulus of the CNJA in particular, several years ago the French authorities developed a policy for structural change ('politique des structures') for agriculture, in addition to the price policy ('politique des prix').
[7] In 1963, agricultural produce constituted 98 per cent of Iceland's exports, 93 per cent of Argentina's, 78 per cent of Australia's, 68 per cent of Ireland's, and 58 per cent of Denmark's.

meat, bacon, butter, and various dairy products in which they are highly specialized.

In the eighteenth century and at the beginning of the nineteenth, British agriculture was particularly successful and was taken as a model by French agronomists. But from the mid-nineteenth century, the United Kingdom began to concentrate on industrial and commercial development; she bought a larger proportion of her food materials from the new countries in exchange for manufactured goods, for whose production she was better adapted. Due to the resulting rural exodus, the United Kingdom now has an agricultural population of only 4 per cent of the total, the lowest in the world. After a bold policy of modernization launched by the government during the second world war – when the alternative was destitution – British agriculture now has generally larger and more efficient farms than the continental ones (the average size is 45 hectares as compared with 18 in France). Production is growing steadily. At the present time, however, it only meets about half the national demand,[8] the United Kingdom being as a result the world's largest food importer. Except in wartime, this is by no means a disadvantage to the British economy. It benefits from the attractive prices of foreign suppliers while at the same time assuring for its own agricultural workers more favourable prices and incomes.[9]

Western Germany, the world's third largest food importer, is in a rather similar position. Importing about a third of its food, the Bonn Republic can pay its peasant producers high prices and encourage the expansion of agriculture with no overproduction problems.

The situation is different in a third group of countries, which, like France, have only recently become exporters, or which export simple food products – mainly cereals – that are subject to marketing problems. The most important of these countries are the United States and Canada, the world's biggest and second biggest exporters of agricultural produce respectively; France comes next, having been

[8] Expressed in money terms, this percentage has been rising constantly since the war, as a result of agricultural policy, which, since the years of hardship in the '40s, has been designed to decrease the United Kingdom's dependence on food imports.
[9] By a system of compensatory subsidies (deficiency payments) filling the gap between market prices and the prices guaranteed to farmers.

a little ahead of the Low Countries since 1963. In these countries, and those that join them in increasing numbers every year, the expansion of agriculture has created some awkward problems. Their agricultural production – the overall result of badly coordinated production by hundreds of thousands of more or less independent farmers – is growing faster for some products than national demand.

Since 1945 the value of agricultural production in France has been increasing four times as fast as the population. After allowing for nutritional improvements with the purchase of more expensive products – meat, dairy produce, fruit, and green vegetables – the margin of goods available for export is still increasing all the time. In the United States, where the problem is incomparably greater, stocks of cereal goods have been accumulating from year to year, reaching their maximum of 150 million tons, or about a quarter of the annual total of world production, in 1957.

For though there are hundreds of millions of people in the world who could make use of the developed countries' surplus production, and even though some of them are starving, very few of them have the purchasing power to be able to pay for the goods. Thus the demand for certain food products (wheat and dairy produce) is less than the supply.

Should we not, therefore, as Alfred Sauvy suggests, refer to it as a market deficiency rather than as overproduction?[10]

4. SHOULD PRODUCTION BE REDUCED OR NEW OPENINGS EXPLORED?

All these countries, and the United States in particular, are now facing a serious dilemma: should they reduce their production, adjusting it gradually to domestic or foreign demand, or should they go on increasing it and try to find a different solution to the problem?

Against its traditions of economic liberalism, the United States government has intervened drastically in the agricultural economy.

[10] The situation which has now arisen on an international scale, *mutatis mutandis*, is analogous to the former 'crises' of the capitalist countries. In the same way, the world agricultural economy needs the impetus for a new economic demand from quarters which cannot now afford to pay market prices.

Its policy of intervention, inaugurated in the 1929 crisis to avoid a slump in wheat and cotton prices, has gradually been extended 'to maintain equilibrium between production and consumption'.[11] Various different methods have been used, such as improvements in marketing and purchase and storage of surpluses by a federal office, and also by restrictions on products in excess supply.

During the war the problem was reversed, the same mechanisms being used to stimulate production. Exactly the same difficulties, however, reappeared in the post-war period. In fact, after a brief respite during the Korean war, the American government adopted between 1954 and 1956 a whole series of important measures, one of which has a direct bearing on the Third World countries. This is Public Law 480 (P.L.480) which authorizes the American government either to give American agricultural surpluses to friendly countries where food is in short supply, or to sell them to friendly countries on special terms, for example by barter agreements, sales for local currencies, or by some kind of long-term credit arrangement.

These measures are very important, since the transactions authorized by P.L.480 now amount to almost a third of America's agricultural exports. In 1965, 80 per cent of the wheat exported by the United States was sold on special terms and only 20 per cent at normal prices. The exception becomes the rule. The value of the food products that were given away amounted to $1,500 millions between 1955 and 1963. But 'P.L.480 was designed as a measure to offset the accumulation of surpluses'[12] and in the words of the law 'to make maximum use of surplus commodities in furtherance of the foreign policy of the United States'. The hope was that the countries aided would gradually become ordinary commercial partners. What will happen when the stocks no longer exist? They have been cut down drastically since 1960,[13] under the combined impact of the P.L.480 transactions, of purchases by socialist countries, and also by a measure, passed in 1956, which has had far more effect on the

---

[11] Agricultural Adjustment Act, 1933.
[12] Robert de Wilde, 'L'Agriculture americaine', *La Documentation française*, January 1965.
[13] Only 80 million tons were left at the end of 1965 and the president of the United States wants to keep a strategic stock-pile of at least 50 million tons.

American agricultural economy than P.L.480. This was the establishment of the Soil Bank.

This measure was designed to reduce excess production. The farmer agrees to a long-term contract undertaking not to produce on land which is put into reserve. The land must be maintained or afforested in exchange for a subsidy. In return for the undertaking, the farmer receives money compensation for his loss of earnings. In other words the Soil Bank finances non-production. Its influence has been considerable, since it has taken over about 12 million hectares, which is equal to a third of the area of cultivated land in France.

Government bodies thus find themselves in a vicious circle. The policy of price support for important products, originally enforced to increase agricultural revenues, often turns out to encourage the production of those crops, namely cereals, for which profitable demand is growing at the slowest rate.[14] Because of their price level it is difficult to sell them abroad and this creates new problems.

Some new direction must be found for national agricultural policies.

[14] Though at the present time these crops are the most useful as a means of combating hunger.

CHAPTER SIX

New directions for Western agriculture

I. SOME PARADOXES OF THE WORLD AGRICULTURAL ECONOMY

It is paradoxical that some people in the world are living at starvation level while others, at a distance of only a few hours' flying time, do not know what to do with their food glut. There is something contradictory in the juxtaposition of costly Malthusian measures to reduce the quantity of surplus produce in some countries with desperate attempts to increase production in others.

But this is not all. By stimulating the production of basic foodstuffs, policies of price support encourage higher and higher production in excess of national demand, as with corn and dairy produce in France and the Common Market countries. These surpluses must be sold in some way or other; but as the Western exporting countries are in competition for world markets of temperate produce, the richer importing countries, mainly Western countries of which the United Kingdom and Federal Germany are the most important, take control of the market.[1]

As a result of competition between exporters, and since the markets concerned are usually residual, dealing with surpluses which vary from year to year, the products are sold at bargain prices bearing no relation to production costs and usually far lower than the prices guaranteed to the producers. In order to dispose of these products governments are therefore forced to subsidize their export.[2]

Another important paradox of international agricultural trade

[1] Inadequate transport is another factor checking the expansion of the corn trade, especially with the Socialist countries.
[2] Thus a kilo of butter bought by 'Interlait', the public authority in charge of the dairy industry, for 8 francs is sold on the English market for 5 francs.

follows from this. The overproducing countries subsidize the economy of the importing countries. The American and French governments help the British and German governments[3] by this simple transfer to keep prices low for their consumers and high for their farmers: this puts the United Kingdom and Germany in a better position as regards industrial competition. These invisible financial transfers involve large sums of money.[4]

This brings us to a third paradox: food production in the overproducing Western countries is determined more by the subsidies to producers than by the actual utility of the products themselves as reflected in production costs or in consumer demand. Thus, in France, for example, with support prices for corn, a farmer with a well located and well equipped farm can make a profit from growing corn, though it is exported at a loss, even though there is a national shortage of beef.

It seems equally paradoxical that national agricultural policies should be so carefully planned, while the international agricultural economy is so incoherent. And so far we are only touching on the contradictions in the marketing of produce from temperate climates. As we shall see, they are no fewer in the case of products from tropical countries (see Part IV). A general reorganization seems to be needed.

2. A PRODUCTION POTENTIAL AVAILABLE ON DEMAND

There are many reasons why the already large productive capacities of Western agricultural systems will go on developing even further. For one thing, the dissemination of more efficient techniques and organizational systems contains a great deal of scope for progress. For another, more progress can be expected from research now under way.

Thus, in France, for example, much agricultural land is still underexploited – such as around 13 million hectares of wild grassland. If land holdings were regrouped and drained where necessary,

[3] And the governments of the USSR and China.
[4] For example, they cost the French economy about 1,000 million francs per year before European control and, according to some estimates, probably brought about 3,000 million into the United Kingdom.

about 6 million hectares could probably be ploughed. If only half of this land were sown with cultivated fodder crops, it would almost double the existing fodder production from ploughed fields. The yield per hectare could thus be vastly increased. The extra fodder production could provide 90 million hectolitres of milk at the rate of 60 hectolitres of milk per hectare. If the remaining land was ploughed and used for corn-growing, producing 4 tons per hectare, an extra 12 million tons would be produced.

What is true of France is even more true of the United States, where production could be increased significantly simply by removing restrictions; the same is true of Canada and many other countries where there is still a margin for increased productivity.

But apart from methods which are now classic, though not yet generally practised, new possibilities of progress for the medium- and long-term are appearing from a more widespread use of sophisticated techniques and organizational systems; in other words, from the industrialization of agriculture.

As we have seen, poultry farming and pig farming are particularly far advanced. As a result of long and careful selective breeding and cross-breeding, the biological species now being used are of a uniformly high productive capacity. Methods of health protection are also widely used and mass treatments for the prevention of disease can be practised. Nutrition has been carefully analysed and low-cost, balanced food rations can now be produced for mass automatic distribution. Finally, environmental needs have been specially studied so that large herds of animals can be sheltered cheaply with the correct conditions for hygiene, ventilation, and heating.

These measures have made it possible to set up pig and poultry farms which, like a modern industry, can produce and deliver standard products in response to demand. But, like industry, they need high investment and a sophisticated technology. This is a constraint as well as the key to the expansion of these forms of production; they are called landless products because they do not require – directly at any rate[5] – a large area of land. The quantity of land

[5] In fact these forms of production do still depend on land, on account of the bias in favour of animal food consisting mainly of cereal. But these types of food are bought outside the farm to an increasing extent. Thus, one of the connecting links between

available does not control their development, as it does vegetable production. The extension of these new forms of production is, therefore, directly dependent on the markets open to them. If the markets seem economically profitable, there is no doubt that capital and technical skill will be invested in them.

What is true for pigs and poultry is beginning to be true for beef cattle and dairy cows. After the 'egg factory' and the 'meat factory', the 'milk factory' is appearing. It consists of several hundred dairy cows, biologically uniform, tended, fed and treated by mass production techniques. The staff can work in shifts, as in a factory, and the cowman is released from the daily slavery of work that begins early in the morning, ends late at night and does not stop on Sundays.

In plant production the most important sector is undoubtedly greenhouse production, which provides the only way of controlling environmental factors, including the carbon dioxide content in the atmosphere. A particular feature of Western agriculture is the development of greenhouses and their extension from the north, where Holland was the first country to use them, to the south.

Autonomous units specializing in the production of eggs, meat, or milk, and similar units for vegetable production, are gradually becoming the basic agricultural units, and agriculture should now be organized around them. Not only the size but also the organization of agricultural production will, therefore, have to be reconsidered.

Will the agricultural concern of the future consist of one highly specialized unit or of a coordinated series of highly specialized units or 'factories'? In either form will it be integrated with para-agricultural industrial firms where capacity for change and investment potential are usually very much higher than for agricultural concerns, even in a cooperative system?

If the age of the peasant is in any case over, the organizational status of the agricultural concern, either neo-capitalist or communal, though decided largely by farmers and their unions, will be

---

agriculture and stock-breeding is disappearing from the farm and coming into the area of relations between different farms and between farming and 'para-agricultural' industry. This is another example of the trend towards a growing division of labour.

equally dependent on government policy, on the incentives it is prepared to give, and on the specific objectives it sets up in its policies related to structural organization. In a free enterprise economy, competition between the two types is not equal.

On the economic level, the industrialized concern must be ready to make innovations. New ideas will be emerging all the time and the concern will constantly need to adjust to them. At the present stage of agronomic research, various important innovations may soon be made, such as artificially induced twin births, and increased yield from photosynthesis, which would be a revolutionary breakthrough.

The more industrialized any branch of agricultural production becomes, and the less dependent it is on the endless number of biological and climatic constraints, the more does it become concentrated into a smaller number of units, well-integrated into the modern supply and distribution networks, and the faster can technical progress spread. In these conditions the potential growth rate can rise, so long as markets develop.

How will Western agriculture develop? As it becomes better equipped and more modern, will it aim, as it will more easily be able to, at a moderate expansion rate, at stabilizing its output, or at a major increase in production?

3. CONVERTING THE NEEDS OF THE THIRD WORLD INTO PROFITABLE MARKETS

As we have seen, the Western countries at present only give food to the Third World when it is surplus and cannot be sold on the international market. Now that economic demand is increasing as a result of purchases by socialist countries,[6] and with policies for the control of production being introduced at the same time, this source of supply may dry up within the next few years.

Will world market trends then be completely reversed? Will the 'buyers' market' become a 'sellers' market', with prices rising to a prohibitive level? At the same time, will the last of the paradoxes given above be eliminated: namely, will the agricultural disputes

[6] In June 1966 the Soviet Union and Canada concluded the biggest contract for corn ever signed, for 9.1 million tons in three years.

between the United Kingdom and the Common Market countries finally be settled, with the United Kingdom having to pay higher prices for her food? In some quarters in Britain there is already some alarm about this trend, which may jeopardize food aid of the American P.L.480 type.

The problem must be posed clearly before it is too late: even if economic demand seems likely to increase, should we let it become the sole factor determining agricultural production in the West? Or should we try to find some other criterion? The United States government seemed to be becoming aware of the problem, since it authorized a 15 per cent increase in crops for 1966–67. Does this mean that it will in the future review its agricultural policy in the context of its aid policy?

In Part V we shall discuss why we judge it essential for world society to convert the most urgent human requirements into economic demand and for all countries to make a concerted effort to set the Third World on the way to accelerated economic growth.

Within this general picture, agricultural interests in Western countries can be identified with those of the peasantry in Africa, Asia, and Latin America. Western agricultural opinion is beginning to realize this: one of the big American farmers' unions[7] voted in favour of P.L.480 and the 1966 Congress of the Fédération française des syndicats d'agriculteurs gave its executive a mandate to take action to 'end the anarchy of world agricultural markets, energetically confronting the problem of world hunger.'[8]

A scheme of this kind is only viable when backed by a world food programme[9] with a large permanent supply of money at its disposal, managed, perhaps, by a world 'office of food economy'.[10] This office should make contracts with the 'overproducing' Western countries, either for the medium or long term, depending on the

[7] The American Farm Bureau Federation (see R. de Wilde, *op. cit.*).
[8] At the Congress of May 17 and 18, 1966, M. Lequertier, director general of the Union nationale des coopératives agricoles de céréales, also made some interesting suggestions for world food cooperation.
[9] Proposed by UNO in 1960, set up by the FAO in 1963, for an experimental period of three years, the existing World Food Programme controls an international fund worth about 100 million dollars, collected from 70 countries, mainly in kind. The materials it distributes are used either as aid, or for programmes for feeding school children, or to finance development projects. See Chapter XII.
[10] Which could be part of a world organization for economic cooperation (Chapter XIII).

product; an international organization would guarantee the contract with a mutual assurance fund; the prices stated in the contract would be established on a logical economic basis to provide genuine guidelines. This means that they would be close to the normal costs of production in the worst-placed regions necessary for the programme, and would take full account of the respective utility of the different products for consumers. The prices would, of course, have to be revised periodically by an impartial commission, made up of representatives from both buying and selling countries and of international arbitrators.

The programme would include cereals, which are easy to produce, transport, and storage; grain; vegetables (beans, soya beans, etc.); and also the three major protein concentrates, powdered milk, fish flour, and yeasts.

Is there any other way of eliminating our first two paradoxes, and at the same time of initiating or accelerating development? Some of the Socialist countries may gradually be able to join in the programme, but, as we shall see, most of them have not yet solved their own agricultural difficulties and food problems.

PART THREE Agricultural Problems in the
Socialist Bloc

CHAPTER SEVEN

The peasantry of Eastern Europe

I. FROM SOCIALISM TO STALINISM

The developed capitalist countries have the largest agricultural surpluses both at the present time and potentially. As we have already seen, if the gap between food and population growth rates goes on widening, the surpluses will not be sufficiently large to make up the deficit in the Third World. The Socialist bloc, particularly China since 1960 and Russia since 1963, is beginning to import large quantities of cereals. In a world-wide perspective, the future of the agriculture and food situation of over one thousand million people must not be overlooked – all the more so because the communists claim that their pattern for development is better than any other and they believe that only they are moving in the 'direction of history'. From a brief summary of the past, we shall attempt to discover whether this claim has any basis in fact.

The political theory of Socialism was developed in the nineteenth century in an urban environment. It launched its main protest against the injustices done to the urban proletariat, who alone paid the heavy price of industrial development, the profits of which, in the early stages, went to other sections of the community. The Socialists did not, and still do not, regard the peasants as members of the proletariat, on the grounds that they themselves are the owners of their means of production – an absurd criterion considering how small or negligible their means of production are. They are not, therefore, regarded as true revolutionaries: only the working class is fit to lead the Revolution. Lenin said that the working class should entrust the leadership to its *avant-garde*, the Party. Despite the vital part the Russian peasants played in the 1905 Revolution, they were only admitted into the party after 1917 as temporary allies, treated as politically inferior, and always suspected of sympathetic reaction towards capitalism.

In 1917, however, the majority of the soldiers who refused to go on fighting, and who thus ensured the triumph of the Bolsheviks, were peasants. They were not granted ownership of land, which was nationalized as soon as the Socialist state was set up.

During the Civil War of 1919–22, due to problems over the supply of food to the army, to the government's decision to pay for agricultural produce with devalued currency, and to the complete lack of industrial goods, the markets were empty. As a result the country was overrun by requisition parties of town workers. This outraged the peasants, who often lost all their reserve stocks and seed, and brought the nation close to famine.

Lenin's N.E.P.[1] revived the countryside, not only by authorizing the most enterprising people to become tenant farmers (possession being granted to each one of them) and to hire workers, but also by restoring the free market. Production increased fast enough to surpass the pre-war level; but consumption in the countryside itself increased even more rapidly, leaving insufficient supplies for the towns, for the army, and for export.

Today, Marxist Socialism is still suffering from the fact that it first appeared in a comparatively backward, autocratic country, surrounded by more developed, hostile countries with the power to destroy it. The threat of Hitlerism forced the Russians to accelerate heavy industry, which requires huge investment, and in the absence of a bourgeois class or access to foreign credit, where could the investments be found but in the rural areas? This explains (but does not justify) Stalin's collectivization policy of 1929. Marxist theory only recommends the collectivization of large holdings where the state could take over from the capitalist limited liability companies. At that time capitalism no longer existed in the Soviet countryside (it is doubtful whether it ever did, since the system was more feudal than capitalist) and in these conditions, collectivization amounted to projecting an analysis of an industrial society on to a peasant environment that had never gone beyond the traditional stage. In

[1] The 'New Economic Policy', which was more liberal.

Marxist terms, it was an attempt to transform the relations of production artificially, but it went much too far.

The landowners had been dispossessed by the nationalization of 1917: this measure was socially justifiable in the case of those parasitic landowners, living off ground-rents, who still regretted the emancipation of the serfs. But if the few well cultivated large estates had been turned into state farms instead of being pillaged by the peasants, they could have served as models for modern techniques. The collectivization of 1929–33, ordering communal cultivation of the fields by producer cooperatives (kolkhoz) was aimed against the rich peasants or 'kulaks'. Some of the kulaks had exploited their poorer colleagues by moneylending or by the terms on which they hired out their horses; or else they underpaid their labourers. But most of them had grown rich on the strength of their knowledge and their ability to organize their production efficiently, as has since been acknowledged in Poland and Hungary.

In the second Civil War of 1929–33, a large proportion of the moderately and even the badly off peasants who still retained individualist tendencies joined the kulaks in their opposition to Soviet power. This aggravated a second famine and caused about half the country's livestock to be slaughtered; at the time of our visit to Russia in the autumn of 1962, the shock caused by this brutal measure still lingered on in the memory of the old kolkhoz members and it is one factor hindering the recovery of agricultural production.

Collectivization was a political measure, guided by theory and dogma; it was also designed to increase governmental and economic control over the peasantry. In the absence of modern means of production, the policy was premature from a technical point of view. Tractors from Stalingrad were produced so slowly that it was quite impossible to allocate one to each of the 25 million peasant holdings (six times as many as there are in the United States in the present day). The cooperative use of communal equipment would have been more appropriate to the modern situation.

Construction costs for the collective stables were too high and the private cowsheds were anyway perfectly adequate. The construction of collective stables achieved virtually nothing and had the unfortunate effect of heterogeneous species of cattle being herded together as well as being taken away from their pasture land. These disadvantages were so obvious that a compromise was reached in 1935 by which most of the remaining livestock was left in peasant ownership; and permission was granted for private landholding on a sufficiently large scale to supply much of the country's animal and horticultural produce. The collective farms paid very badly, but did provide fodder for the privately owned livestock. In the general conditions of scarcity – which are still not over – the high, free-market prices favoured the peasants living near urban centres.

After the War and the destruction which came with it, a period of rapid reconstruction began. It was not followed by an agricultural revival. The prices of forced deliveries were sometimes fixed at such a low level that for potatoes, for instance, they did not always cover the expenses of transport to the official depots. Rigid restraints of this kind must always be accompanied by a burdensome mechanism for control and repression; everything must be regulated from above. The far-distant central authority was very badly informed as to the real situation. For example, it was not until after there had been five virtually non-existent cotton harvests, between 1949 and 1953, that the uselessness of growing cotton in the Ukraine or on the Hungarian plain was realized.

2. RECOVERY UNDER KHRUSHCHEV

In September 1953, after the Russian Revolution had been congratulating itself for a third of a century on its success in spite of the mediocrity of its results, Nikita Khrushchev made an epoch-making speech; for the first time in public he emphasized the difficult situation of Soviet agriculture: 'Stock-breeding in Siberia produces less now than it did in 1913'. During the secret struggle for succession after Stalin's death the Party had to relax its control over the collective farms. The policy of destalinization was inaugurated in March 1956, with far-reaching measures of liberalization.

As compulsory deliveries were reduced and then discontinued, and as prices for agricultural produce rose, collective farmwork appeared more attractive. The State could then confine itself to fixing how much essential material it should provide, without intervening in the detail of crop-sowing. The general assembly of each producer cooperative could take a real part in choosing its president and could dismiss the less efficient of the Party appointees. The suppression of the machine and tractor depots[2] increased the autonomy of the co-operatives and re-established the unity of work organization. The right to private holdings and stock was reinstated after having been largely curtailed in the last years of Stalinism.

The peasants began to take more interest in their work and were allowed a little more initiative and autonomy in the collectives: the period between 1953 and 1958 was consequently the time of the most rapid expansion of Soviet agricultural production: a 50 per cent increase in five years. Of course 1958 was a good year climatically, and initially the 42 million hectares of new land, with its fertile leafmould soil, provided an abundant harvest. The increase, however, particularly of animal, horticultural, and industrial produce, would never have been so great without the political factors just mentioned.

A rapid reversal came in 1958–66, and expansion halted abruptly. The harvests of 1963 and 1965 were certainly affected by cold and drought, but near stagnation in a sixth of the world, over a period of at least eight years, cannot be explained by climatic hazards. The Party, back in firm control in 1957, was again issuing absolute commands. The 'campaigns' or orders for agricultural progress, were far too generalized for such a vast country, and often put too much emphasis on one single problem, which, though relevant in some places, was inevitably of secondary importance for much of the country. For instance, Khrushchev ordered maize to be planted too far to the north; and fields to be ploughed before being treated with fertilizers, a mistake if farming is to become more intensive. The three fodder crops (peas, maize, and beet), which he ordered to be planted everywhere from the Baltic to Central Asia, were not successful in all localities. Private holdings and private ownership of livestock were again politically suspect and restricted until the political downfall of Mr Khrushchev.

Khrushchev's successors made a new experiment in liberalization,

---

[2] Which managed the heavy machinery, collected the produce, controlled political action, and kept the peasants under the control of the state.

this time extending it to the whole economy. The rights to private stock farming and land holdings were again reinstated. The State increased its agricultural investments, whereas it had previously left up to 85 per cent to the kolkhoz.[3] Rejected in their entirety by Bukharin in 1920, the traditional economic laws of the market, which can still be valid in a socialist régime, are being rediscovered one at a time in the USSR; although, clearly, they can have a retarding impact, to ignore them altogether would have a disastrous effect, which would become worse the more developed the economy.

The rate of return on capital investment is generally a better index of efficiency than the quantitative fulfilment of production targets, since quantity is sometimes obtained at the expense of quality. Russian paper mills concentrated on producing thick paper so as to make up their quota, whereas in use surface quality is more important. Profit cannot play a proper role until prices, hitherto fixed arbitrarily, are brought nearer to production costs, and until normal interest rates are paid on state investments. Interest rates could be partly fixed, favouring certain kinds of production, and partly, as happens in Yugoslavia, settled by a sort of competition for money between different forms of production.

Ground-rent, payable to the State, must be reintroduced; valid economic calculations cannot be made without it, otherwise rich areas or areas near towns are always given an unfair advantage. In the Soviet system taxes are dependent on production and this discourages intensive farming, whereas a fixed tax per hectare would encourage it. The commissions for improving economic mechanisms set up in the People's Democracies will rediscover the economic laws necessary for socialist régimes faster than the Soviet Union; it is more difficult for this gigantic state to abandon its dogmatic principles. Its government is still unwilling to face the consequences of thoroughgoing destalinization because its position as a world power and as an ideological leader imposes some inflexibility.

The Soviet agricultural labour force will certainly continue production on the incentives given to it in the Khrushchev period. But

[3] Since the time of writing, I have heard that my study *Sovkhoz, Kolkhoz ou le problématique communisme* has been translated into Russian; about two thousand copies were printed and distributed to all specialists. But the average collective farm worker is not allowed to read the criticisms: simple faith must be protected.

progress is still being held back because enterprises are too concentrated, decisions are taken by a centralized bureaucracy, and individual initiative is discouraged.[4] The peasant will work harder the less he feels despised, the more he is allowed his dignity and freedom of thought as a human being and as a producer participating in the organization of his work, and the more he is granted respect and the freedom to use his initiative in projects with an increasing measure of autonomy. The broad outlines of a modified form of planning can be maintained at the same time.

3. THE EFFECT OF STALIN'S FOREIGN POLICY[5]

Soviet authoritarianism can be explained partly as a defensive response to attacks by the Allies in their attempts to isolate the régime in 1918–21 and partly by the need to suppress internal revolts such as Makhno and Kronstadt. Subsequently, the Soviet Union won strategic footholds throughout Eastern Europe from Poland to Bulgaria (1944–45), and the Party everywhere assumed absolute power which, by early 1948, reached as far as Prague.

Stalinism was bitterly resented as a foreign dictatorship, particularly in Rumania where there is a proverb, 'All things Russian are swinish'. It was more acceptable in Bulgaria, which has a tradition of friendship with Russia, and where there was already an active peasant cooperative movement.

By the agricultural reform of 1945, East European territories belonging to Germans, to collaborators and to the owners of *latifundia*[6] were shared out. If the owner remained, he was never left with more than 57 hectares; though in Hungary this was often 50 and sometimes only 20, and in Bulgaria and Yugoslavia it was 35.

[4] *Results in 1965*

	Forecasts in the Seven Year Plan for 1965	Actual Production in 1965
Cereals (Millions of Tons)	164 to 180	120.5
Milk (Millions of Tons)	100 to 105	72.4
Meat (Millions of Tons)	at least 16	9.6
Eggs (Millions)	37,000	29,000

[5] See in particular R. Dumont's historical works: *Economie agricole dans le monde*, 1953, chaps. XIV to XVI (East Germany, Hungary, Czechoslovakia); *Révolution dans les campagnes chinoises*, 1957, chap. XV (Rumania); *Terres vivantes*, 1961, chaps. XIV and XV (Rumania and Poland) – translated as *Lands Alive*, The Merlin Press, London, 1965 and The Monthly Review Press, New York, 1966.
[6] Large under-used estates.

The desire for property was so deeply rooted in the peasants and agricultural workers benefiting from the redistribution, that production was quickly resumed; the only exceptions were the large estates, which had been very well cultivated, like Esterhazy in Hungary. The resumption of production was also helped by the network of former cooperative systems, though their directors were dismissed unless they were absolutely submissive. Poland had given up rationing in 1949, before France, though the food situation was far worse there. Hungary did not give up rationing for several more years and Czechoslovakia took even longer.

To begin with, after the war, when sharing out the land, the Communist Party managers in most of these countries promised the peasants ownership 'in perpetuity'. Party students who explained to their countrymen how the Soviet kolkhoz worked were expelled from the Agronomic University of Budapest in 1947. I have discovered that there were three small, semi-clandestine agricultural cooperatives in Hungary in March 1948.

In June 1948 there was a sudden, complete reversal. The congress of the 'Cominform' of the USSR criticized Eastern Europe, Yugoslavia in particular (Tito was not amenable to Stalin's orders), for 'avoiding the problems of the class struggle and of the restriction of capitalist elements in the countryside'. This criticism would have been more valid if it had been concentrated on the other People's Democracies, since Yugoslavia (with Bulgaria) was then the furthest advanced along the road to collectivization. But generally the system of individual agriculture in the people's democracies was no more than a façade. Using the Cominform as a cover, Stalin was intent on rapid collectivization.

In a speech at Kecskemet on August 20, 1948, the Hungarian dictator Rákosi, a former exile in Russia, took up the Stalinist line: 'The old-fashioned system of individual agriculture is based on the principle of the survival of the fittest; the "kulaks" are destroying the working peasantry . . . which has chosen the road to co-operation . . .' In fact, most of the peasants were extremely reluctant to make this choice and had to be encouraged by economic and political pressure. Well-off and even moderately well-off peasants were taxed so heavily by means of duties and compulsory deliveries at steeply graduated rates that many of them were forced to join cooperatives. In 1952, some of the Hungarian kulaks had their farms, houses, livestock, and equipment confiscated and cooperatives of non-landowning workers were set up in their place.

The vast majority of the Eastern European peasantry responded with passive resistance. In Hungary alone, more than 100,000 hectares of agricultural land were still lying fallow in 1952. That year the index of vegetable production in Hungary fell to 87, compared with 143 and 135 for 1951 and 1953 (100 in 1949); this cannot be entirely attributed to drought. Imre Nagy – whose tragic end in 1956 made him world-famous – was brought to power in June, 1953 to deal with this serious situation. On July 4, 1953 he announced: 'The rapid development of heavy industry has been holding back the development of agriculture ... our peasants have been justifiably outraged by oppression and numerous abuses ... in violation of the principle of free consent. The government will give workers permission to leave their cooperatives; these will even be dissolved if the majority so chooses'.

Soon afterwards Rákosi, who had stayed in power with Nagy, gave a cunning interpretation of this speech – claiming that it had been misunderstood and thereby intimidating all those who had been preparing to leave the kolkhoz. Back in power after the fall of Nagy, he renewed administrative, police and economic pressures for compulsory collectivization. Then came the revolution of October, 1956, which although launched by young people, students, and writers, was welcomed by a large number of peasants.

In July, 1956, I found the peasantry of Rumania resisting collectivization inch by inch. Shortly after coming to power in October, 1956, Gomulka emphasized that in the Stalinist Era, then drawing to a close, the value of production per acre of farmland in Poland was 622 zlotys[7] for private farms, 517 in cooperatives, and 394 in state farms – in exactly inverse proportion to the aid granted by the state. Finally breaking Stalin's rule of silence, he dared to announce: 'The destruction of a large number of agricultural holdings, classed as "kulak", constitutes a special page in the catastrophe of the ill-considered agricultural policy of the period which has just ended'.

[7] At that time the zloty was worth 21 francs at the official rate.

Stalin died in March, 1953 and was denounced three years later at the 20th Congress of the Communist Party of the USSR. He was also challenged in Eastern Europe, where his policy of giving priority to heavy industry in small countries with insufficient coal and mineral resources had proved disastrous for the economy as a whole and for agriculture in particular.

Compulsory collectivization before modern means of production were available did not allow for the fact that the peasant, once enrolled, regarded himself as a factory-worker; he wanted to work only eight hours a day, instead of the twelve he had given to his own land. Once the supreme wisdom of Stalin had been denounced, the roads to socialism could diverge; this allowed for competition, a necessary condition of progress. With the failure of the Soviet system, a certain amount of decollectivization became necessary, as much on the economic level as on the psychological.

4. THE POLISH ROAD

In Poland the peasants were really free to leave the cooperatives, as is proved by the fact that many were almost abandoned and they now cover less than 1 per cent of agricultural land. State farms account for 13 per cent of it, but unlike Yugoslavia their yields are not really different from those of other kinds of farms. Agricultural progress is now sought in a system of individual peasant holdings, inside a state which is still staunchly socialist.

Of course, the liberal spirit of October, 1956, which rallied the entire nation behind Gomulka for several months, soon diminished. But compulsory collectivization is no longer considered, even for the distant future. The kulak, once an outcast, is now the object of public congratulation and is praised as being a model farmer.

This preservation of the small holdings can certainly be justified for a time by the extremely slow decrease of the agricultural population (39 per cent of the total population in 1962 compared with 60 per cent of the total population in 1938 and 55 per cent in 1955). Rural employment should not be decreased too fast, when there are only 3 hectares of farm land per worker. Mechanization brings a large increase in productivity per hour of work, but little increase per hectare; here the limiting factor on output is the land rather than man. Mechanization can, therefore, considerably reduce employment in these circumstances.

The policy of giving absolute priority to mechanization, though justifiable in the depopulated virgin lands north of Kazakhstan, was debatable even for the overpopulated rural areas of the USSR and the valleys of the Caucasus or Moldavia. We saw in 1956 that the use of tractors in the Transylvanian kolkhoz reduced the average rate of employment on collectives to less than 100 days per year. In the overpopulated south-east of Poland, absolute priority should have been given not to mechanization but to other ways of intensifying agriculture; increasing the yield per acre but not reducing employment too rapidly.

In Eastern Europe, as in the USSR, great efforts are now being made to increase the production of fodder crops; plans forecast that they would double in five years. (However, the effects of the principle of giving priority to mechanization still linger on.) In Hungary an 18-year-old tractor driver earns almost double the starting salary of a 23-year-old agronomist. In Poland the State still levies compulsory deliveries at reduced prices, but then refunds the profit from this supplementary tax to the village from which it was exacted, on condition that an agricultural society is set up, that subscriptions go partly towards working capital, and that the society devotes three-quarters of the money it has raised to the purchase of tractors and agricultural machinery. This method of compulsory collective accumulation, directed by the State, albeit in the framework of a peasant economy, would seem much more attractive if the societies were allowed to make their investments themselves; for instance, if they could give priority to plantations, greenhouses, sprinklers, silos, service roads, or processing buildings.

The State has other means of action at its disposal, since it is in charge of most land improvements and of electrification. While industry received instructions from the plan, individualist agriculture is controlled through the medium of prices, to which the peasants have been very responsive. The State processing factory makes contracts with the production groups, a kind of contractual vertical integration. Thus, industry advances the means of production (seed, fertilizers), and gives the peasants credit for investment; the societies provide the machines and other collective fixed capital; and the peasant's contributions are the land and buildings, which he still owns, and, of course, his work.

Some of the peasants are, of course, still underemployed or underproductive because their farms are too small, particularly since, for some inexplicable reason, amalgamation is making little headway; this reduces the productivity of the tractors. Development towards large holdings has thus been sidestepped for the time being; the farm buildings under construction are too small and will soon be outdated by the requirements of modern industrialized agriculture.

For modernization, investments must be large and must, therefore, be made economically; first of all the superfluous labour force must be redeployed; and the peasants must then be convinced of the advantages of a good collective system. This will be difficult on account of the lasting shock caused by Stalinist collectivization. After a period of rapid increase of almost 4 per cent per year, from 1956 to 1960, the growth of Polish agricultural production is already falling off: it grew only 14 per cent in the five years from 1961 to 1965, in spite of increased investment.

In a description of Stalinism and the present trends Claude Roy wrote: 'Deterioration in strength and energy, waste, slow communications, abuses of authority and "couldn't care less" attitudes are the characteristics of regimented and Socialist countries. But Poland is honestly and sometimes effectively trying to break away from this pattern without abandoning the social justice which is true Socialism. Liberty has been a good investment in the agricultural sector'.[8]

5. THE YUGOSLAV ROAD

In an attempt to prove to Stalin that the Yugoslavs were still *avant-garde* communists in spite of their 'excommunication' in June, 1948, the government accelerated compulsory collectivization later the same year. In 1951 the country was on the verge of famine, which was only warded off by American aid. By 1953 anyone who wished to go was free to leave the peasant work cooperatives, whose num-

[8] 'La Pologne sans lunettes roses', *Le Nouvel Observateur*, December 8th, 1965.

bers have been gradually declining (though more slowly than in Poland) and have now almost disappeared. More recently, the State has been concentrating the vast majority of its investment on the Socialist sector, consisting of 300 combines and self-managed agricultural units, former state farms. Some of these units are very large, over 20,000 hectares; many are connected to processing factories. With 15 per cent of the agricultural land, this sector provides almost 40 per cent of Yugoslav agricultural production, and twice as much of the commercial corn crop. By the time this sector grows to 3 million hectares, 30 per cent of the agricultural land, it will be able to feed the non-agricultural population and make a large contribution to the export market. These combines work the country's most fertile land, particularly the chernozem soils north of Belgrade. This sector is expanding slowly, purchasing land at low prices, often between 4 and 40 dollars per hectare, a price which bears no relation to its intrinsic value as a means of production. Production has been increased rapidly by widespread use of Italian types of corn, hybrid maize, fertilizer, by an advanced technology and large scale investment. It is undeniably better than in the Soviet or Polish kolkhoz. However, a large number of state farms incur a loss, which can be partly explained by the faulty price mechanism that has for a long time given preference to industry at the expense of agriculture.

Harvests in Yugoslavia between 1961 and 1965 were 50 per cent greater than they had been ten years earlier, between 1951 and 1955. As in Poland after 1956 and in the USSR, rapid growth can most easily be obtained by correcting a previous, bad agricultural policy. The average harvest for 1963–4 was only 3 per cent above the 1959–60 average. The rise in production was greater than in Poland but it is levelling off more quickly.

Though climate may be one determining factor, insufficient attention to the peasant's interests is no less decisive. Since 1957 they have been able to obtain credit if they make production contracts; however, these loans are still only 3 per cent of the total expenditure on agriculture though the peasants still cultivate most of the land. The motive behind this approach is mainly political: the government wants to increase production without compulsory collectivization. The mere prospect of collectivization can still cause panic.

In September, 1963, Danilo Dolci questioned some peasants[9] near Belgrade about their attitude to collectivization. He obtained some interesting answers: 'We would rather work on our own and sell our goods on our own. . . . In cooperatives, some people work, but others are idle. I have to work there every day when they want me to. On my own farm, I work when I want to. . . . This policy frightens me; we are poor, and I do not want to go to prison for this. . . . We are afraid to give the land to the cooperative, because we are afraid of dying of hunger'. In such a poor country, this last fear is no metaphor: it evokes vivid memories.

There is also an economic reason: investments give better returns if made in fertile lands, managed by good technicians, than they would in the peasant areas in the mountains of Bosnia and Montenegro, where the economy is still at subsistence level. However, after studying Dalmatia in October, 1965, I concluded that different policies are required for at least two completely separate peasant sectors. The subsistence farms in the mountains are best left alone; their economic possibilities are practically non-existent and the young people are leaving all the time, sometimes to go abroad. By contrast there are fertile plains in the interior of the Karstio mountains: some have been irrigated and are used for growing early vegetables (Gruda), others for vines (Potonaje, Gindac wine), which produce a good income for the peasants.

But, unlike Poland, the proportion of income invested either in service and processing cooperatives or in the farm holdings seemed quite inadequate. The small number of new orchards and vineyards are more than offset by fallow lands and abandoned olive-groves. This presents a sharp contrast to the major developments in the great Hungarian plain, particularly as the traditional method of spacing, which is unsuitable for machinery, has been used in the new plantations. In Hungary the vineyards have been planted with spaces between the rows wide enough for tractors to be used.[10]

---

[9] *Enquetes sur un monde nouveau*, Maspero, 1965. 'At last they dare tell a foreigner that they are frightened'.
[10] The usual kind of agricultural cooperative, however, of the necessary stages of commercialization is a new form of peasant structure, which could usefully be studied by the backward countries. For there is no reason for them to adopt the Soviet model.

As for the cooperatives, the sums raised by subscriptions from agricultural workers is negligible – about 25 US cents per head. The local collective provides the vast majority of the capital. The average peasant wage is much higher than that of the agronomic adviser, who only earns 60,000 dinars (42 US dollars) per month. In the producers' council, representation is proportional to total net revenue, which tends to under-represent the peasant – another form of anti-rural discrimination. Incomes, instead of being invested, were spent on improving rural housing and buying motor bicycles and even cars. Lack of confidence in the future is the main factor hindering peasant investment. Unlike Polish peasants, the Yugoslavs do not seem to be sure of keeping their land, and many say they are not satisfied with their cooperatives. But these are mainly the effects of underdevelopment: any final judgment on the system, such as the hasty, dogmatic statements of the Chinese, are presumptuous at this stage.

Furthermore, with the rapid rural exodus,[11] and some degree of modernization, the limit of 10 hectares set for individual holdings is out of date, especially in the case of dry, infertile land.[12] Yugoslavia must be commended for achieving a measure of workers' control; but in the workers' councils, the political members often have the last word, and treat Party directives as more important than technical advice.

How far will the political climate allow workers' control[13] to spread? The economic reform of 1965 brought prices closer to production costs and emphasized the autonomy of the holdings, by reducing the subsidies which had been financed by inflation. Subsidies will be replaced both by loans, granted according to the economic viability of a project and its impact on the foreign exchange position, and also by self-financing. However, in Socialist régimes

[11] Seventy-six per cent were agricultural workers in 1939; 49 per cent in 1962, producing 30 per cent of the national income.
[12] Ten hectares of modern heated greenhouses costing over 2 million US dollars constitute a capitalist enterprise. As environment becomes artificial, the notion of surface area, only being valid in uniform conditions, loses its importance. But the anti-kulak prejudice which has disappeared in Poland and Hungary seems to have survived in Yugoslavia, to the detriment of production.
[13] A. Meister, *Socialisme et autogestion, l'experience yougoslave*, ed. du Seuil, 1964. The imprisonment of Djilas, after his questioning of the 'new class', shows that freedom is still only relative.

the conflict between freedom and control, most frankly faced in Yugoslavia, has not yet been solved. But the operation of market rules in a planned economy, a completely new departure, opens up many possibilities; many of those who disparaged it at the outset have now adopted it.[14]

6. THE HUNGARIAN ROAD

After our visit to Poland in 1959, we emphasized the superiority of that country's peasant solution (in spite of its hazards) to compulsory collectivization on Stalinist lines, as in Rumania. After a study of the situation in Hungary in September, 1965, our conclusions on the future of cooperative production became less sweeping. In 1957–8, 18 per cent of the land was still in a collective system, in addition to the 14 per cent worked by state farms.

In 1959 Kadar's government turned its attention to the country, to experiment with new types of agricultural cooperative. He tried to persuade the rich peasants and the most influential farm workers in the villages that the new system was in their interests: 'In a modern economy, peasant agriculture will not lead to progress'. Not only was the kulak no longer ostracized but his qualities were officially recognized. In Poland he works to grow rich, but in Hungary he is singled out to take charge of organizing the new cooperatives, and is given complete freedom if the peasants in his village trust him – as they usually do.

There are a vast number of cooperatives (3,400) of various types[15] in Hungary, each freely organized by its General Assembly, which can choose its own president. Ground-rent is first of all reintroduced, though not in its entirety, and used for the benefit of cooperative members, who remain in possession of their own land.[16]

On collective farms, the maize fields are ploughed and sown by tractor before they are divided up into portions and the other stages

---

[14] B. Rosier finds this judgement of the Yugoslav experiment rather harsh. He may be right, in the light of more recent trends.

[15] Individual peasants make up 3 per cent of the population. No measures have been taken to reduce their numbers but they are gradually disappearing in the course of natural economic trends.

[16] So as to transfer this rent to the nation, I would only have reintroduced it for the present owners, without making it hereditary.

of work are assigned to different peasant families, who share the profits of the harvest. This eliminates tedious checks on the amount of work done by each member, and the supervision – which is impossible in practical terms – of the quality of the work. The former system required a large collective bureaucracy and created an authoritarian atmosphere. Payment for weeding and manual reaping in kind is at the rate of 25–33 per cent of the grain – which seems little, and wages are equally low. When weedkiller eliminates weeding, payment for harvest alone will be 13 per cent of the produce.

The unstable sands of the Great Plain, between the river Danube and the river Tisza, have long been fixed by vines which are planted close together and trained over individual props, interspersed with different kinds of fruit trees. When the peasants felt that the land was going to be taken away from them for collectivization, they soon stopped fertilizing it and neglected its upkeep. 'Special' cooperatives, so-called to avoid the general impression of inferiority, were then established. The peasant, then able to keep plantations for his own benefit, soon started tending, fertilizing and treating them properly; and their yields are increasing.

This does not mean that they have lost sight of the future; the cooperatives levy a tax of a tenth of gross production to finance new plantations, this time with widely spaced rows (2.4 metres, sometimes 3.2, following the so-called Lanz-Moser system). The new plantations are mechanized and managed collectively. Thus, every year, at least 4 per cent of old vines are replaced by new ones, and the old peasants are gradually disappearing at the same time. Collectivization will be complete in 15 to 20 years' time, with no difficulties and with apparently general consent.

In areas where the population is very widely scattered in 'tanyas' (houses which were originally shepherds' huts), and where the soil is very heterogeneous, the cooperative works the old vines on a share-cropping basis. It pays the land tax, and pays rent to its members, the former landowners. But the rent is sometimes only 30 per cent of the previous rate. The cooperative provides fertilizers, sulphates, and sulphur. The share-cropping cooperative worker does all his work by hand or with a horse and receives 40 per cent of the wine grape harvest and 50 per cent of the value of the exported grapes. Here as well modern orchards and vineyards are gradually being replanted so that they can be mechanized on a collective basis.

The General Assembly decides on the size of the areas for private holdings, which are sometimes as much as 5,700 square metres (or 1 per cent) per family. There is usually no limit set for privately owned livestock.

Some of the peasants have kept one or two cows. These are good producers when they are properly looked after in traditional stables; large investment in collective stables is unnecessary. This is important, because in the collective stables built to a fixed model by the State the cows are still tied up; they must, therefore, be fed separately (as if they were in a restaurant). This means that there must be one worker for every eight to twelve cows, instead of one for 50 to 80 in the free stalls (cafeterias) in the United States, New Zealand, and Western Europe.[17] Of course winters in Hungary are cold but the same system can be used in enclosed stables; a good model can be found in Alfa-Laval, south of Stockholm, where the animals are kept in small stalls on wooden laths which can be cleaned out by hosing the manure into a tank below.

In contrast to the Soviet Union, however, private stock and holdings are rapidly on the wane in Hungary. Here the agricultural population is decreasing faster, now being less than 30 per cent of the total, compared with 32 per cent in the USSR in 1965. Since food supplies are more reliable in the Hungarian villages, it is easier for workers to abandon private farming, particularly so for young tractor drivers, specialists, and technicians. The decrease has been even more rapid than was expected; this means that investment loans will have to be higher than was forecast.

The Yugoslav peasants of Voivodina still think that rural life in Hungary is a nightmare; we did not have this impression. Progress still lags, and I made a number of suggestions to the Hungarian Institute of Economy. After consultations between Hungarian colleagues they were duplicated by the Institute of Rural Economy. This is the first time that my criticisms (which have the reputation of being biting) have been circulated in a communist country. With

[17] In 1946 D. R. Bergman and I pointed out to our rural engineers the advantages of free stabling in waste areas. These advantages were understood as soon as the reconstruction work was finished. Before we cast the first stone at socialist bureaucracy . . .

more free discussion, possibilities for progress are growing fast in these countries, although no one can claim to have found a solution to all their problems.

7. THE CONDITIONS FOR ECONOMIC PROGRESS

In Budapest Erdei Ferencz told us that it has now been agreed everywhere from the People's Democracies to the USSR that it is detrimental to impose highly detailed plans on a unit of production, whether agricultural or industrial. Detailed planning demands control by a burdensome, dangerous bureaucracy, which defends its own privileges and thus abuses power. It would be preferable to organize life on a more commercial basis, such as the making of contracts and the fixing of some prices, while at the same time creating the conditions of competition within a controlled market. This would increase autonomy and responsibility in the productive units, and increase their risk of failure as well; but they would be making their own decisions.

Opinions begin to differ on the question of whether these powers of decision should be given to the workers' councils, as in Yugoslavia, or to the managers as in the USSR. The Russian system could lead to that abuse of economic power which comes when there is no adequate counterweight. Socialist as well as capitalist economies need real entrepreneurs with energy and initiative; not to invest their own money (any more than do the 'managers' of modern capitalism) but to take risks and lose their jobs if they fail – for instance, if a badly run State-enterprise finally becomes insolvent. Such a dismissal would have to involve a very significant loss of both prestige (it would have to be made public) and of livelihood (which would, therefore, have to be appreciably higher than average).

In practice, incentives are lacking. For instance, Burgert, the manager of a farm at Balbona in Hungary – a true agricultural factory employing 2,000 workers – earns less than twice the salary of his youngest tractor driver. If he were dismissed he could earn the same salary elsewhere. He himself may be a completely dedicated worker. Others, taking a less altruistic view, would put into their work only what they got out of it. For managers like this a knack of stalling and forestalling the higher bureaucracy is essential. The most conformist and amenable (though not necessarily the most whole-hearted or efficient) managers have the best careers – which, of course, leads to an entirely inappropriate system of advancement, and an absence of real sanctions against inefficiency. But the declaration that an enterprise is insolvent can only be justified on solid economic grounds; this demands that prices, interest rates, etc. should be rationalized. Insolvency is a rational indication of inefficiency only within a rational price-structure.

In Hungary the semi-archaic kolkhoz stables are largely financed by the State, which provides loans for 25 or 30 years at an interest rate of 1 per cent. Here, as in China, repayment periods should not be of more than 5 or 7 years at the most, except perhaps for plantations and hydraulic installations. The interest rate should never be less than 5 per cent, increasing in proportion to the time of repayment, so that each cooperative has a direct incentive to repay quickly. The 'sovkhoz' (state farm), since it pays no interest, does not try to make optimum use of the means of production obtained with state loans. As a result, the sovkhoz uses twice as much horse-power per worker as the kolkhoz.

There are many other problems which we cannot study in detail in an overall survey. We have already pointed out that it is better to have a fixed land-tax per hectare, equivalent to a differential ground-rent, based on the natural fertility of the soil and the economic advantages of the location. Means of production which are too heavily subsidized are inevitably wasted; an example is the fruit tree plants so generously distributed by the French government from the Maghreb to Madagascar.

Water is free in the USSR. A watering device we saw in Kazakhstan could halve the quantity of water needed for irrigation in comparison with naturally flowing water; thus the area of irrigated land could be doubled by a single dam. The sovkhoz uses this device on state credit. The kolkhoz uses it much less; it has no incentive to save 3,000 cubic metres of water per hectare, since water is free. Yet for the State, installations for the collection of water are very expensive.[18]

Although the great priority given to industry in Hungary ensures

[18] *Sovkhoz, kolkhoz, ou le problématique communisme.*

that it is efficiently staffed, and has more credit and better equipment than agricultural ventures, its present low-quality machinery (restocked after the war on the Soviet model) limits exports to backward countries – who pay mainly in tropical goods. In order to purchase Western tools,[19] so vital to modernization, Hungary must sell agricultural produce and this, therefore, should receive priority.

If the rate of progress is to be more rapid, the economic structure as a whole must be reconsidered, on the example of the Committee for the reform of the economic mechanism of Budapest. The resulting discussion will inevitably come up against political problems, which must be faced without too much diffidence. Progress in the socialist economy is thus indissolubly linked with political liberalization. This in no way means a return to capitalism and private ownership of the principal means of production. But increased initiative and autonomy can only have their full effect in a more relaxed political climate, as has already been seen in Yugoslavia.

The place of the peasantry in a Socialist society must also be reconsidered. Peasants have been very much discouraged by exploitation, lack of respect, and even contempt until now. In the highly specialized 'industrialized' agriculture of the future (for example, poultry farming in Brittany) the workers will really be technicians; and the peasant is thus in the process of disappearing. But this will take time, and it is advisable to grant him more freedom and consideration in the meanwhile.

8. IF THE CORN SHORTAGE CONTINUES THE SOVIET UNION WILL BE DOMINATED BY THE UNITED STATES

The USSR has not fulfilled a single one of its agricultural plans since 1929. In 1962 I realized that none of the schemes for material prosperity, the basis for the transition to Communism predicted for 1980, would be achieved. The huge cereal imports following the bad harvests of 1963 and 1965 are a dangerous handicap to modernization in the USSR. If this agricultural inferiority continues, it could even endanger her political independence.

---

[19] It would be in our interest to give more and more generous credit loans to purchase them with, so as to help them throw off the hold of Soviet power.

The 13 million tons of corn imported in 1963-4 cost about 1,000 million dollars. Insufficient corn reserves in spite of good harvests in 1962 and 1964 can also be attributed to the low cost of bread, for much of it was fed to livestock, particularly in the area around Moscow, where the prices of supplies from the kolkhoz were extremely attractive. If destalinization is delayed, that is, if economic errors are not corrected forthwith, the demand for corn could rise again in five or six years. World population, however, is growing faster than the cereals supply.

In a free-market system world cereal prices would rise very quickly, thereby increasing the economic dependence of the USSR on its great rival. The United States could even stipulate, more or less directly, political conditions for the sale of food products. In the growing world economy a less unequal mechanism for the general allocation of resources would reveal that there is an enormous wheat shortage now concealed by lack of purchasing power. A world authority for the distribution of scarce resources could lodge protests against countries which are not using their production potential to the full; if the deficit continues, the USSR would come into this category.

Utopian visions? After all Egypt has been forced to make concessions to the United States, since she had to import half her corn in 1965 (it had been a quarter, ten years earlier). Since 1962 the Soviet Union has been withdrawing everywhere before the United States, from Berlin to Cuba, from the Congo to Santo Domingo, and above all in Vietnam, and not only for military reasons. The Soviet capacity for aid is falling fast, which may well aggravate the poor countries' unilateral dependence.

Of course there is great deal of scope for further development in Socialist agriculture. Eastern Europe, better able to increase the size of its farms than Western Europe, and more or less free from Soviet control, should easily be able to realize her potentialities. The undogmatic Hungarian road to collectivization could stimulate rapid progress, particularly if the whole economic mechanism is reexamined and reorganized. The enthusiasm of the producers must be aroused, and for this a measure of political freedom is needed. When carried out by an enlightened authority a plan can stimulate initiative through autonomy and decentralized decisions. Freedom of expression has no need to compromise the authority required for the protection of the common good.

This does not mean that freedom should be impaired. Fortunately socialist humour is beginning to re-emerge. In Cuba the manager of a firm, showing his balance sheet, is portrayed as saying 'The situation is pretty good; however, it is not a complete disaster.' In the USSR, in a kolkhoz assembly, the agenda includes the building of a stable and the construction of communism. The president opens the meeting: 'Since we have not yet received the nails for building the stable, we will go straight on to the second item on the agenda, the construction of communism.' And in Warsaw: 'By the year 2000 every Pole will have his own helicopter. Why? So as to get to Kharkov more easily if we hear that there are shoes there.'

But we should now move on to the problems currently facing Socialism in agriculture in the less developed countries, starting with Asia.

CHAPTER EIGHT
Development: a vital condition for Socialism

I. CHINA

At an early stage in history, primitive nomadic agriculture caused serious erosion in the hills of China. The country's vast population then had to be fed from the low-lying valley of the Wei, a tributary of the Yellow River. This made her the first country to practise intensive agriculture and forced her to carry on a desperate search for any kind of natural fertilizer. As the west and centre of the country are mountains and desert, the Chinese had to go down into the east, where the plains were eroded and the rivers still unsettled in their course. A vast system of dykes was built as a protection against flooding and irrigation networks were built in the Red Valley of Szechuan[1] before the birth of Christ. These works were carried out by rural communities, long used to collective systems and willing to do the necessary tasks. (During this period, India was a tribute-paying Chinese possession.)

The extortionate levies exacted by the landowner, moneylender and mandarin on the one hand, and the comparative scarcity of land and money on the other, caused frequent peasant revolts; some of them were powerful enough to overthrow dynasties (for example, the Ming Dynasty – A.D. 1368–1644), though not to establish an organized government. The Confucian respect for order and tradition became a further obstacle to economic development. After having been very much in advance of Europe in the late Middle Ages, China dropped back in the seventeenth century, when her population began a very gradual expansion. No adequate explana-

[1] See Han Suyin, *The Crippled Tree*. Jonathan Cape, London, and Putnam, New York, 1965.

tion of China's population explosion can be found, in the absence of a technological revolution, as was the case in Europe. Early intensive agriculture, particularly the systematically planted and irrigated rice-fields, careful market-gardening, and maize-growing, allowed this expansion to take place, but could not then support it. The growth of population overtook the growth of resources as soon as the central power began to weaken. Nineteenth-century China can thus be taken as an early example of underdevelopment, in that its population was growing faster than its economy. These conditions were favourable for semi-colonization by Europe and Japan and for the republican and communist revolutions, all of them consequences of overpopulation with inadequate and little industrialization. The Communists organized the last revolution. It failed in the city and only won through in the countryside (almost by a miracle) – through peasant guerrilla warfare.[2]

The Communist government of 1949 had made a detailed study of the mistakes of the Russian revolution. In order to avoid the collapse of production, it tried to preserve bourgeois elements within the system – the few industrial (even capitalist) cadres, artisans, civil servants, traders, etc. The only group it refused to tolerate was the non-working landowning class, which was completely dispossessed by agrarian reform. The government planned to win the support of the mass of rural workers, including the rich peasants, by appealing to their nationalism. It wanted to start off by making them 'unconscious Socialists' through a policy of very slow, gradual collectivization of the traditional systems of cooperation, first on a seasonal and then on a permanent basis.

In the summer of 1955, 15 per cent of the peasants were employed in semi-socialist co-operatives where ground-rent was retained, as proposed by the party in December, 1953. Chairman Mao then ordered an abrupt acceleration, in sharp contrast with the previous caution. In China, collectivization advanced further in eight months than it had in four years in the USSR. It took place without civil wars, famine, or large-scale slaughter of livestock. Soon, however, the movement became an attack on the rich peasant, now cut off from any share in the organization, like the former landed

[2] Isaac Deutscher, 'Le Maoisme', *Les Temps modernes*, September 1964.

proprietor. In 1957, 740,000 socialist co-operatives, paying salary only for work, farmed China's 107 million hectares of agricultural land.

China may have obtained better results in eight years than the USSR did between 1917 and 1925, but her achievements are still not good enough in view of the population increase brought about by widespread health measures. Without the skills of the kulaks, cooperative harvests failed to reach the high level rashly promised during the recruitment campaigns; such failures also point to peasant hostility and unforeseen slackness in collective work. Alarmed by food shortages, the government started propaganda for birth control in 1956.

Throughout the country, 1958 started with arduous attempts at water conservation. In a burst of enthusiasm the government thought it could abandon its neo-Malthusian policy and the new slogan was 'One more mouth to feed, but two more hands to work'. The party line, the Great Leap Forward, meant the end of planned growth in any real sense of the term; the sole aim was the breaking of existing records in every sphere. No further attention was paid to economic laws or to technological possibilities; yet another popular slogan was 'Politics is in command'. Each collective was told to build and supply its own small-scale blast-furnace, although these proved largely unusable.

Experiments with the amalgamation of cooperatives resulted in their being joined, by September or October, 1958, into 26,500 rural people's communes, each consisting of an average of 4,000 hectares of farmland with 4,500 families. Even long after the revolution, any step forward could be made only through the class struggle. Communalization was thus launched as an attack on the richer peasants. Less than a year before official propaganda had been congratulating itself on the fact that the vast majority of the Chinese rural population had reached the standard of living of the 'rich middle' peasants.

'Communism is paradise, the people's commune is the ladder to it... Six years' hard work for ten thousand years of happiness.' With such slogans the new communes blazed their way through the stages to communism, distributing free food, the first practical application of the famous dictum to each according to his needs. If this practice had been continued, it could easily have had the dangerous effect of increasing the birth rate. There was over-investment, over-industrialization, over-centralization, boundless optimism, a premature announcement of bumper harvests. The enthusiasm of the newly founded communes ended rudely in 1959: the country was on the verge of famine.

The old mandarins had seen famines as an essential means of cutting down population surpluses which the country would be unable to feed in normal conditions. They used to criticize the missionaries for their determined efforts to help the starving people. This was realism when production was virtually at a standstill. The Communist government, on the other hand, gritted its teeth and met scarcity with the cry 'Let no one die of hunger'. (By contrast, in the winter of 1965-6, the starving people living in the streets of New Delhi could see rich Indians coming out of gargantuan feasts.) The blast-furnaces were the first to be abandoned, followed by all the unprofitable workshops, projects which had been designed to give the communes an unusual degree of autarchy.[3]

The measures of 1959-62 corrected the situation, at the cost of substantial ideological concessions. Ownership of many means of production was returned to subdivisions of the commune, first to the brigade then the team, although the avowed political objective was still constant evolution towards national or state ownership. Incomes were now only granted on socialist principles in direct relation to work and so large families were the worst fed; the government no longer felt reluctant to penalize them by giving them fewer ration cards; an extra mouth is no advantage if the two hands are underproductive. This economic pressure for birth control backed up renewed propaganda for contraception; abortion became common. The Third World would do well to give careful thought to this example, and also to the example of government austerity; we cannot say as much for China's dogmatism.

Since 1962 the food situation has been improving fairly rapidly in the big towns; enormous projects for the intensification of agriculture have been set up around them, comprising irrigation, plantations, and electrification. Cheap vegetables are in good supply;

[3] In anticipation of atomic war?

supplies of fruit and animal produce have increased but are more expensive; continued cereal and textile rationing are, therefore, made tolerable. I was struck by the number of installations that had been set up between my two visits in 1955 and 1964 – irrigation works, terracing, reinforcement of dykes, drainage, reafforestation, electrification, mechanical pumping, and so on.

On the other hand, the harvests as a whole do not seem to have increased in anything like the same proportion; the level of nutrition seems no higher than it was in 1955. To avoid taking too much corn from the overpopulated countryside, provisions for the towns are supplemented by imports of 5 million or 6 million tons of corn per year. Hardly any rice is exported now, and very little soya beans – much less than before the communes. Nevertheless, of all the large Afro-Asian countries, China is still the only one successfully emerging from underdevelopment with no outside aid whatsoever. All the Soviet loans have been repaid, down to the last cartridge for the Korean war.

China will soon be a great industrial and nuclear power. She will either have to reduce her present rate of population growth, if this is really 2 per cent per year, or face serious food shortages. If she is aiming at faster development, population growth will have to be brought down to about 1 per cent, and even then the standard of living cannot rise at all rapidly, except on the cultural level, which of course counts for something. China is, therefore, trying to perpetuate the revolutionary situation and keep the class struggle alive artificially, perhaps with the intention of concealing strong peasant hostility. Apart from the fact that full benefit cannot be derived from the irrigation works owing to lack of fertilizer and technical knowledge, peasant hostility goes a long way towards explaining the very low productivity of the enormous land improvements.

China would nevertheless like to build communism quickly; but of course it cannot be built in China in the condition of extreme plenty which Marx takes as his precondition. Indeed, even a comfortable standard of living is now regarded officially as suspect, because it lowers the 'revolutionary tone' which can only be maintained in austerity. It is impossible for a foreign visitor to assess the popularity of the new régime among the mass of Chinese peasants.

I came across both hostility and outbursts of enthusiasm; in general, keenness for work seems to be lower in the country than in the town, as can be seen from the fact that 500 or 600 man-days were required to cultivate one hectare of rice-field for a single agricultural season.

Will China ever follow the example of the USSR and move towards relative liberalization? With the spread of education, this seems a likely development. But the speed at which China moves in this direction – and it is essential that she should do so in the reasonably near future – will depend very largely on Western attitudes. It is, therefore, very much in our interest to contribute to Chinese economic development with technical aid and equipment loans, once China has been admitted to the United Nations. Otherwise we cannot totally dismiss even the possibility of a Sino-Japanese bloc working towards world supremacy. This should prompt us to strengthen international solidarity and to start drawing up the laws of a United World.

If China gives up her attachment to dogma and controls her birth rate more successfully, she could raise her standard of living faster than the rest of the Third World and could provide them with a better 'model' for development than the Soviet Union. China started her communist revolution in similar conditions and was quicker and more definite in her rejection of the absolute priority of heavy industry.

2. NORTH VIETNAM AND NORTH KOREA

Quite apart from the bombing which discredits the United States in the eyes of most of the Third World countries,[4] North Vietnam faces a more difficult food situation and has a much lower standard of living than China. A very rapid reconstruction after the war against the French and its disruptions brought about a sharp increase in harvests, although only qualified approval can be given to the agrarian reform after 1954, when in every village the landowners were brought to trial. The formation of socialist and semi-socialist

[4] Apart from chap. I of *Chine Surpeuplée*, see our report to the government of North Vietnam, published in *France-Asie*, January 1966.

producers' cooperatives from 1959 was followed by a slightly slower expansion.

I have not, however, observed any major economic errors comparable to those of the other socialist countries. But in the deltas, which are overpopulated even now, the law of diminishing returns on labour generally prevails since labour is in excess supply compared with the other factors of production. The amount of labour input per hectare has probably increased much faster than rice yield. Thus, in spite of hard work, the food situation in Hanoi has been deteriorating year by year ever since 1960.

Socialism is thus held back; individual peasants still make up 12 per cent of the population and only a third of the cooperatives are socialist; there is nothing comparable to the Chinese communes. And no one has thought of following neighbouring China's example of birth control. But then, China has not had to face more than twenty years of war.

Agricultural growth is probably even faster in North Korea, in spite of the massive destruction of the war. North Korea has vast power and mineral resources and had already been to some extent industrialized by Japan. Its technical level was higher than that of China. Modern techniques had already been disseminated through the countryside by the Japanese. The speed of reconstruction, however, is really a tribute to outstanding courage and energy: the ability of the Koreans is truly astonishing – in the South fairly good progress should be made and the Northern leaders, too, are very astute. Although the policy of North Korea may be largely derived from its powerful neighbour, there is nothing reminiscent of China's 'collective folly' during the Great Leap in 1958. The North Korean agricultural cooperatives have been enlarged; between 80 and 300 families occupy 500 hectares of farmland. In addition to its higher level of industrialization, Korea has twice as much land per worker as China, which is another reason for its superior position. All the agricultural cooperatives are of the socialist type and members pay no ground-rent. Like communes (though they operate on a smaller scale) they manage their own trade, credit arrangements, and health services. Male members are bound to give the cooperative 230 days of work per year and female members 180 days. In all, each peasant worked an average of 345 days per year from 1960 to 1963, compared with 301 days in 1957.[5]

In agriculture and probably in industry, too, North Korea leads the socialist bloc. Food production has probably doubled in the last twenty years, in spite of the destruction of the war; though 1944 was, of course, a very low starting point. The area of irrigated land has increased sevenfold since then and now represents perhaps 40 per cent of the agricultural land. The industrialization of agriculture has also gone ahead: in 1964 for its 200,000 hectares of farmland, North Korea had 20,000 '15 horse-power units' of tractor power (which means many less than 20,000 tractors), although China, which is vastly bigger, has only five or six times as much tractor power. Japan introduced the North Koreans to fertilizer and ever since independence high priority has been given to the chemical fertilizer industry – 750,000 tons of fertilizer were manufactured in 1964. A common dictum of President Kim Il Sung is 'Fertilizers mean rice and rice means socialism'. In addition, by 1964, 81 per cent of the peasants' homes had electricity.

While China has about 200 million tons of basic foodstuffs for perhaps 700 million inhabitants, North Korea has about 5 million for a population of 11 million; this is 56 per cent more per head than in China. This is in spite of the fact that the proportion of peasants fell from 74 per cent in 1946 to 43 per cent in 1963, while the proportion of non-agricultural workers rose from 18 per cent to 55 per cent. These statistics show how much faster development has been in North Korea than in China. Nevertheless, the targets of the next plan seem rather rash; they include catching up with Japan in seven years and increasing industry at the rate of 18 per cent per year. Agricultural progress has been slowing down since 1961; the rate of population growth has been increasing and is now nearly 3 per cent per year.

3. THE HISTORY OF THE CUBAN REVOLUTION

Though patriotism may have been as important in Cuba as it was in China, the revolution there was at first politically suspect, since it

[5] Bernard Couret, *Le Monde diplomatique*, December 1965, p. 6.

started with no support from either workers or peasants. The first guerrilla war was fought by a small band of young city dwellers, students, and members of the intelligentsia. After some hostility the first manual labourers to join them were the peasants of the Sierra Maestra. When the guerrillas, originally bourgeois idealists, came into contact with the poverty of the countryside, of which they had been almost unaware, their views took a more radical turn; from their humanist position they began to delve more deeply into Marxist-Leninist texts.

The workers of the capital were the last to join. Once the new government had cast off its bourgeois wing in late 1959, it began a more revolutionary implementation of what had been, in principle, a very reformist agrarian law (leaving 400 hectares to each great landowner and promising compensation). But it kept its independence from the communist régimes of the old world. The former *latifundia* were not divided up, on the grounds that their employees were members of the proletariat rather than aspiring peasants. Although we have personally seen some exceptions, this view was, on the whole, correct.

Cuba wanted to make itself the shop window for Revolution in the American continent; it had to prove in material terms to the Central and South American rural proletariat that the question was no longer simply one of slogans or of struggles for personal advancement. The Cubans, therefore, aimed at securing a rapid, immediate increase in the workers' standard of living; in towns by lowering rents, in the country by raising wages and by selling seasonal produce more cheaply in 'people's shops'. The number of days worked increased so fast that unemployment, which had until then been high, was eradicated in less than three years. In the first two years of the Revolution, the workers' general purchasing power rose by 60 per cent, but production by only 10 per cent.

The Cubans forgot that it is impossible for more to be distributed than is produced; and the United States' blockade accentuated the problem. The inflationary policy aggravated the general scarcity and soon made rationing necessary, particularly when production began to decrease in 1961. If a worker could earn enough to buy his rations in ten days' work per month, he had no incentive to do any more work. By 1963 absenteeism was rampant, although condemned as a 'betrayal of the homeland'.

The great expropriated estates had been referred to as cooperatives since 1959, but they were not given any definite structure until 1961. Soviet and Chinese writings had emphasized that ownership by the whole nation is preferable to cooperative ownership by a group of interested workers. The enormous people's farms which were then formed received all their credit from the budget, had to forecast all their expenditure a year in advance, and hand over all their income to the Treasury. With even less autonomy than the sovkhoz, they were controlled from above as much in their daily management as in the supply and sale of their products. In the absence of any economic or financial independence, there were no incentives for profit-making, and so no profits were made.

Enthusiasm began to wane as soon as Cuba achieved full employment, for daily salaries were not generally dependent on work. 'A worker earns two pesos for one peso's work', a Soviet colleague told us. With sugar as the only crop, land and labour were under-used and major food imports were necessary; when the sugar production policy was completely reversed, however, the best sugar plantations, even those situated near factories, were destroyed. Each 'granja del pueblo' (people's farm) then began to diversify its crops, growing 20 or 35 different types, with production dispersed throughout the island, which is 750 miles long and which, anyway, had poor transport facilities. Farms and districts should have specialized so as to minimize the transport problems, aggravated by the blockade, and to restrict demand for machinery and training in new techniques.

Yield from the new crops was poor, and by 1963 the productivity of the working day had dropped by almost one-half in 4 years; 1963 was the nadir, with sugar production down to 3.8 million tons compared with 5.5 million in 1953–8 and 6.9 million in 1961. Favourable sales contracts with the Socialist countries provided an incentive to restore priority to cane sugar; the groups of granjas were granted some autonomy and 6 million tons were harvested in 1965. There are plans for producing 10 million tons of sugar in 1970. This target will certainly not be reached, since production fell again in 1966 to about 4.5 million tons, and 1,000 million pesos[6] would have to be invested; with the present capacity it would be difficult to produce more than 7 million tons.

The restoration of sugar, with stock-breeding in second place, seems a wise move, but in some places it is being carried out quite indiscriminately. Food crops are being neglected and root crops are still in short supply. This is the result of too much bureaucracy and centralization in both production and distribution. Fidel Castro finally took corrective measures in October, 1965. With free local markets and more initiative and independence in the granjas, supplies should improve quickly – on condition that each worker is paid for his work and not simply for his presence; this is now being slowly put into effect.

4. SOCIALISM AS A MEANS OF DEVELOPMENT

Cuba's hasty nationalization measures in 1960 were guided more by anti-Americanism than by careful economic thinking. Because of the black market, it seemed desirable to extend state control to retail trade. But why include family businesses, crafts and service industries, hairdressers, and restaurants? Che Guevara rejected the temptation to use material self-interest as a means of promoting accelerated economic development.[7] He talked of the new man whom we ought to create, who could be adapted to his theoretical plan. He protested violently when I suggested that the 'cooperators' of 1960 should be given a sense of collective joint ownership. He wanted only to increase their sense of responsibility. The perfect man, a utopian dream, will never exist. Society must be adapted to human beings as they are, good and bad at once. They may improve, but only slowly.

Apart from a few government members, not even the most ardent Cuban revolutionaries were prepared to make a complete sacrifice. It was, therefore, a mistake to give up (except for a few small peasant groups) the producers' cooperatives with free membership in favour

---

[6] The peso was formerly worth a dollar; its domestic purchasing power has dropped appreciably. See 'Cuba a l'age de raison', by M. Niedergant, Le Monde, May 12, 1966.
[7] Le Socialisme et l'homme a Cuba, Maspero, 1966.

of the state system. Within the state system there could have been autonomy in daily purchasing and selling decisions, with broad regional specialization (the logical consequence of diversified production on a national scale) as determined in the plan. The system could then have made a meaningful contribution to necessary investments instead of leaving them all to the State, avoiding many of the hazards referred to above. If work had been paid for according to its real value, inflation and consequently rationing and absenteeism would have been reduced. If people could have earned money by the local free sale of food, shortages would have been curbed more quickly and supplies obtained at lower prices than on the black market.

The shortage of qualified accountants is an even more serious difficulty than the scarcity of technicians. It was possible to mitigate the lack of technical knowledge by distributing simple, clear information leaflets as widely as possible in the granjas. But without exact accounts for every small work unit and for each form of production, it is difficult to see where the main errors arise. The government remains completely in the dark, with no information to help it to correct its technical or economic mistakes. This is definitely an essential weakness of socialist régimes. If profit, the invisible hand, is eliminated, some deliberate method of correcting economic mistakes must replace it. A signalling system of this kind would be easier if people running the autonomous cooperatives had to suffer for their mistaken predictions. On the whole, the state system has provided an easy way out.

If Cuba's mistakes could be analysed openly they could serve as a valuable lesson. Revolution now needs effective agricultural reform and industrialization. A guerrilla war can no longer accomplish the whole process. Socialism should be regarded as one particular form of development; like any other system its primary needs are financial and intellectual investment, more capital and technical knowledge. The young South Americans who call themselves revolutionaries should be doing more to prepare themselves for their duties as technicians, economists, and accountants, so that their countries may from the outset develop more successfully than Cuba; the Soviet Union will not be able to give other countries as much aid *per capita*.

Cuba sets a good example on many fronts, as in its excellent literacy campaign, its revolutionary enthusiasm, its comparatively free atmosphere, and, most of all, in the integrity of its leaders. Castro's dialogues in the people's assemblies look impressive, though he can control discussion as he likes. But Cuba has had to pay too high a price for Castro's economic training, mainly acquired through his mistakes, many of which could have been avoided had he been less ambitious at the outset. The cost could still be offset if other Latin American countries learn in future from Cuba's example. This is why we have felt morally obliged to show the whole picture, at the risk of offending our friends in Cuba,[8] as we have already offended our African and Russian friends and will offend our Chinese friends. Propaganda and misplaced compliments are the most insidious of communism's early diseases.

5. PREMATURE SOCIALISM

Samir Amin[9] spent some years working in Mali's Ministry of Planning; now, no longer willing to take any responsibility for present events, he is teaching for the United Nations at Dakar. He considers that socialism cannot be built in tropical Africa until after twenty or thirty years of capital accumulation. With a virtually Neolithic agricultural system and a population explosion unmatched by adequate economic progress, the food situation in Africa is deteriorating rapidly.[10] The rich countries of the Coast may be increasing their food imports instead of buying machinery; but in Mali, for instance, shortages and the black market have already taken hold.

Mali followed the ill-advised course of creating a national currency, and chose inflation as a short cut to expansion – so the Mali franc lost virtually all its value. In spite of its poverty, Mali threw itself into prestige building projects, such as the presidential palace, which in all probability cannot pay its own electricity bill; from this inflationary policy sprang the government's difficulties. In 1964 the 35 National Companies' deficits were probably over 5,000 million

[8] *Cuba, socialisme et développement*, ed. du Seuil, 1964; revised edition 1968.
[9] *Ghana, Guinée, Mali*, 'Tiers-Monde', P.U.F., 1965.
[10] The FAO report of 1965 singles it out as 'particularly disappointing'.

CFA francs.[11] The losses of the import-export company alone probably account for a good third of this; to finance the deficit it will draw on the accumulated fund of past profits of the private companies which it replaced. Once, in a single day of business, the Ministry of Transport made 1,200 CFA francs and spent 367,000. Most of the buses broke down and the vast majority of the passengers never paid their fare. Since there is no work and virtually nothing in the shops, Bamako is the only African capital where the population is not on the increase. For this reason, 40 per cent of the settlers have left the Niger Office, from which they can no longer export their profits to Upper Volta, even if that is where they came from, except by indirect methods (taking out livestock and fish); furthermore they have to sell their paddy (unhusked rice) at the taxed price. They have been replaced by mechanized rice-growing companies, whose deficits are mounting and whose accounts are even more badly kept than those of the Cuban granjas.

Samir Amin writes that there is less slackness and corruption in Mali than in Ghana or Guinea.[12] Nevertheless, one district of Bamako, known as the ministerial villa area, was built on state loans and let to diplomats. The villa area produces a source of considerable income for the houseowners, who are ministers or top civil servants, the only people with salaries high enough to provide security for the building loans. Members of the government have many different ways of earning money. Times have indeed changed since Jean-Marie Kone made his colleagues in the ministry go and work in the groundnut fields. Economic failure is so acute that the present team will probably not stay in power much longer. The commercial bourgeoisie are already preparing for their comeback. The common people, who have nothing left, are unlikely to raise any objections. But Africa always has surprises in store.

In Guinea, since 1960, more and more of the National Companies have gone bankrupt. This coastal country is much richer than Mali in both mineral resources and agricultural potential. But socialism needs a minimum of political and administrative organization, and consequently some degree of development – as well as a high

[11] The CFA franc is worth two centimes (two-fifths of a US cent).
[12] V. R. Cornevin, 'Le socialisme guinéen est menacé par des difficultés de tous ordres', in Le Monde diplomatique, April 1966.

standard of morality, as the Chinese government has had to learn in its arduous struggle. The free granting of independence in Africa did not provide the same training; not that we recommend thirty years' civil war!

Algeria is another African country which has embraced socialism. But here also success has been elusive. According to estimates by G. Lazarev, production on Algeria's self-managed farms, which had been abandoned by the French settlers, was in 1963 about one-third below the level of 1959. This may seem a sharp drop; it is even worse than it seems since the number of working days has probably increased by 50 per cent or even doubled. This would mean that the productivity of the working day has decreased even more than in the Cuban granjas, where we estimated that in 1963 it was half what it had been in 1959. Productivity has risen in Cuba recently, but no such improvement has taken place as yet in Algeria. The working day is only about six hours on many of the farms; corruption among officials is frequent, and theft of materials has become a common practice. Small élites have consequently grown up in the country, often with an income ten times as high as most of the fellahin, who live in appalling poverty, close to famine in some areas.

A general example of indolence is set by veterans of the war, who assumed that Ben Bella's socialism granted them the right to take it easy. It would be a good idea to collect these 'djounouds' together on the same farms, where they would not be able to live off other people's work[13]; they would have to produce at least enough to live on themselves. Self-management is an excellent principle, on condition that the organizers are competent and qualified and that the workers are devoted to their collective; Daniel Guérin has not emphasized this last point sufficiently strongly. In a comparatively underdeveloped country, a certain amount of discipline should be exercised from above. Wages cannot be paid to those who do not do even the minimum amount of work.

Democracy and socialism are not miracle solutions; there are no miracle solutions. Before the nineteenth century they never existed in Europe for the masses before a certain level of development had been reached. Africa and South Asia should not rush towards these

[13] This was probably beginning to happen at least as early as the summer of 1966.

goals; they should nationalize only those enterprises which they can manage efficiently, in such a way as to be able to invest the profits. This does not mean that they must reproduce all the abuses of the early stages of capitalism.

Other leaders, like Senghor[14] in Senegal, talk about African socialism, saying that it is 'founded on the French Utopians and has taken the concepts of economic planning and dialectics from Marx. The class struggle within a country is less important than the struggle between the rich and "proletarian" nations.' But though this form of socialism may claim to follow Teilhard de Chardin, it retains privileges as anachronistic as those of the Mourid priests who enslave their serfs (tabipes). This is a travesty of the ideas of socialism, which were originally designed to reduce social inequality and wipe out alienation.[15]

In view of the population explosion in the Third World, socialism must make development and faster economic progress its main concerns. In the initial stages particularly, these aims can hardly be reconciled with extreme egalitarianism.

African governments can prepare the way for the last stages in the construction of socialism by accumulating as much capital as possible through taxation. Although at present they do levy taxes the money is all spent on a privileged, almost parasitic, class.[16] They could raise even more money, but only at the risk of putting themselves in the hands of the foreign powers who once balanced their budgets and still guarantee the vast majority of their investments, although, for example, the Common Market countries are now reducing their aid.

6. THE VICTORY OF SOCIALISM IS NOT INEVITABLE

If socialism is to prevail and to derive the full benefits of planning, it must correct its economic mistakes as soon as possible. Initiative

[14] In an interview with Ania Francos in *Jeune Afrique*, December 19, 1965.
[15] 'It would be more accurate to call it exploitation', as J.-M. Domenach said, *Esprit*, December 1965.
[16] In *L'Economie du Maghreb*, éd. de Minuit, 1966, Samir Amin estimates that production in Algeria has fallen by about 36 per cent and that administrative spending in 1963 came to 35 per cent of gross domestic product; expenditure on the army alone was 10 per cent of G.D.P.

must be stimulated; socialist projects must have more freedom in their management and some of the laws of market competition must be reintroduced. Socialism is still in its infancy; its first practical demonstrations are only at the experimental stage. It will only advance fast enough if it makes a rational economic reassessment of its organization, the respective roles of the Party technicians, producers, and consumers. It must stop justifying privileges on dogmatic principles derived, more or less honestly, from what are often very outdated 'sacred' texts of Marxist-Leninism. As soon as it seems possible for some of the Party's directives to be proved wrong after rational examination, the group in power fights back, for its 'supreme wisdom', the ideological basis of its limitless power, would be held in question; but for the sake of progress it must be questioned.

Economic structure, the size of the projects, the most desirable balance between local initiative and centralization, the level at which general or specific decisions should be taken, and so on, all depend largely on the stage of development already reached and the type of operations under consideration. It would be dangerous to try to organize non-mechanized agriculture in the same way as heavy industry. Central Africa and Albania do not need the same system as Czechoslovakia, which because it is more developed has been more harmed by economic Stalinism.

The progress of socialism will be determined by the rate of its economic and political liberalization. This last point will cast doubt on the absolute power which the managerial class, the 'national proto-socialist bureaucracy', has given itself. This class will try to oppose liberalization, claiming erroneously to represent the truest and best expression of the wishes of the working class. If its claims were true, it would mean that peasants, technicians, intellectuals, industrial workers, service workers, and civil servants were cut off from any political power. Even now, the peasants have to bear too much of the cost of industrialization.

Claiming to free man from capitalist exploitation, Stalinism with its monolithic and compulsory ideology subjected him to the most rigorous oppression. The hold is now slackening, but so slowly that the economic victory of socialism over neo-capitalism cannot be predicted with any certainty. Neo-capitalism is advancing steadily and is proving more flexible and more capable of rapid economic progress.

Socialism cannot claim mass popular support while it still imposes restrictions. Workers' and peasants' sons often have better opportunities for advancement in a socialist régime, but the human individual is less respected than in the English and Scandinavian democracies. What is the intellectual to do, when conformism in Moscow is so rewarding and heresy so dangerous?

The Americans are in no position to talk about oppressed peoples, at any rate before solving their own colour problem, and evacuating the Dominican Republic and Vietnam. All the same, the assumption that it is absolutely necessary to have collective ownership of the means of production has not yet been proved true; it emphatically does not mean copying the Soviet economic structure. Fortunately this structure is in a state of radical change.

We still believe in an ideal of the solidarity of man which is both communal and individual, a form of socialism that would attempt to build a less unequal world economy, which while respecting the individual would at the same time work towards accelerated development.

In most parts of the world, it will only be possible to accelerate development if agriculture is accorded a higher priority. If we want to overcome hunger, industry should initially be put to the service of agriculture as it has been in China. The peasant should be made to feel happy working in collectives that are as autonomous in their day to day management and in the detailed planning of their output as in their purchasing and selling decisions. In time, the collective will grow to the appropriate size for its level of mechanization. The Chinese system and the special Hungarian cooperatives are beginning to move in this direction.

The organization of the socialist economy should be flexible and dynamic enough to adapt itself more closely to the development of new techniques and machinery, and also to basic human needs. Technical progress tends to increase industrial concentration; socialism demands greater solidarity; the individual hopes for greater liberty. For these reasons we prefer freely established voluntary communities, roughly on the lines of the Polish associations and Yugoslav cooperatives and, best of all, French communal agriculture.

Rather than nationalization we recommend ownership of the land by local collectives, which are better able to use it to maximum advantage. The nation would be in no way prevented from upholding the supremacy of the common good, as long as its methods were more humanly acceptable than bureaucratic and police oppression. Economic controls can be more flexible if they result from free market forces along with a certain amount of price-fixing. This practice is developing on both sides of what was once the Iron Curtain (now, fortunately, less rigid). The consumer should also have some influence on what is produced, particularly in the case of perishable goods such as animal and horticultural produce. It is sometimes difficult to say just where the beneficial free market ends and harmful speculation begins; only practical experience will give the answer.

Socialism must discard the dogmas of its past as quickly as possible and reject its totalitarianism. If it can accommodate an outlook which is individualist as well as universalist, it will come to represent a great hope for mankind, a vital counterweight to the abuses of capitalism. Competition between the two systems could be extremely useful, as a means of forcing both to improve and often to move closer together – though hardly to unite.

More study[17] must be devoted to finding out which forms of socialism are appropriate to which places; this will be determined by their stages of development, their principal forms of production, and their historical and psychological backgrounds. Unless the socialist countries take immediate steps to correct their mistakes and defects, particularly in agriculture, they will have to continue importing food; and they will be in serious danger of becoming dependent upon North America. Far from reducing the world food shortage, they would worsen it. Unless immediate corrective measures are taken, underestimation of the food problem and failure in agriculture

---

[17] In *Planification et croissance accélérée*, Maspero, 1964, Ch. Bettelheim only touches on all the difficulties which have arisen in Guinea and Cuba in the first stages of planning. He certainly knew the problems, however, and an analysis of their causes would be extremely useful in future revolutions.

will reduce – indeed have already reduced – the political prestige of the socialist countries in the Third World.

At the World Population Congress in Belgrade in September, 1965, the Soviet delegates, presenting their traditional view, condemned birth control. 'All we need do', they said in essence, 'is to increase agricultural production; this presents no problems'. Why does the Soviet Union wait so long before setting the example? Perhaps it is counting on the population explosion to increase revolutionary tensions in the Third World.

This hope would be more in keeping with Chinese policy. Socialism will never be an easy way out. It will constantly have to reassess its aims and fight against the ever-present threat of injustice, oppression, and dogma.

If the two developed blocs, the capitalist and the socialist, could achieve some degree of peaceful coexistence, a necessary preliminary for negotiating gradual disarmament, new resources large enough to help the Third World would soon become available. The division of the world between two ideologies is now repeating itself in the form of a split between the rich and the poor. China and the USSR are diverging steadily; so are the North Atlantic countries and the Third World. Some form of coexistence between the rich North and the poor South must definitely be brought about if this split is not to become more dangerous than the East–West division, which is now being resolved by greater understanding between the USSR and the USA. If China became the leader of a revolutionary Third World, the rich countries in both camps would have cause for alarm. The most enlightened understand that it is in their interests to reduce social injustice in the world.

We now go on to examine the possible future of the Third World: it can increase its own efforts to promote work, training, and savings, and so to become more self-sufficient. The developed countries could give effective help if they could be made to realize their moral obligations, which, for the first time in the history of mankind, coincide with their own long-term interests.

PART FOUR The Third World must rely
mainly on its own resources

CHAPTER NINE
Privileged minorities in Africa

Although agricultural production is increasing in the developed countries only North America, Australasia, and France produce worthwhile surpluses. On the whole, European countries are still importing countries. The socialist bloc is underproductive, and its requirements are increasing. The Third World will not be able to wipe out hunger and poverty unless it can increase its own production. It must now develop in its turn, in far more difficult circumstances than those of Europe in recent centuries. Before examining the agricultural problems of Africa, South America and Asia, we will touch briefly on their fundamental problem: that is, the training of active, skilled workers.

I. MORE TECHNICAL EDUCATION AND URBAN AUSTERITY

Slavery and colonization were instrumental in, though not essential to, European development. Neither could have arisen, however, without the complicity of privileged minorities in the conquered countries. Such minorities exist everywhere. They were, and indeed still are, necessary for development. Those who devoted themselves to organizing society early in its history, promoting philosophy and science and the education of the young, had to be relieved of servile work. But while some members of the privileged class sought power or wealth through the practice or patronage of productive activities, making themselves useful to society, others lived a life of luxury off the work of conquered tribes, who in this way were brought to their current state of stagnation.

Since a basic characteristic of underdevelopment is that growth of population overtakes that of production, developing countries need machinery and consequently capital investment. But the most vital prerequisite for progress in production is the training of technical staff in industry and agriculture, commerce and finance. The mass of workers must, therefore, be given some kind of basic training to render their work more productive.

'Mobilize unused resources' advises Gabriel Ardant, the French economist. But first of all, the most useful and scarce of what the Chinese call the 'concealed productive forces' (for example, technology and modern equipment) must be brought into use. If Ardant had studied the results of Morocco's Promotion Nationale in greater detail, he would have noticed that heavy expenditure did not produce satisfactory returns in the absence of enthusiasm and technical knowledge. In January, 1963, near Aures in Algeria, a Christian organization for technical aid began a reafforestation project; the slope on which this was located was too dry, technical mistakes were numerous, and as a result productivity was about 90 per cent lower than it should have been. Goodwill is no substitute for knowledge and equipment.

The people's work will not be useful unless they are aware of the benefits they can derive from it, unless they really want to improve their position, and unless the social system is such that the workers can profit from their labour. A minimum of technical skill is another factor necessary for satisfactory productivity, and technical training should, therefore, come first in the scale of priorities. In Africa, Latin America, and Asia, the Europeans inculcated into the people a greater feeling of respect for legal (defence of property) and literary knowledge than for other branches of learning. The new states, following our example, concentrate to a large extent on luxury education – and manual work tends to be looked down on in those parts of the world where its status should be highest.

Mass education of the young must not have the detrimental effect of causing unemployment or dissatisfaction. Close links must be established between education on the one hand and manual work and professional training of all kinds on the other – agricultural, craft, industrial and commercial training. The socialist countries provide the best model here: the programme of each teaching unit should be linked to the plan by an education scheme stipulating that every pupil must be trained in relation to his future career. The administration, an increasingly parasitic body, must not become any more overcrowded than it is already. The educational system should be geared to turning out more efficient workers, together with the technicians and staff who are so vital for the development of production.[1]

An increase in the salary of manual and technical workers would have to constitute one aspect of this reform. Wages, however, must not rise in advance of productivity and there is still often a need for greater urban austerity, and for reducing the privileges of the ruling minority who waste their country's currency on luxury imports. This is easier said than done, since the trained and qualified will probably have more opportunities for emigrating to rich countries in future. There are already some Africans who have stayed in Europe; and some South Americans, Indians, and Cubans are settling in the United States. Perhaps increased power, prestige, and responsibility could provide some compensation for low incomes; but special rights are always a difficult issue. This is a universal problem, which can only be solved by international measures.[2] At the moment, the poor countries are helping the rich ones, paying themselves for the upbringing of their children and then letting them go abroad as unskilled workers as soon as they are old enough to be productive. The semi-developed countries of Eastern Europe spend money on training skilled workers, many of whom leave for the West. Western Europe provides the United States with trained workers. Of course, Berlin walls cannot be built everywhere.

Although it is just as important as the education of the young, the professional training of adults is badly neglected and mismanaged; it should be given top priority. When really comprehensive and

---

[1] The Dacko government in the Central African Republic and the Bureau pour le dévoloppement de la productivité agricole (BPDA) had drawn up a reform of this kind but it was rejected when Colonel Bokassa took power, as were other austerity measures designed to reduce the unfair privileges of the civil service. In Upper Volta the trade union leaders boasted in January 1966, that they had annulled the finance bill as it 'reduced our purchasing power'. In this case, the trade unions are the minorities who exploit the peasants and had better be careful when the latter realize it. But these unions were right to protest at ministerial corruption.

[2] As an incentive to students to return to their country of origin, it has been suggested making the local University give students from backward areas a diploma on their return for the studies they had done abroad.

adapted to the level of development, intensive training for a period of several months or even weeks could have an immediate effect on production; its cost would be recouped very quickly. The economic value of expenditure on general education is often emphasized rather dogmatically in various departments of UNESCO, but this theory is mainly applicable to developed countries. For many poor countries general education is still a luxury expenditure (as in Tanzania or at the University of Ghana at Accra), where it has the ultimate effect of crowding the streets of Ibadan, Dakar, or Brazzaville with lazy and eventually delinquent young people.

2. THE PLANTATIONS AND PEASANTS OF THE AFRICAN FOREST REGION

In the green forests growing all along the western coast and in parts of central Africa the climate is damp and agricultural potential often high. When the so-called 'virgin' forest is replaced by plantations, when the soil is protected from erosion and from the sun – which destroys the humus quickly – when methods of cultivation are good and fertilizer is used, harvests are excellent. The peasants of Ghana and Nigeria, the Ivory Coast and Cameroun, together with some of the neighbouring African countries, produce 70 per cent of the world's cocoa supply,[3] which in the nineteenth century was an American monopoly. Robusta coffee was developed later, under French tariff protection and though it will never offer serious competition to the Arabica coffees produced in Colombia and Brazil, it has become fairly important, constituting one-quarter of world production.

Although African peasants have always been mainly responsible for growing these crops, working in conjunction with a network of technical service industries which provided them with seedlings, rubber trees, oil palms (or Elaeis) in Guinea, and sugar cane were grown mainly in great commercial plantations, backed by European capital; the largest of these are in the Congo (Kinshasa). Bananas, an export crop, and pineapples were originally introduced by

[3] See Osende Afana, *L'Economie de l'Ouest africain*, Maspero, 1966. On March 15, 1966, Afana was ambushed and executed by the maquis of Cameroun.

white settlers and have in some cases been taken over by African peasants.

All these forms of production have caused an increase in the volume of Africa's agricultural exports; but, as a result of falling prices, their purchasing power has not increased to any significant extent. Furthermore, although the growers of these crops have caused an increased demand for food, there has been no correspond-ing increase in food production. In consequence, food imports have risen sharply in Africa (especially Ghana); the continent, therefore, has less money available for the purchase of machinery. Increasing food production would do more to improve the balance of payments by reducing imports than increasing the export of goods whose market is already saturated. This does not mean that every agricul-tural district should try to be self-sufficient. Since the south of Ghana is so well suited to cocoa-growing, it should continue to specialize. It could also produce various perishable goods, such as most fruits, vegetables, eggs, and poultry; but the most sensible system would be for it to buy most of its food from other parts of the country or from neighbouring states.

As we shall see, the African savannah does not have such good prospects, since it is further from the coast and industrialization presents more problems. Production in this area should, therefore, be protected until it can become competitive. The savannah now sends oxen, meat, dried and smoked fish to the coastal countries. It may at some time be able to add cane sugar, from the Niara Valley in the Congo,[4] for example, then cereals, onions, other vegetables and fruit, either fresh, dried (like the delicious lichees from Canton in China), or tinned.

The agriculture of the forest area could be developed substantially with plantations replacing the unproductive natural forest. At some point man-made forests would have to be planted in order to satisfy the increasing demand both in Africa and in Europe. There is no obvious reason for abandoning the large plantation system, which requires large capital investment and advanced technical inputs,

[4] 150,000 tons of sugar will be produced in 1970, as the capitalist company SIAN has set up Sosuniari, a company with mixed public and private ownership; as Lacouture said in Ghana, an excellent plan is the construction of 'African socialism with the help of western capitalism'.

even if these come from abroad.[5] Africa should not take any hasty decisions to abandon primary production as, for instance, Cuba did with cane sugar; when the emphasis on sugar production was restored two or three years later Cuba had already paid dearly for her mistake.

Foreigners are less willing to invest their money in Africa now than previously. It is, therefore, both essential and desirable that local private and, more important, public, money should constitute a large part of investment in Africa. The Ivory Coast is developing state plantations of oil palms with the aid of European capital, and the co-operative plantations in the south-west of Dahomey are also financed by European money. These quasi-industrial concerns pay their African employees a regular daily wage, which is sometimes regarded as preferable to the unreliable profits of an independent producer at the mercy of both climatic hazards and price fluctuations. These plantations provide an excellent foundation for such vital preliminaries to modernization as professional training and disciplined work. Ideally, the organization of the plantations should be taken over by Africans, but only if this can be carried out without lowering production. The process must not be too hasty, since many young Africans still balk at the hard work expected by plantation overseers.

Coffee and cocoa production is still largely controlled by peasants and there seems no reason for making any change. In Western Cameroun, however, the cocoa yield from large plantations (Corporations) has sometimes been ten times as high as the national average. At the present stage, the most desirable trend seems to be a gradual changeover to medium-sized plantations with wage-earning employees, since they have better possibilities for technical progress and large investment than a peasant system. At some point it will be possible to think in terms of communal agriculture or even producers' co-operatives; given present attitudes any such system would be premature.[6] We would rather recommend various kinds

[5] P. Bairoch points out, however, that 'the productivity of food-growing agriculture is on the whole higher in countries where plantations have comparatively little importance' for plantations always take the best land. When they are extended, therefore, a corresponding effort should be made to increase food production. Cf. *Développement et Civilisation*, March 1966.

[6] In January 1966, we warned Pascal Lissouba, the prime minister of Congo (Brazzaville), against a project for a cooperative village in which the profits would be distributed

of limited co-operatives for service industries (supplies, sales, and pest control), conceived and organized by the most determined and active peasants – I almost said 'kulaks'.

The land-tenure system, now often tribal, should advance in such a way as to encourage investment; that is, to provide a better guarantee that those who have planted, improved, or invested in the land should have the rights of ownership.[7] A trend to be avoided at all costs is the formation of a parasitic class of non-working land-owners, living off rents from the land and the appropriation of agricultural profits which they subsequently invest in land specula-tion. In Africa this would aggravate the tendency towards the South American pattern, as can already be noted in Abidjan. This city's wealth is founded on processing and selling agricultural goods, and on the wasteful expenditure of foreign aid.

Thus the forest regions of Africa have an extremely high potential for increased agricultural production, both for export and for the domestic market. They could develop their ricefields instead of buying so much flour; they could produce far more fruit and vege-tables and, above all, animal produce – thus moving away from complete reliance on coffee- and cocoa-growing, both of which are forms of production where a rapid increase in output could easily have the effect of lowering total revenue.[8] The problem of the tropical savannahs is much harder to solve.[9]

3. THE SAVANNAHS

Though infertility, poor soil, and an unreliable climate are the

---

partly according to the size of family, therefore according to needs. Attempts to send town-dwellers back to the land were another potential cause of failure, aggravated by the fact that training had until then been predominantly military. Such a project might easily cost the budget as much as the cooperative villages in the Central African Republic, where Israeli advisers caused many technical errors by putting too much emphasis on tractors. There is a grave danger that premature projects of this kind may discredit the idea of socialism in the countryside.

[7] See our report to the United Nations: *Le Développement agricole africain*, coll. 'Tiers-Monde', P.U.F., 1965.

[8] Ghana's cocoa market has been improved by huge purchases by the USSR. I had recommended these a long time ago. If they had taken place sooner, Nkrumah's position might have been different from what it is today.

[9] All these subjects are treated in more detail in *False Start in Africa*, André Deutsch, London and Frederick A. Praeger, New York, 1966.

general rule there are fortunately some important exceptions. Parts of East Africa, from Ethiopia to Kenya (and further south) have rich volcanic mountains with fertile soil, sometimes at a high altitude where the climate is temperate with the right amount of rainfall. The English settlers in Kenya developed Arabica coffee, tea, and highly productive dairy-farming, for which European strains of cattle were used. Ethiopia could follow Kenya's example and increase the productivity of much of her land, but landowners levy up to 80 per cent of the harvest as rent and the 250 villages which make up her agricultural capital are seriously underdeveloped. East Africa is the most suitable area for the production of milk derivatives (the best source of first-class proteins) and may one day be able to provide a large proportion of the continent's supply.

The region could also provide corn to produce bread, which is easy to transport and is now becoming a symbol of civilization in Africa. It could also supply tinned fruit and temperate-climate vegetables, while at the same time exporting tropical fruit, flowers, and early winter vegetables to Europe. But here it will be in competition with West Africa which is nearer to European markets and, of course, none of these ideas could work without a reduction in the cost of transport.

There are fertile humid savannahs on the edge of the forests from Bouaké in the Ivory Coast to Grimari in the Central African Republic, where a fallow period is no longer always necessary. More difficult problems are presented by the modernization of the other flat savannahs, where the rainy season is shorter and the soil generally poor. Their subsistence economy is based on sorghum, millet and more recently (and particularly in the east) maize. The Europeans have recently started to plant industrial crops such as groundnuts and cotton. Those modern agricultural techniques perfected here ought to be easy to disseminate, since the principles have been summarized in a few simple pages[10]; but progress is still too slow.

Now that groundnuts are becoming Senegal's main crop, the Senegalese are dependent upon increasingly large imports of rice and corn for their survival; shortages before each new harvest are

[10] Consult the research institutes for cotton (IRCT) and oil (IRHO), 11, Square Pétrarque, Paris 16e.

becoming more and more extreme. The situation could be much improved, however, by proper weeding with hoes: at the moment, large areas of the millet fields, which are sown annually, are smothered with weeds. Senegal's first plan concentrated on the diversification of agriculture, but has not yet succeeded in promoting it.

Ex-president David Dacko of the Central African Republic, who invited me to Bangui in July, 1965, wanted like so many others to modernize agriculture immediately, mainly by means of mechanization and irrigation.[11] Tractors, however, have already caused a number of failures in tropical Africa, from the groundnut scheme in Tanganyika (1945–52) to the C.G.O.T. (Compagnie Générale des Oleagineux Tropicaux) in the Casamance in Senegal (1948–55). They are much too expensive while crop yields are still so poor.

In tropical climates where the rainy season is short, the success of the cotton harvest depends entirely on early sowing. On the frontier of Chad and Cameroun, in Toubouri, 800 kgs per hectare are obtained from sowing on June 1, 400 kgs from sowing on July 1 and 100 kgs from sowing on August 1, when conditions are similar in all other respects. This vital point is really one of discipline, plain and simple, rather than one of method.

The next question is the protection of crops against weeds, insects, and disease. Chemical fertilizers often double yields, but they are very expensive, particularly in the interior of the continent, where they cost 70 per cent more than they do in Europe. Since agricultural prices are lower, again on account of transportation costs, the use of fertilizers is not economic except for very good crops, sown early, and carefully tended. Agricultural progress does not proceed, as Khrushchev believed, through disconnected isolated steps, which take account of only one factor at a time; it proceeds through a conjunction of all the various factors necessary for success. Early sowing, however, offers so much scope for improvement that it could be recommended as a single first step. In 1965–66, it could have raised the cotton harvest in the Central African Republic from 26,000 tons to 50,000.

[11] Dacko rejected my report. It appeared in the *Annales de l'Institut agronomique*, 1966, with the title 'Le Difficile développement agricole de la Republique centrafricaine'.

Animal traction, by oxen or donkeys, makes ploughing easier and faster at the end of the dry season when the earth is hard, thereby facilitating earlier sowing. But investment outlay on animals and equipment is high; like fertilizer, animal traction is only economic when yields are good. It could often be given priority over chemical fertilization, particularly if foreign exchange is in short supply. Any attempt to formulate a system of priorities is complicated by the fact that some factors are complementary.

Except in the great plantations of the forest zone, where agricultural discipline is very strict and there are good possibilities for the upkeep of machinery, tropical Africa is not, on the whole, ready for mechanical traction. Tractors, tractor equipment, spare parts and motor fuel would constitute a heavy drain on scarce foreign exchange and white mechanics would have to be paid high wages for maintenance. Tractors can be brought into general use when yields have grown substantially. Good African mechanics would have to be trained and paid reasonable salaries and the tractors would have to be manufactured in the country itself. Given these considerations, the tractor will not come into general use in Africa until 1980, and later still in backward areas. The highest priority should, therefore, be given to instruction in early sowing, the care of crops, and animal traction, together with insecticides, fungicides, and fertilizers. The dangerous gap between rates of population growth (2.5 per cent) and food production (1.7 per cent), observed in Africa since 1958, can only be narrowed by more relevant experiments in these fields. Progress is slow, since the peasant feels despised, even crushed, by the privileged urban minority – whether in Mali or Upper Volta, Ghana or the Ivory Coast. The farm worker has virtually no hope of bettering his social position; his main ambition is to put his son into the upper caste by giving him an education and the élite class uses the army to enforce its privileges.

The agricultural adviser should be the main instigator of technical progress. But in Africa he is a comparatively underestimated official and all he wants is a position in the capital, after a period in Europe. He is not nearly so well treated as his colleagues in the Health and Education Departments, in contrast to Russia where agronomic advisers are regarded as directly productive and are consequently better paid. In Africa their devotion to the general good and to the peasantry often seems qualified by an uncooperative environment and by their low status and inadequate training.[12] In many current projects in French-speaking Africa, such as SATEC (Société d'Assistance Technique et de Crédit) in the groundnut-growing area of Senegal, young French technicians have recently been brought back to carry out the organizational work. These technicians, however, do not know the languages, customs, and attitudes of the various countries. They are only given one day's instruction in the basic methods of modernizing groundnut-growing, yet they are expected to promote more regular and conscientious methods of work. It would be impossible for European technicians and agronomists to organize the work of the entire peasant population of Africa. There are not enough of them and if there were they would deprive young Africans of a valuable means of practical training and social advancement. Africa must not continue to allow her development to be directed by foreign capital and technical skill.

4. IRRIGATION IS STILL PREMATURE IN ALL BUT DESERT AREAS

Africa is full of great irrigation works, starting with Gezira on the Upper Nile near the capital of Sudan: surrounded by desert and having few other resources, the Sudanese have long been using the fertilizing waters of the Nile for irrigating alluvial soils, especially for the growing of cotton. Working on the basis of long, careful studies carried out by the English, they have achieved magnificent results, and long fibre cotton is now Sudan's main export.

At the other end of the scale, the Niger Office in Mali can be used as an example of what to avoid: the serious famine of 1914 gave an incentive for research into ways of stabilizing the harvest. Belime, the main instigator of the project, noticed that the delta contained some mouths which were dry and which could easily be converted into natural irrigation canals. The French School of Soil Science was not yet operative at this time (not, in fact, till after 1945) and the dam was finished, just before the war, without the benefit of

[12] An African agronomist wanted to make his men work instead of spending most of their time hunting. He was quickly repudiated by a weak, demagogic government.

preliminary studies of soil type being made.[13] The dam irrigates old alluvial soil which is very uneven in quality, too hard to plough and difficult to drain. On account of summer rains, 4,000 cubic metres of water must be drained from the land in a short space of time; this is impossible without a more expensive drainage network – the irrigation canals only hold 2,500 cubic metres. The people embarked on cotton- and rice-growing before obtaining the right varieties of plant and studying the correct cultivation techniques. Yields did not reach a reasonable level until 1958.

West of Segou, dry fields, if properly treated, produce almost as good harvests as irrigated fields and at far less cost. Yields are sometimes almost 2 tons of raw cotton per hectare, with averages of 800 kgs in the progressive villages. This area of Mali is not desert; the flooding system irrigating the ricefields along the main valley of the river has been controlled with very simple dyke and overflow constructions. The Niger Office intended to employ in this area the surplus population among the 'mossiss' people of Upper Volta but the two countries are now divided by a linguistic and monetary frontier.

Unlike the settlers in Gezira, those in Mali have never enforced the very strict sanitary precautions necessary for the control of insects and diseases which prey on cotton. Mekki Abbas, the organizer of the Gezira project, came back from a visit to the Office, disgusted by the carelessness he had seen. After investment costs of over 2,000 US dollars per hectare, the first areas to be cultivated have already had to be abandoned. Banguineda near Bamako and most of the rice-growing district of Kolongo in the valley of the Niger are now overgrown with wild red rice. Furthermore, the Niger Office has always been in debt and France was unable to support it. In recent years, annual losses have been well over 2 million US dollars and Mali is, anyway, in a weak situation economically. Taking 40 per cent of the country's agricultural budget, the Niger Office contributes only 10 per cent of production. Lesser and middle-rank organizers in Mali have shown no enthusiasm for work and the prevalent demagogy fails to drive them on; unfortunately, this form of 'socialism' has done nothing to inculcate the administrative class

---

[13] In soil science (pedology) soil types are classified according to their evolution, as influenced by climate, vegetation, crop-growing, etc.

with any sense of professional conscience; they still have the mentality of the privileged.[14]

Hydraulic works in Africa could also be used to produce electric power for industrialization. Electricity can be obtained at very low cost, at present from the Zambezi and the Volta, and in the future from the Konkoure in Guinea, the Kouilou, and especially from the lower Congo. But irrigation is often the most costly factor of production: it does not become economic until crops are good. It should, therefore, be promoted first in those areas, such as Egypt, where the people could not survive without it. In other places, its economic value must be compared with other factors of agricultural modernization.

Foreign aid, a form of dying colonialism, is usually put into prestige projects. The Richard Toll project in Senegal, however, has been a disaster and the small rice-growing projects in Upper Volta and in the Ivory Coast are operating far below their full capacity. The best way of making sure that such projects are run effectively would be to ask the people to carry out some of the work without payment. Their guaranteed right to ownership of land, improved in this way, would then depend upon the work they had done.

Africa's Atlantic coast is very rich in fish, particularly in the north off Morocco and Mauritania and in the south off Angola and South Africa. Fishing is now developing fast, and much of the produce is used to make fish meal for European animals. Since this substance has a very high protein content and is easy to preserve and transport, it offers an economic way of supplementing protein deficiencies in the predominantly vegetarian African diet. Thus the sated Europeans are wasting these proteins by turning them into useless products, taking them out of the mouths of African women and children who need them so urgently. Some day it will be blindingly clear to everyone that distribution of food according to monetary wealth alone is a fundamental injustice. The sovereignty of money will appear as immoral as slavery or prostitution.[15]

[14] We do not include an existing agricultural project for a dam in the Sankarani, a tributary of the Niger, by means of which irrigation works could be extended.
[15] The same goes for Peru's fishing trade, when the Indians of the Andes have such bad protein deficiencies. See the film *Un cri* by Armand Chartier, at the Ministry of Agriculture's cinema in Paris.

5. THE DRAMATIC SITUATION IN NORTH AFRICA

South East Asia, from Java to India, is the world's most ominous breeding-ground for imminent widespread famine. Moreover, in Africa too, from Egypt to Morocco, more and more people are falling victim to the debilitating effects of undernourishment. The results of an inquiry into nutrition conducted in Morocco in 1965 have not been published; but it showed that the calorie intake of a tenth of the population, mostly living in the shanty towns of Casablanca and other cities, was often as low as 1,600 per day; 30 per cent of the population, the poorest country dwellers, farm-workers, share-croppers, and smallholders, had a normal intake of only 1,700 or 1,800 calories per day. The standard of living of civil servants and of people in the Gharb, on the other hand, had risen slightly.

Even the most deliberately optimistic forecasts on the future of population and production in North Africa come to the conclusion that deficits are on the increase. Since independence, Morocco and Tunisia have probably increased their food supply by only 1 per cent and 2 per cent per year respectively, while their population growth rates are certainly over 3 per cent and 2.8 per cent – Morocco's could be as high as 3.5 per cent by 1970. The food situation has been seriously aggravated by the drought of 1966 and people are dying of hunger on the borders of the desert. In absolute terms, Algerian production is falling, and according to unpublished calculations, production on the self-managed farms expropriated from settlers probably fell by about 43 per cent between 1960 and 1964.[16]

Egypt has announced fairly large increases in agricultural produc-tion, but this is apparently contradicted by her increased cereal imports, which now constitute half the total consumption, as opposed to a quarter ten years ago, and still do not cover total demand. The recent rate of agricultural growth could be about 2 per cent per year, compared with population growth of 3 per cent. And only about 10,000 new industrial jobs were created per year on average between 1952 and 1964.

[16] As I told President Ben Bella in January 1963; I advised him to try to make some colons stay on for five years, during which time they could have trained their successors. Before the war, I once told Algerian students that more of them should be studying to become agronomists, but with no success.

It would require a tremendous effort to raise the Maghreb's agricultural growth rate to an average of 1.5 per cent per year, and really exceptional efforts to raise it to 2.5 per cent. An enormous campaign for education in birth control would have to be launched for population growth to be reduced from 3.2 to 2.7 per cent per year. Tunisia and Egypt have made timid beginnings, Morocco has begun to move in this direction, but Algeria remains undecided. Whatever the nature of the régime, the privileged town-dwellers show no concern for the peasants' ever-increasing poverty. People were dying of hunger in Algeria after the dry winter of 1965-6.

In this region irrigation comes into its own – on condition that the coastal plains, where potential is high, as well as the expensive dam reservoirs now quickly silting up, are first used to the full, which was never the case in French Algeria. If the Aswan dam irrigated 500,000 hectares, intensive agriculture could produce enough food for 5 million more people. But the dam and secondary irrigation networks will not be completely finished until towards 1980; meanwhile, population is increasing by one million each year. If no corrective measures are taken, the increase might be more than one and a half million each year in fifteen years' time. Egypt would then be in danger of losing more of her economic and, consequently, political independence. Desalination of seawater is another possibility, but it is too soon to know when its cost will be sufficiently economic for use in irrigation.

In the meantime, agricultural progress should be accelerated by all possible means. After the agriculture near the coast has been intensified, the scheme of 'rural renewal', put forward by the forestry service, would halt erosion on the hills by means of ditches, embankments, and plantations of trees along the contour lines. Bush plantations would be more suitable than annual crops because of the irregularity of winter rains, especially when they are heavy. Forage trees and other intensive fodder crops could be complemented by stock-breeding of dairy cows, sheep, with improved meat and wool yields, and dairy goats; goats should be kept in stables or in a fenced field, so that they do not destroy the remaining vegetation.

There is great potential everywhere for increased production with more intensive agriculture.[17] It cannot be realized, however, before a certain level of development is reached, as the experience of Japan and Mexico has shown. The first steps are the hardest and slowest and the Third World has difficult problems ahead.

Some people say that other countries should model themselves on Israel. This is not easy, because Israel's population includes highly qualified immigrants and she has received enormous amounts of capital from abroad. Moreover, as a result of their struggle for existence, the Israelis have developed an iron will which enables them to overcome both natural and human obstacles and to build a democratic society to which the whole population feels actively committed. Nevertheless new rural communities which would arouse enthusiasm for work should be set up in other countries; the self-managed farms in Algeria have failed to promote this enthusiasm.

6. BASIC PROBLEMS: THE POPULATION EXPLOSION AND PRIVILEGED MINORITIES

The essence of Africa's problem is that the peasant does not feel committed, does not feel that his work furthers his own interests or those of his country. Independence sparked off a feeling of enthusiasm, which could have been used to further economic development but was in fact completely wasted. Whatever the economy or form of government – socialist, liberal, military (becoming more and more common), one-party, or pseudo-democratic – there are always unfairly privileged minorities. In some places the privileged class consists mainly of politicians and members of the administration; in other places it is traders and members of the professions. Everywhere, they exploit the peasantry. The same, of course, was true of Europe; but the European bourgeoisie, in revolt against feudalism, did develop production. In Africa the minority[18] causes such a drain on national revenue that it limits investment, destroys any chance

---

[17] See our report to President Ben Bella in L'Algérie indépendante, coll. 'Tiers monde', P.U.F., 1963.
[18] In Economie du Maghreb, ed. de Minuit, 1966, Samir Amin shows that public spending in Tunisia is increasing twice as fast as production, now being 28 per cent of gross domestic product.

of rapid development, and places economic independence in jeopardy. A country cannot be economically independent when the vast majority of its equipment is supplied by foreign aid. Progress has been most rapid in Ghana and the Ivory Coast, but Samir Amin has already pointed out its limitations.

On September 2, 1964, journalists in Dakar criticized me for expecting too much of Africa. 'You want her to do as much in one generation,' they said to me, 'as Europe did in two or three thousand years. This is impossible; it will require a complete transformation in mental attitudes; it will take several generations. Give us time and space; let us draw breath.' Of course nothing valuable is accomplished hastily and badly studied projects all fail, as the experience of the last few years has shown. 'Africa is under-populated, so why do you bring up the subject of birth control?' Underpopulation is, of course, a hindrance to development when 'economic archipelagoes' are separated by huge areas of empty country. The population explosion might, therefore, seem acceptable if not desirable, but only for those countries capable of facing it squarely, that is, of accelerating agricultural progress to overtake population growth. In recent years very few African countries have succeeded in doing this in food production (South Africa is the exception!), though some have increased their exports. If our friends in Dakar want to stay out of trouble and justify their lack of progress they have no alternative but to bring down the birth rate as quickly as possible. Some officials have refused to make any choice, preferring laziness and privilege.

A large number of African students call themselves revolutionaries, but their life style is hardly suitable for militants. In our discussions in 1961–2 they refused everything at once: foreign aid, decreases in the salary of officials, any concerted attempt to increase peasant production, and birth control. They thus revealed themselves completely ignorant of the hard facts of development. The recent difficulties in Guinea and Mali should destroy their holy belief in the miracle of effortless socialism.

We have fought colonialism, racism, apartheid in South Africa, and rebellion in Rhodesia. In all the countries which regard themselves as independent but which are in fact still subsidized, we can

see the emergence of another equally insidious form of segregation –
based on power and money.[19] And being less highly trained, this
'new class', as Djilas would call it, is not always as efficient as the
previous one. It has no compunction about using any available
means to keep itself in power, including military coups d'état, and
the use of foreign troops, as in Gabon and East Africa, as well as
imprisonment and assassination of opponents. The students of
Casablanca in March 1965, and Mehdi Ben Barka, are well known
but by no means the only examples.

In 1966 Africa's future seemed even blacker than it did in 1962,
when we finished *False Start in Africa* with a plea for twenty years
to overcome underdevelopment in the world. In specifying this
short period of time, we imagined that everyone – peasants and
rulers in poor countries, public opinion and governments of rich
countries – would combine their efforts to this end. This is not the
way things have turned out and the privileged lobbies, firmly
ensconced in power, are taking full advantage of the situation, whatever their political complexion. In order to challenge their power,
which now has no effective counterwight, the peasants would have
to form cohesive and determined pressure groups.

7. INTRA-AFRICAN RACISM AND BALKANIZATION

Like the proletariat in Europe in the nineteenth century, the
peasantry in Africa in the twentieth century, constituting 80 per cent
of the population, is the most representative class. If it demands and
receives more suitable education and more equipment, then cuts will
necessarily have to be made in the abuses of the privileged, such as
luxury building and imports. Governments could expect the rural
population to work harder in return.

Modern Africa will never become a reality while the peasants
devote only 500 or 1,000 hours work per year to agricultural production. Ministers would obtain better results if they drove cheap

[19] In *Jeune Afrique*, January 2, 1966, Abel Eyinga wrote: 'Repression of the people is
taking the place of dialogue, absolute power by one tribe or one individual is replacing
government by the will of the people ... I appeal to the French people and to their
leader to help us to build a democratic, efficient Africa, which is ready to enter the
20th century, *by not opposing necessary changes*'.

Citroëns or Jeeps instead of Cadillacs or Mercedes, and particularly if they sometimes took up Jean-Marie Kone's hoe, as Mobutu has recently suggested.

Revolution still remains a possible answer: though this depends on the type of revolution, its organizers, and whether it is more like Chinese communism at its most heroic than the anarchy of the Congo. Certainly the abuses and corruption of the young Congolese Simbas were not more excessive than those of their former rulers. But they had no cause to wipe out all educated Africans, as they did in some centres. The massacres of the Hutu élites in Burundi, of the Tutsis in Rwanda, and the negroes in southern Sudan, represent a pernicious form of intra-African racism; quite apart from humanitarian considerations, by wiping out all trained personnel they reduce the chances of development.

'Revolution' is not a magic word any more than 'socialism' and 'democracy'. It will only succeed if it inspires and organizes the mass of the population into disciplined and enthusiastic workers, and the rulers into honest and devoted duty – in other words if it succeeds in promoting development. Now more than ever before, let Mali and Guinea take note, revolution without development is a betrayal of that revolution, even, or particularly, in Africa.

The countryside cannot develop to any significant extent without industrial projects that provide locally produced tools for agricultural modernization and for the processing of agricultural output. Africa should be thinking in terms of exporting metals instead of crude minerals, and cloth and oil products instead of raw cotton and oilseeds. If industrialization is to be economically viable, then states must agree to combine to provide the necessary capital and an initial market.[20] Europe should be buying manufactured goods, not raw materials, from backward countries.

In Africa, as Jean Rous[21] puts it, 'Population is increasing faster than food production, the terms of trade are deteriorating, the price of raw materials is still settled by the large monopolies. . . . After the failure of the forces of progress, we are now witnessing the rise of neo-colonialism. . . . Africa is in danger of following South

[20] See the work of the United Nations Economic Commission for Africa and my report to this Commission, *Le développement agricole africain*, P.U.F., 1965.
[21] *Jeune Afrique*, January 23, 1966.

America. . . .[22] Cooperation must give priority to the modernization of the countryside, the diversification of crops, training, reducing unemployment, increasing production and productivity, encouraging regional integration associated with more flexible
monetary areas.' A repetition of events in the Congo has to some
extent been avoided by the Balkanization of the large colonial group-
ings. In French West Africa and French Equatorial Africa the
French government was in favour of it, some elements doubtless
following the divide and rule principle. The position of France and
the EEC countries would be just as strong if they spent more public
money on financing industrial equipment in Africa.[23]

[22] A danger which I pointed out in *False Start in Africa*, chap. XVII: 'South Ameri-
canisation and a Rash Type of Socialism'.
[23] The inadequacy of such schemes was the basic reason – there were other more personal ones – for my resignation from the executive committee of the Fonds d'aide et de
coopération (FAC) in autumn 1961. This fund financed for the same price as a productive sawmill, a palace for the National Assembly at Bangui, opposite the old one which
was still in very good condition. As soon as it was finished, at the end of 1965, the new
government dissolved the National Assembly.

CHAPTER TEN

Latifundia *in Latin America: an obstacle to progress*

I. THE RICH AGAINST THE NATION

Before political independence from Spain and Portugal at the beginning of the nineteenth century, Central and South America gave the superficial impression of being richer and more prosperous than the north of the continent. But the luxurious towns and richly gilded churches were only a veneer. Even on the prosperous sugar plantations in Antilles and the Nordeste of Brazil slaves lived in abject poverty, and conditions were twice as bad on the quasi-autarchic feudal estates of the interior. In the south of Brazil the pioneers enjoyed a long period of prosperity on the coffee belt, which stretches from Rio de Janeiro to the north of Parana, though at the cost of destroying the fertility of soils which are better than those of Africa.

During the same period, in the north of the continent, rough New England farmers worked infertile land in a less favourable climate, but here the workers owned their land. Their more modern agricultural methods, into which machines were introduced at an early date (the combine-harvester was invented over a century ago), became the foundation for a rapidly expanding industrial sector. Enterprising industrialists were blessed with good resources: coal at ground level, oil near the surface, and capital from Europe. The frontier pioneers opened up the prairies and soon succeeded in providing Europe with cheap corn. Meanwhile the Southern states, which still practised slavery, wanted to preserve free trade to enable them to buy capital and consumer goods at favourable prices from Europe. It is easy to see how the American Civil War arose, resulting in the replacement of the slave system with an industrial economy.

Unfortunately, the plantation system can still be found, often virtually unchanged, throughout the south of the American continent. The slaves may have become paid workers, but they are no better treated. When I was in Pernambuco and Algoas in 1958, I felt that they were perhaps even worse fed than their predecessors. At least slaves had some market value which had to be preserved. The *latifundiaries* hold a virtual monopoly over a scarce factor of production: fertile soil. Corrupt landowners neglect and sometimes even paralyse this vital factor of economic development, leaving it as extensive pasture land or allowing it to lie fallow in the hope that its value will rise. They are thus doing their country harm, indeed betraying it.

Important advances around the beginning of the century did much to improve agriculture in Argentina, but since 1940 development has been so slow that population growth has overtaken production growth in much of this fertile and underpopulated country. In consequence, exports must be held back, mechanization delayed and progress towards industrial development generally impeded; industry in Argentina is lagging behind that of Southern Brazil, Mexico, and even Chile.

The large capitalist plantations, stretching from Puerto Rico to Jamaica and from Central America to the coast of Peru, have often achieved important technical advances in the production of sugar cane, cotton, bananas, and so on, but coffee-growing overworks the land and stock-breeding does quite the reverse. The Indians of the Andes, who live in mountains so high that any work demands painful effort, have a wretched standard of living, continuously aggravated by population growth. In Bolivia even agrarian reform has not worked; it should have included structural reorganization, credit loans, and redeployment of the population into the eastern plains on the far side of the Andes, apart from the usual education campaign.

Revolt is breaking out among the other Indian communities; they have been deprived of more and more of their land ever since the Spanish conquest and they are becoming increasingly overcrowded. A priest is leading the *Violencia* rising in Colombia,[1] Castroist

[1] Camillo Torrés, who died in combat, used to say: 'Any analysis of the situation in Colombia shows that a revolution is needed to feed the hungry, clothe the naked and fulfil the wishes of our people'. This quotation is taken from *Esprit*, May 1966, in which

guerillas are fighting in Venezuela, and the inhabitants of Peru are joining the same cause. Production for export has expanded quickly in some sectors – except corn and meat in Argentina – sometimes even to the point where the price was forced down, as in the case of coffee in Brazil, Colombia and Central America; but the price of coffee has since been supported by an international price agreement.

Malthusian processes check the increased consumption that should be the main objective of food production if shortages are to be eliminated. Food production, however, has not kept up with population growth: there has, therefore, been a drop in food exports and sometimes in the standard of nutrition, particularly in the Nordeste of Brazil and the Andes; there has also been an increase in food imports and in some countries the currency has been devalued. A further consequence is the flight of capital to the United States and Switzerland, which reduces local investment by the country's inhabitants. The Alliance for Progress[2] is pouring water into a leaking bucket.

The improvements which are made still benefit predominantly the privileged classes, who have the best of everything from Acapulco in Mexico to Copacabana, one of the famous beaches in Rio de Janeiro. The proceeds from coffee, a highly productive and lucrative crop in the red basalt earth, go entirely into buildings and luxury hotels or land speculation. An aerial view of the outskirts of Rio and São Paulo shows a thick network of useless roads. They are built with the purpose of increasing the value of future, often hypothetical building sites, whose price is expected to rise. This means that market gardeners and fruit growers are being pushed back too far from the towns, with obvious consequences.

One capitalist from São Paulo bought half a million hectares of good land in the Matto Grosso (specially chosen by soil scientists) simply because he knew that a railway would be built there. This has since been built and crosses 67 miles of the estate. But the land is not put to any useful purpose, because it was bought for the

---

J. Givet also expresses his concern at seeing the machine-gun becoming the emblem of the Third World at Cuba's Tricontinental Conference.
[2] A development plan for the South American economy, suggested by President Kennedy, which was intended to be supported mainly by money from the US.

owner's grandson in the hopes that public investment would increase its value a hundred or a thousand fold in the meantime. The areas which should be exploited first, however, are not those which have been bought up simply to be taken out of production, but those which are poorer and further away from the means of communication; for the people who live in those areas have inadequate resources and cannot wait for speculative profits.

Due to the chaotic transportation and market systems, and to weak purchasing power, local prices are not high enough to offer an incentive to marginal producers. The marketplaces of the big towns, Rio, São Paulo, Recife, and Bahia, therefore, are not adequately stocked; some people are in a permanent state of need and undernourishment creates an apathy that arrests work and development. Many villages can be seen to be suffering from terrible hardship.

Given the size of the continent, the real situation is, of course, much more complex than it seems from this brief outline. Though many areas are fertile and underpopulated, cultivated land constitutes only 2 per cent of its total; large expanses of pasture are appallingly under-used. This continent could be feeding one thousand million inhabitants more adequately than China could at the end of this century. Nevertheless, a large proportion of its 230 million inhabitants are very badly fed now. The countries surrounding the Rio de la Plata are an exception, but, though still well in the lead, they are also now marking time.

2. 'ASSISTANCE' FROM NORTH AMERICAN INVESTMENT

North American capital has been an extremely useful aid to development in some places, acting as a catalyst to industrialization: in Mexico, for example, capital investment supplemented tourist expenditure and large horticultural purchases. Capital was more commonly invested in cheap raw materials for the North American market, such as iron ore and oil in Venezuela, tin in Bolivia, and copper in Chile; also in coffee, cocoa, and bananas. Though hardly smaller in numbers of buyers, the Northern market is very much larger than the Southern in terms of value, average purchasing power being enormously higher.

South America's troubles arise from the alliance between the privileged minorities in the countries themselves and the powerful North American companies established there. The rich are entirely content to defend a status quo in which prospects for development are few. Aware of the requirements of modern technology, Celso Furtado reminds us[3]: 'In the present situation in Latin America, the rule tends to be monopoly and a gradual concentration of incomes. The only hope for development lies in systematic, deliberate action on the part of central governments; it will never proceed through the mechanism of the market. But the United States is afraid of a change of economic policy, which would constitute the only escape from the North American sphere of influence short of subversive action. United States "security" demands the preservation of the social status quo. . . . Action to promote development is therefore virtually non-existent. The private North American firms operating in these countries enjoy a privileged position in comparison with those in the United States. They are outside the anti-trust laws, have politico-military protection, and many privileges. They will automatically become super-powers. The central decision-making bodies of the national states will soon become secondary.'

Agricultural development, like economic development generally in South America, cannot move forward unless it is freed from the double domination of corrupt native minorities in league with the great North American companies. In January, 1960, a summer school run by the National University of Santiago in Chile made an inquiry into the economic integration of rural Latin America into the twentieth century world. Since I had seen rural society and agricultural systems reminiscent of the Spanish Estremadura of the sixteenth century in central southern Chile, I made the slightly ironic suggestion that they should aim at very gradual evolution in stages.

A reformist policy could take an increase in land-tax as its logical beginning; this was advised by the eighteenth-century physiocrats and proved effective throughout the world, from Europe to Japan. Thus a *latifundiary*, who only kept 8,000 sheep on 8,000 hectares of fertile land, halfway between Santiago and Valparaiso, part of which

[3] *Le Monde*, January 5, 1966.

could have been irrigated, would have been forced to increase his stock gradually to, say, five sheep per hectare. This might be possible in theory,[4] if he had to pay land-tax to the value of one sheep per hectare. 'That's all very well,' an agronomist from Recife in Brazil said to me; 'your suggestion would be reasonable in a European context. You forget that our politicians value their lives. The ones who seem rather zealous about collecting the present low land-taxes often have "accidents" on pedestrian crossings. It is no coincidence that this never happens to their more complaisant colleagues.' Pressures of this kind make gradual change impossible and drive the people to revolution.

When the United States rejected Fidel Castro's offers of negotiation in April, 1959, it pushed him into the arms of the Russians. Its attitude put another obstacle in the path of reform, which was made even more difficult by the Bay of Pigs invasion in 1961, then by the occupation of Santo Domingo (America's Budapest) in 1965. 'Reform is a blind alley, which does not even have the advantage of being the least dangerous policy. Castro's Cuba never suffered as serious an attack as the reformists of Santo Domingo.'[5]

3. MEXICO: 'SABOTAGED' AGRARIAN REFORM IS BETTER THAN NO REFORM AT ALL

The peasants on the Mexican *latifundia* were so exploited and oppressed as to be stripped of all their dignity. The Institutional Revolutionary Party (PRI) came to power after the bloody and destructive revolt of 1911–21. It has remained in power ever since – with some compromises. Having promised 'land and liberty', it began to distribute part of the great estates to all the rural population of the nearby villages on the central plateau. This gesture was basically social and was bound to fail in economic terms because the peasants were not granted enough land to enable them to set up viable farms. Many did not know how to farm, or did not have the financial means to do so. Redistribution virtually stopped between 1928 and 1934 since it was holding back production; it was taken up

[4] René Dumont, *Living Lands*, Merlin Press, London, 1965, p. 88, and The Monthly Review Press, New York, 1966.
[5] Elena de la Souchère, *Le Monde diplomatique*, January 1966.

again between 1934 and 1940 under the stimulus of Lazaro Cardenas of the left wing of the PRI. He wanted to give the peasants instruction and credit loans in addition to the land, and he made the allotments larger instead of giving one small one to everyone. Eventually he nationalized the petroleum industry and at this point Anglo-Saxon capitalism aligned itself against him.

Reform slowed down again when the right wing of the PRI returned to power in 1940. Of course the redistributed land was not taken away, since the recipients had hot tempers and were quick to use their machetes, especially when fortified with drink. But most of the roads and irrigation works served large estates that were still privately-owned and largely financed by credit loans. Prompted by their disquieting memories of the terrible massacres of 1915–20, the landowners carried out a campaign for the intensification of agriculture, exploiting markets in the United States and in their own towns where industrialization was advancing rapidly.

The rate of agricultural progress achieved in Mexico between 1940 and 1955 seems to be unique, not only for Latin America but for the whole of the Third World. Production almost tripled in fifteen years. Opponents of reform have pointed out that these results were obtained essentially from the estates which remained in the hands of the large landowners, but this can easily be answered by the fact that Mexico is the only Latin American country where progress has been so rapid, and the only one which embarked on thoroughgoing agricultural reform before Cuba (1959–63). The landowners and public authorities had been goaded to extra effort by their fear of reprisals by the peasant masses and this can be seen as an essential spur to progress. The landowners wanted to raise their standard of living to the level it had reached before the reform. Their estates had shrunk somewhat and they had, therefore, no alternative but to intensify the use of the land, for which the public authorities furnished large amounts of credit for irrigation and training.

Ever since 1955, the landowners' fear of the peasants has been waning, and simultaneously progress has been slowing down; memories are dying, the right wing of the PRI has strengthened its influence and corruption is spreading. Mexico's agricultural growth rate was probably little more than 2 per cent[6] for the ten years between 1955 and 1965; and now population is probably increasing at about 3.8 per cent. Confident of the government's real views beneath its pseudo-revolutionary declarations, the *latifundiaries* are once more making inroads into the collective farms ('ejidos') established by the redistribution of the *latifundia* during the reform. They pay very low wages, unaware that this curtails their markets. Mexico should now concentrate on developing production on the rest of the land, which was intended for collective ownership by the villages but is in fact usually cultivated in uneconomically small separate units. Though some of these are in infertile areas, intensification would be possible on many of them – on condition that domestic purchasing power is advanced by industry.

4. THE *MINIFUNDIUM* AND THE IMPASSE OF THE ALLIANCE FOR PROGRESS

Large *latifundia* are a major cause of underproduction in agriculture; this is especially noticeable when they involve the raising of oxen in open fields. In the llanos of western Guarico in Venezuela, I noticed that yields were as low as 4 kgs liveweight per hectare per year. With a series of economic improvements, yields could be brought up to 200 kgs – or even 1,000 kgs if there were large investment including irrigation and use of the best new alluvial soils close to the banks of rivers.[7]

The small estate, however – the *minifundium* of the Venezuelan *conuco*, and the Brazilian *caboclo* or Chilean *inquilino* – puts another significant brake on agricultural advance. Its owner is usually a pariah, living apart from society, with more or less uncertain rights to cultivate a strip on a great estate; or he may reclaim a corner of tropical forest, using the same methods as the Bantu of Central Africa. He lives at virtually subsistence level, sometimes selling only one or two animals a year, just enough to find money for salt, oil,

[6] Cf. Ballesteros, *Partisans*, October 1965. He pointed out that the great landowners have kept the best land, evaded the law by giving pieces of land to their children, and taken advantage of the irrigation works. In any further attempt at reform, mountain or semi-desert land would be distributed; the colonization of tropical areas has, on the whole, failed.

[7] *Living Lands*, Chapter I–VII.

paraffin, matches and cloth. Investment is impossible with this type of agriculture. How would he find the money, with productivity so low? In the absence of agricultural surpluses of any size, his purchasing power and demand for industrial products are minimal; this limits general prospects for development. The *minifundia* owner represents an even more primitive state of development than the *latifundia* – especially where the latter is well-managed, like the estates of the Bookers group in Guyana. This can also be seen particularly clearly in Haiti, where Paul Moral shows that the 'destruction of the large holding (sugar cane, cotton) and the failure of all attempts to re-establish it (bananas, rice) are disastrous methods of decolonization, from the economic point of view . . . the triumph of the subsistence farm at the cost of economic disorganization at both a regional and a national level.'[8] Paul Moral is disturbed at seeing that 'many parts of black Africa seem to be following Haiti's trend: going from village ownership to individual ownership, from the extended family to the nuclear family, but with polygamy, communal work, and local solidarity still continuing'.

The distribution of the well cultivated *latifundia* – and there are some – into little subsistence units may well result in decreased production and always results in increased rural consumption; the town's food supplies, therefore, become even more unreliable. It might be best to keep the *latifundia* as units of production; but first, fiscal measures should be introduced to make them intensify their agriculture. The next stage could be the establishment of enterprises with joint private and public ownership; this would be a means of preparing for a changeover to producers' cooperatives. after mechanization, but only when the majority of the workers really want it. There is nothing intrinsically undesirable about the large estate; indeed, it is better suited to the requirements of modernization. It is the under-use of large estates which must be changed, and also the excessive political power granted to their owners – a power which is usually contrary to the interests of society as a whole, and which delays development. None of these measures can be put into practical effect unless the power is taken away from

[8] 'Le "facies agraire" haitien', colloquium CNRS-Institute of Latin America, on *Les problèmes agraires des Amériques latines*, Paris, October 1965; it contains a number of interesting ideas.

the *latifundiaries*. This is what happened in Cuba, although here sudden ill-prepared structural changes caused a drop in production. The Alliance for Progress has reached an impasse and, as we have seen, agricultural growth in Mexico is dropping behind population growth. J. Jouvin shows[9] that 'Food production *per capita* for local consumption has been dropping continuously since 1959 in Latin America as a whole. Production in 1964 was 8 per cent lower than production in 1954.'

Kennedy's Alliance suggested initial structural, fiscal and agrarian reforms. But in April, 1964, President Johnson immediately sided with an attack by reactionary interests on President Goulart, who wanted to expropriate the estates near roads and railways. The measure may have been clumsy; but, as Marcel Niedergang[10] asked, was the United States acting in its own best interests when it aligned itself openly with those landowners most hostile to economic progress? Those whom the gods wish to destroy, they first make mad. This dictum has never been so apt.

5. EDUARDO FREI IN CHILE

South American reformists, unwilling to accept protection from the United States, concerned about problems of development but reluctant to follow Castro's example of rebellion on Marxist lines, saw a new hope arise in Chile. The Christian Democrats won the presidency, with the support of the Right, which was apprehensive about Allende's Popular Front. But, contrary to all expectations, they brought back legislative elections, to the disadvantage of extremists on both sides. The 'Chilianization' of the copper mines, formerly owned by North American trusts, cannot be regarded as nationalization, since any direct conflict with the United States, such as Cuba's in 1960, was carefully avoided. Since then long strikes have weakened President Frei's authority.

The outline statement for agrarian reform in Chile which Frei proposed to Parliament points out that whereas agricultural production increased by 2 per cent per year between 1939 and 1965,

[9] 'La place de l'agriculture dans le développement économique récent d'Amérique latine', as note 8.
[10] *Les vingt Amériques latines*, Plon, 1965.

population increased by 2.26 per cent. The balance of trade in food, which was 13 million dollars in surplus in 1939, showed a deficit of 104 million dollars in 1961–3, and 120 million in 1964. Frei's plan is a moderate reformist one in that it includes graded but fairly substantial compensation for landowners. This will reduce the ability of the beneficiaries to invest and they will have to repay money for the land allotted to them by the reform. Consequently, it will be difficult for them to modernize agricultural methods. The state should see that the compensation payments are reinvested in industry or in agriculture to avoid restricting development.

The Chilean plan proposes a maximum size for agricultural holdings of 80 hectares of irrigated land, or the equivalent in other land; but it will probably leave 320 hectares of irrigated land for those landowners who treat their workers well and raise good crops. I would have been less generous with compensation but would have allowed 320 hectares to any *latifundiary* who already cultivated his own land and asked for five or six years' grace in which to achieve yields 50 per cent higher than the regional average. Only those who reached the target in time would be allowed to keep their 320 hectares; this is a good size for modernization, particularly for irrigated crops.

Thus, as in Mexico, the *latifundiaries*, with this incentive for intensification, would compensate for the predictable drop in production on some of the new holdings. The reform is moving too slowly: it should first deal with neglected areas[11] which are not realizing their high production potentials, particularly those where communications are good. Before opening up the distant forest areas, production in most parts of the continent should be intensified on good accessible land. This must be the first move, rather than the abandoning of coffee plantations or allowing extensive stock-breeding near roads and railways.[12]

If Chile is to be any more successful than Mexico, however, a concerted effort must be made on the holdings distributed to former

[11] Peru expropriated the American estates first of all, which is understandable from a political point of view; but they are the best cultivated and production will drop substantially, as in Algeria and on the Esterhazy estate in Hungary. It would be better to start with the pastureland of the *llanos*, and the most fertile fallow land.
[12] In British Honduras, estates beside roads and railways were taxed at a higher rate, as as incentive to intensification.

tenants or *inquilinos*. Instead of trying to make them landowners, in the hope that they would be more conservative, the reform should have given ownership of the land to local collectives. Agricultural workers must first be trained, given equipment, and brought into an organized system. One possibility would be to follow Israel's example, and have competition between various types of agricultural holding, with cooperatives gradually becoming predominant. The tenants on the nationalized land must be given guarantees both of their rights to stay as long as they cultivate the land well and of their rights to compensation for their investments if they leave; those who chose to stay could still join the cooperative villages and use the communal services (collective equipment and credit, cooperative sales, purchase and processing).

Egalitarianism will never lead to success. Larger holdings could, therefore, be assigned to those workers who had formerly obtained the best results on the small plots which they had been given as part of their salaries. The others would be better off as employed workers and some plots would be large enough to employ three or four men. This measure is strictly in the interests of production: a great many of the *inquilinos* are virtually illiterate and do not have the necessary education to become overseers. Cuba's example shows that state farms should be for the purpose of experimentation only, and should definitely have as much autonomy as possible.

Agrarian reform should thus be regarded as an economic measure, with increased production as its principal aim. This is the only possible way of integrating town and country workers; and it also has political significance, since an essential part of it would be the removal of power from a corrupt, privileged class – although those members of it who worked for the common good would not be made to suffer. Recent visitors to Chile have been disturbed by the power of the landowners to form a strong pressure group on the right wing of the Christian Democrat party. The party stands as a defender of the sanctity of property – an alibi for any form of corruption. Will Eduardo Frei be strong enough to break free from the stranglehold of the United States (given a more sensible attitude in Washington[13])

[13] This condition can be borne in mind as a working hypothesis, though too much wealth and power always corrupt the shrewdness and integrity of both individuals and states.

without any complete political rupture, while, at the same time, controlling Chile's own privileged minority? Jean Mayer feels it is unlikely; he regards Frei as 'the last hope of liberal capitalism'.[14]

If Europe were not so much under the sway of the United States – and under the control of its own monopolies – it would be better able to help South America to break free from its double bondage. At the time of De Gaulle's visit to South America, however, no mention was made of the essential barrier to progress, the indigenous privileged class. An over-conciliatory programme for reform would lead to an impasse – a sort of 'Alliance without Progress'. The movement must take some revolutionary measures[15] if any positive results are to be achieved. The logical conclusion is that any effective reform must include a preliminary revolutionary stage, when the main obstacles to progress are cleared away. This does not mean that all Cuba's economic errors need to be repeated. But, even at the cost of some mistakes, any attempt at improvement is better than slow engulfment or that contempt which is scarcely tolerable to the Latin temperament.

Peasant revolt is not only a fight against exploitation but also a search for dignity: 'In societies like those of South America, where the peasant is deprived of any rights, oppressed and hardly treated as a human being, any movement which tells him that he is a human being with rights should succeed. If you question the peasants about communism they will reply, even though they have barely heard of it, that communists are men who demand their rights. In 1962 a militant evangelist in Peru explained social revolution to me in biblical terms—"Christ was on the side of the peasants, as can be seen in the Gospels." '[16]

6. USEFUL COMPETITION: BETTER ORGANIZED REVOLUTION VERSUS BOLDER REFORMISM

Reform can work, so long as it is decisive enough to curb the power of the privileged and to break free from the hold of the United

[14] *Esprit*, June 1966.
[15] As I reminded the Chileans in January 1960, great landowners only obey the existing laws when revolution is in the air (*Living Lands*, Chap. V).
[16] E. Hobsbawm, 'Problémes agraires a la Convencion' (Peru), colloquium 1965, as note 8.

States. Chile's experiment may be one of South America's last chances for reform. Revolution is called for when the existing régime is an oppressive dictatorship, such as that of Batista's Cuba, Paraguay, Brazil, or Haiti. The most reactionary dictatorships survive, however, even in conditions of general poverty. They would surely be unable to last for long if neighbouring countries were moving forward more rapidly in a true spirit of freedom.

They could be boycotted – but only 'subversive' Cuba is given this treatment. In Latin America and the Caribbean authoritarianism has recently been spreading under the watchful eye of the United States. Once the protector of 'democracies' friendly to US capital the USA is now an active enemy of the communists. Its free-world image is becoming rather tarnished as its main concern becomes the defence of wealth. From the plateaux of the Andes to the ports of the Nordeste, Algoas or Recife, the tragedy of hunger will never be conquered until there are new governments better prepared for the difficult tasks of economic progress.

Through either reform or revolution, absolute priority must in future be given to development: technical staff must be trained and suitable institutional frameworks created. This is not a matter of political truth or universal solutions. At every stage, each individual situation must be studied, with reference to the level of development already reached, to the historical tradition, to available resources, and future possibilities, among a great many other factors.

Industrialization, aimed to begin with at saving foreign exchange, caters, therefore, only to the local needs of very small countries. For reasons of efficiency, factories in future must expand and find wider markets. Countries will, therefore, have to draw up regional agreements between themselves to avoid duplication in their plans for the manufacture of producer goods. At a later stage they will have to establish free trade areas and customs or economic unions, like the one beginning in Central America. These unions could not, without danger, include both the United States 'shark' and the twenty South American 'sardines'. The small countries must form a united front against unfavourable agreements with their over-powerful neighbour.

With much higher agricultural productivity *per capita* than Africa or Asia,[17] South America should achieve economic 'take-off' much more easily. But industrialization has tended to concentrate on luxury consumer goods, such as private cars, instead of investment goods, such as fertilizer, machinery, and the other requirements for agricultural modernization. This pattern will not change as long as the profit motive takes precedence over the common good.

In a difficult political situation, an old professor safe in his office can hardly advise the young to resort to violence. He cannot possibly know the countries well enough to be able to judge when conditions are ripe for success. But neither has he any right to condemn violence – particularly, say, to young Christian trade unionists who have just come out of prison; or in any situation where men's dignity is outraged – deprived 'of both bread and books' as the Mexican peasant-general Zapata put it in 1917.

7. GREATER EFFICIENCY OF WORK: A PRE-REVOLUTIONARY ACT

We must do our best to make the youth of these countries realize what development involves. Development cannot continue to be led by lawyers and poets. It needs engineers, technicians, agronomists, skilled workers, and farmers – all of whom must be able to do better than their predecessors – not to mention organizers, economists, and accountants; in their absence socialized projects are carried on in the dark, and mistakes cannot be rapidly corrected. This has been the basic weakness of socialist economies.

Revolution provides heroic causes, but development needs humble sacrifices – which are more thankless though more vital for success. Some young people believe that nothing can be done without revolution. We refuse to accept this view. In January, 1966, we advised the South Americans at the University of Louvain – like the Africans in Paris in 1961–3 – to start by training themselves for concrete, productive, and useful economic employment. Better organized production and development, and greater professional efficiency are in themselves steps towards revolution. 'Under the

[17] Almost twice as high (excluding Argentina) and three times, with Argentina included, according to P. Bairoch.

present régime we can do nothing to prepare ourselves for the work of the future.' This is not true, since these South Americans are studying at the University of Louvain. The Institutes of Agronomy of the State of São Paulo in Brazil are hardly ever full. 'If we went there we would not get good jobs.' Where is their revolutionary ardour or spirit of sacrifice, if their main objective is to earn a lot of money as soon as possible? The Cuban revolution would never have taken place if Fidel and his companions had not had a revolutionary ideology for which they were ready to sacrifice their lives: many did so. Let us not give hasty support to those who will not even sacrifice their comfort.

While preparing for the tasks of the future, no one must expect miracles to proceed automatically from the construction of socialism; we now know all the difficulties involved. Population growth has overtaken agricultural development and even planned revolution will come across difficulties in its structural reforms. South America, like Africa, is largely underpopulated. But until agriculture catches up, birth control will hasten economic development, and, therefore, make it easier to break free from the domination of the United States and its allies, the privileged minorities.

As in Africa, the birth rate could be allowed to start rising again once development had begun and industrial and agricultural production had overtaken population growth. Areas which are overcrowded already, like the Caribbean, part of Central America, the high plateaux of Mexico, and the Andes in Brazil's Nordeste, should be much more cautious. The dry *sertão* is a particularly clear case: it should not be given any priority since other regions of the country will be much easier to develop.

If the world is to free itself from hunger, Africa and Latin America must accelerate their development; endless problems will arise and we have tried to mention some of them. Natural potential is better in South America than it is in much of Africa, and the area is in any case more developed. But its political problems seem much greater because of its closer proximity to the foremost world economic power with its overwhelming ambitions.[18]

[18] In August 1966, during a conference in Mexico on agrarian reform, I showed that at the present rate Central and South America will have a population of over 1,000 million within a century; it has little more than 30 million hectares of arable land. The

Everywhere in the world, backward countries will find it more and more difficult to catch up, and underdeveloped economies will find it harder to 'take off'. In overpopulated areas, where all the good land is already in use and intensification is ever more costly, it is becoming increasingly difficult to raise agricultural productivity, though this is the only possible way of promoting development.

---

agrarian specialists are campaigning for 'the land for those who work it' – a pre-capitalist concept which encourages the proliferation of subsistence *minifundia*. They should be campaigning for better wages in the large holdings or for firmly established producers' cooperatives. In September 1966, the great stock-breeders of Nicaragua produced on average 15 kgs of meat (live) per hectare, but experiments have shown that 700 kgs is possible. They are absentees; their overseers are often illiterate – and the revolver and cartridge belt are their hallmarks. Three times a day, 365 days a year, the peons eat a pancake of pure maize flour, four ounces of beans and a cup of coffee. The hacienda Hamiona, a coffee and stock farm near Matagalpa, refuses even to *sell* milk to the peons' children.

CHAPTER ELEVEN

India and South East Asia: the first footholds of famine

I. INDIA[1]

The threat of famine in India is no hypothesis for the future, it is a sad reality. In the report I submitted to the United Nations in 1959, as an 'evaluation' of community development, I forecast that acute scarcities would strike India in 1965-6. At the same time, Ford Foundation experts stated that in the absence of some radical change India's supply of food grains would be 28 million tons short of the quantity required to cover human needs, estimated at 110 million tons.

Adopting very low standards of nutrition, India's Third Plan set its production target for cereals and pulses, which are more important in India than in any other country, at 100 million tons. Over 80 million tons have been produced in some good years since 1960 and in 1964-5, 88,000,000 tons were produced; but in 1965-6 the figure fell to 71,000,000, the result of serious drought. It is, however, important to emphasize that the highest yields after the heaviest monsoons are still very much below the minimum estimate of human requirements. A climatic factor may have aggravated the situation, but the permanent state of India's agricultural production is one of widespread, massive, lasting, chronic shortage. In December, 1959, I had good reason to use the title 'India's Agricultural Defeat' for an article I wrote in the *New Statesman*. If everyone had admitted that the first battle had been lost, there would have been more chance of averting the complete failure of the present time.

[1] Cf. G. Etienne, *L'Agriculture indienne*, 'Tiers-Monde', P.U.F., 1966.

Though useful as a temporary measure, American food aid does nothing to improve the long-term position. Indeed, by concealing the seriousness of the situation, it allows the government to neglect the organizational reforms (such as those we suggested in 1959) necessary to rectify matters. The largest 'democracy' in the world has so far only succeeded in building a mere semblance (some say caricature) of Western democracy. On New Year's Day, 1959, the Prime Minister of Uttar Pradesh told us that as an astrologist he could predict that the end of the world would take place on February 5, 1962. When Nehru told him to draw up his state's Third Plan for 1961-6, he answered that he would go up to February 5 inclusive – exactly to the last day. Some electors still queue up to kiss the feet of their representative, regarding him as their lord. India, which receives more aid than any other country in the world, nonetheless holds the most terrifying and ominous threat of famine.

This is an old story, which has been continuous throughout the course of history. With a sparse population and land largely covered by savannah and forest, for much of her early history India practised sheep-breeding – meat eating was then permitted – and nomadic agriculture, with long fallow periods preserving the fertility of the soil. The slow, insidious growth of the population has not stimulated the determined search for fertilizers carried on by the Chinese, or any significant intensification of crops. When forests are destroyed, dried dung has to be burned for heating and cooking and, therefore, cannot be used as manure. As the scavenger is utterly despised, no one can collect faecal material for use as fertilizer. When the soil's organic content is poor, it is less resistant to drought. In the area south of Agra the soil has now degenerated so that millet must be grown instead of wheat. The whole Deccan peninsula has been ravaged by erosion. People now say that India is infertile; it would be truer to say that the soil has been impoverished by bad cultivation.

India has too many cattle and now that the savannahs are culti-vated and no longer available for grazing it is less and less able to feed them. Ploughed fields now constitute more than 40 per cent of India's total surface area compared with 11 per cent in China. Except in the rather westernized Punjab, however, there has been virtually no increase in forage crops. The tragic aspect of this situation proceeds not so much from the ban on eating sacred cows[2] as from the fact that the cows are so badly fed that they produce very little milk while the country suffers from serious protein deficiencies.[3] For the same reason, the oxen are not strong enough to do the necessary amount of work and there should be a revolution in feeding methods. At least there is no religious argument against birth control for cows.

Rural overpopulation is increasing steadily. Until after independence, India was the only country where the agricultural population was still rising not only in actual numbers but in proportion to the rest of the population. When British industry destroyed the textile-producing artisan sector, most of the spinners and weavers went back to the land. The average farm-holding has grown smaller everywhere: in some places it has been reduced from six to two hectares, as in the east of Uttar Pradesh, north of Varanasi or Benares. Even in good years the country people there are pitifully poor.

Share-cropping has inflicted a death wound on Indian agriculture. In the Mediterranean the system of paying rent with a portion of the harvest impeded agricultural progress, whereas a fixed rent for farming rights, with the agricultural worker keeping the entire harvest, accelerated production in north-west Europe, particularly in the British Isles. Moreover, European landowners used to plough back at least part of their profits – in buildings, plantations, roads, and water control. And they used to supply all or part of the working capital, such as animals and machinery as well as advances for seed and fertilizers.

The Indian landowner of the eighteenth century still had the powers of a feudal lord and could exact statutory labour; he did not, however, have the right to evict his tenants, who were holders of a real hereditary right of cultivation. There was no justification for Lord Cornwallis's measure of 1793, by which a group of people known as the *zemindars*, until then only responsible for the collection and payment of taxes, were given ownership of land. In such

---

[2] Apart from Muslims and Christians, the pariahs eat them, and, therefore, incur general contempt.
[3] A doctor, treating a child with kwashiorkor, prescribed very expensive medicines. He ended by saying, 'If only he could eat two small eggs a week, he would get better.'

ways, Cornwallis carefully built up a circle of collaborators benefiting from colonial rule and, therefore, likely to defend it. He doubtless hoped that at least some of the ground-rent collected would be used to finance agricultural progress, as had happened in England, but he forgot that the privileged Hindu minorities, accustomed to living in a conquered country off the tribute paid by their subjects, would think of their own luxury first. The words *Golconda* and *maharajah* conjure up images of fabulous wealth; we forget the unspeakable hardship they entailed. These *zemindars* and the *talukhars*, who were in similar position, could now exercise the rights of a Western landowner in addition to their rights as feudal lords, and could evict their workers as they pleased.

With this new right, far beyond the common practice of Indian tradition, and with increased population pressure, they could extend their claims still further. In the eighteenth century, the wheat harvest, the only harvest of any size, was usually divided out into three equal parts. The landowner took one, in return for his land; the share-cropper took another, in return for his labour; and the third part went to whichever of the two had supplied the means of production – the harness, tools, fertilizer, seed, water, and so on. The share-cropper now usually supplies both the labour and the working capital but receives only half the harvest instead of two-thirds. His social position has sunk still further as farms have been getting much smaller. With rice-yields per hectare only 40 or 50 per cent the size of China's and 20 per cent of Japan's, a large section of India's peasantry must be regarded as totally destitute.

The workers' self-interest dictates that their crop-growing should be as extensive as possible, using labour and capital to the minimum and using land, the only factor in production supplied by the landlord, to the maximum. The worker usually pays for chemical fertilizer himself, and the landlord graciously accepts half of the increased harvest derived from it without making any contribution to its cost. The workers, therefore, stop using fertilizer as soon as they have done their accounts – except in the rare cases where the landlord pays for half of it.

The peasants' credit needs are supplied by moneylenders and speculative merchants who charge exorbitant interest rates – I even noticed rates of 15 per cent per week near Hyderabad.[4] Credit co-operatives cannot expand as much as would be desirable, since they only distribute public funds and do not receive peasants' deposits.

The caste system, though abolished by law, still survives in custom, particularly in the country. Young people of low caste have no hope of being granted any real social advancement or even simple human dignity. Shortages, and the resulting black-market prices, offer good opportunities for speculation. American food aid is not always distributed entirely without profit to the middlemen. Corruption is rampant, and with it, nepotism, inefficiency and idleness among many of the middle ranks. Many of the Indian civil servants, with their intolerable pretentiousness and pride, symbolize the most unacceptable form of privileged minority. For example, a Brahmin agricultural adviser told me that he could not go into ricefields in case his shoes got muddy.

By the agrarian reform carried out during the First Indian Plan, land was bought back from the *zemindars* at high prices, though it had been distributed to them for nothing, and no measure was introduced to ensure that the compensation was used for investment. It could, therefore, be spent on gold and jewellery, building and other luxury expenditure – not to mention foreign travel and the export of capital. The land was not even given back to 'those who work it', for a whole series of middlemen came between the landlords and the labourers. By increasing the number of landowners, this reform also increased the number of parasites. The village's poorest inhabitants are eager to buy the only luxury they can afford on their low wages[5] – the luxury of idleness. And the rich do not even manage their own property: they can afford overseers.

2. PROFIT FROM HUNGER

The Indian government prides itself on its social expenditure – for instance, the fine houses it has built for some of the pariahs – the *harrijans* or sons of God, as Mahatma Gandhi called them. The

[4] And even 100 per cent per week, the rate exacted for late interest payments. See *Living Lands* by R. Dumont.
[5] One rupee or 20 US cents per day (food not provided), with cereal prices higher than they are in Europe.

money would have been better spent on new, irrigated ricefields; and the buildings could then have been financed by savings out of the profits. A great landowner from the south of Madras disagreed with me. He said: 'If the total area of cultivated land were increased, land rent would fall and as a landowner I should lose money. With more ricefields, employment would rise, then wages might rise as well and I would lose more money. If more grain were produced as a result of the changes, prices would fall; the whole project is against my interests and I oppose it.' The argument of the common good would clearly do nothing to sway this kind of thinking.[6] Like some South American *latifundiaries*, such people will never understand anything short of armed revolt. I listened in amazement to a shameless account of the enormous advantages to be derived from want, a description of the profits to be made from famine. And I realized that continued famine was very much in the interests of the privileged class, a powerful interest within the Congress Party.

The Nizam of Hyderabad, I was told, probably made an income of almost a million dollars a year from his compensation payments. Not surprisingly, some people are reluctant to increase aid to India: here, even more than in Africa, aid will have the effect of increasing the power of the privileged, many of whom are not far from being common criminals. This is the final blow to any hopes for development. The only answer would seem to be revolution, Chinese-style but less dogmatic. Would it be able to solve India's agricultural problems? There is room for doubt unless something is done about overpopulation.

An immediate halt in the population explosion is more vitally necessary in India than anywhere else in the world, in view of the enormous difficulties – technical, economic, and, more serious still, political and human – which obstruct rapid agricultural expansion of any kind. Since independence the annual rate of population growth has doubled, rising from 1.2 per cent to 2.4 per cent. Family planning clinics may have affected a few million people, but the eradication of malaria and other fatal illnesses has affected almost all of

---

[6] All the same I did ask him if he was a member of the Communist Party, whereupon he disclaimed this violently and said he was anti-communist. 'But your arguments could well be used as communist propaganda,' I answered. This did seem to make him think.

India's 500 million inhabitants. The death rate is dropping much faster than the birth rate.

India's potentials for agricultural progress, though still vast, will be very difficult to exploit. The irrigation networks in the northern and central parts of China are inoperative throughout the long winters in which vegetation cannot survive. In India, the irrigation networks are in tropical and subtropical zones, and could, therefore, produce two or three harvests a year. But, as I saw in the Damodar Valley near Calcutta, water is badly wasted in the rainy season, due to imperfect installations, such as channels without sluice gates, absence of side canals, too shallow dykes in the ricefields, and so on. The peasant, paying for his irrigation according to the area of his land, has no incentive to save water; a tax proportional to the actual volume of water used would give him a motive to save it.

In the war against hunger (which will soon have to be waged on a world-wide scale), India will be our testing ground for techniques to be tried out and perfected. The United States is using the seriousness of the food situation to obtain some political recompense – notably in demanding support for its 'filthy war' in Vietnam. Food aid should be distributed in such a way as not to discourage local producers. A Cereals Office would have to be set up to stabilize prices, provided that the Indian administration were efficient enough and, more important, honest enough, to manage it; unfortunately, this does not yet seem to be the case.

At the present time world aid consists mainly of gifts of food but as soon as possible these should be replaced by gifts of machinery for irrigation, fertilizer, and factories to manufacture fertilizer, weedkiller and insecticide; agronomists, technicians and instructors are needed at all levels to see that the equipment is properly used. How can these initiators of progress, the Gram Sevak, 'servants of the village' in community development,[7] be inspired to devote them-

[7] In the United Nations some people have presented Community development as the most effective weapon against communism. The results obtained in India give good grounds for doubt. It was introduced widely in 1952 after the failure of propaganda of the 'agricultural extension' type and with the aim of affecting health, education, production, and so on. The unfortunate Gram Sevak had to give corrective advice on 64 different points: latrines, vaccinations, chimneys, literacy, management of the municipal budget, cooperatives, agricultural loans, technical advice, etc. to between 1,500 and 2,000 families. The advice mainly dealt with administrative buildings, sanitation, wells, and roads. In our report we showed how inadequate the achievements of this policy had

selves body and soul to their task? The whole structure of society will have to be altered, and a whole mass of prejudices combated – not only prejudices about sacred cows, but also about castes, share-cropping, moneylending, corruption and speculation. Work and knowledge should earn more respect than wealth; in India, this in itself means revolution.

Other parts of South East Asia are also giving cause for concern. While India and Ceylon did little enough to increase their *per capita* food resources[8] up to 1964–5, the agricultural situation is even worse in other countries.

3. A RECESSION IN FOOD SUPPLIES: PAKISTAN, THE PHILIPPINES, INDONESIA

'The increase in production during the decade has lagged markedly behind population growth in Indonesia, Pakistan, and the Philip-pines.'[9] Let us first draw attention to the fact that production has just begun to rise in Pakistan, particularly in the west; this improve-ment seems to be connected to the fact that corruption has been radically reduced. It does not mean that the whole problem has been solved or even that the difficulties are becoming less serious. The modernization and mobilization of the overpopulated Bengal Delta presented problems long before it became East Pakistan. In the Indus valley, for example, expensive drainage systems are required to remove the salt which is forced to the surface by flooding; these will become more and more costly.

No significant progress can be observed in the Philippines, where there is no real attempt at systematized irrigation and harvests are, therefore, irregular. Here again, the recent population increase has done nothing to stimulate any significant reform of the land system or intensification of agriculture in the Chinese style. Attention is still focused on export crops which, like sugar, are bought at preferential prices by the United States.

---

been (chap. iv). For Congress, the party in power and the landowners' party, did not want to take any effective action which would be contrary to the interests of the privileged.

[8] That is, in the official statistics; in fact they have probably hardly increased at all.

[9] 'The state of food and agriculture, 1965', edited by the FAO in Rome.

By contrast, Java, in Indonesia, overpopulated from an early date in history, carries on its traditional, intensive crop-growing, organizing its ricefields to produce two or even three harvests a year. Working in association with Dutch agronomists, the Indonesian peasants were beating world records for sugar-cane yields in 1934, with a national average of 17 tons of sugar per hectare for half a million hectares. And the rubber, oil palm, tea, and coffee plantations were regarded as models of their kind by all the young agronomists in Asia (I was in Tonkin at the time).

Since independence, the situation has continuously deteriorated. Many of the plantations are neglected; no new ones have been set up, and sugar yields have dropped to 11 tons per hectare. The large outer islands, where population is sparse, earn one-sixth of the foreign exchange for machinery imports they did before independence;[10] but on the whole, they are still reasonably fed. The drama is concentrated in Java, which, with its small surface area, holds 70 per cent of the whole population, now over 100 millions, and it has no industry in any way comparable, for instance, to Japan's.

Famine is spreading insidiously in the south and centre of the island; in spite of official denials this area has not been free from starvation since 1963. Massive emigration to the other islands and accelerated industrialization might provide a solution. All the resources of the country would have to be mobilized in order to set up the necessary infrastructure and land-reclamation works, apart from the resettlement of at least one million settlers per year – the annual population increase in Java alone must be about 2 millions per year. Sukarno tried to use his aggressive foreign policy to maintain an uneasy political unity between three opposing forces – nationalism, Islam, and communism.

The fight against *Neocolim* – colonialism, neo-colonialism and imperialism – has thus passed from New Guinea to North Borneo through a sharp confrontation with the Malaysian Federation which was set up in London in 1963. The fight between the army and the communist party for the presidential succession ended in the

[10] Between 1950 and 1965 agricultural exports probably fell from $1,200 million to $200 million.

autumn and winter of 1965-6, with the systematic massacre of communist adherents and sympathizers. Even though something like four people out of every thousand were massacred (a horrifying total) the food problem remained unsolved. Here, as everywhere, we have reason to doubt the army's ability to organize efficient economic development. It may be able to overthrow the government; this is not so difficult; but unless it can perform some proper function in society, it will not keep its power except by totalitarian methods.

4. 'FORTUNATE' ASIA

'Fortunate' Asia was a geographer's name for the least congested part of Asia, comprising the rice-exporting countries of Burma, Thailand, and Cochin-China, and the countries producing rubber and other colonial goods – Sumatra and Malaya. Though South Vietnam has been torn apart by war, Cambodia has managed to remain neutral, as a result of Norodom Sihanouk's clever diplomacy. Though the old provinces south-west of Pnomh Penh are becoming gradually overpopulated, they are still farming in the Indian style, producing only one harvest per year, with yields of less than one ton of paddy per hectare.

Cambodia is moving towards socialism, nationalizing its banks and its import-export trade. But it does not possess socialism's main political prerequisite – honesty. Corruption is spreading in the ministries and has even reached the royal family. The spending power of the civil servants will, therefore, be increased and they will be tempted to more corrupt practices by the dream of owning a Mercedes or a villa. Until now, corrupt practices in South East Asia have been connected to some extent with American aid, the one supporting the other. Cambodia has had the courage to refuse aid from America. She must next strengthen her courage for the more difficult task of wiping out her own privileged class.

After a really bad monsoon, China and, especially, India have bought their rice from 'Fortunate' Asia. These countries even sent rice to France, since the colonial government, through its discriminating tariff took Indo-China's rice away from the people of

South East Asia to feed French poultry. Today these rice surpluses are diminishing rapidly and Burma will no longer be able to fulfil her traditional function of making up India's food deficit.

Fortunately, in recent years, food production in Malaysia, Thailand, Formosa, South Korea and Japan has run ahead of population growth. Agricultural production in Japan probably increased by 90 per cent between 1938 and 1962. But this country cannot be regarded as part of the Third World. Being developed, progress is no longer so difficult, as has been shown in the case of France. In both Korea and Formosa, American aid and the tradition of Japanese influence provided favourable conditions for more rapid agricultural modernization. But in the long term, these little oases of prosperity will be quite unable to resolve the food problem for the seething masses of South East Asia. Unless current blunders are corrected in the near future, this area is in immediate danger of sinking into terrifying, widespread famine.

5. FAMILY PLANNING, SUPPORTED BY ECONOMIC PRESSURE FOR BIRTH CONTROL

Latin America and Africa, being on the whole underpopulated, can exploit both of the two great factors for agricultural growth: extension of cultivated land and increased yields. By contrast, apart from Sumatra, Borneo, the Celebes, Malaysia and some small pockets here and there, South East Asia will not be able to effect any sizeable increase in her area of ploughed land. The intensification of agriculture still offers a wide margin for progress, particularly in India, but the rate of progress obtainable from this one factor is very low in the initial stages, as can be seen from a comparison of India's growth rates with those of Japan.

This fact is further proved by the very poor results that China has obtained since 1957 after the most thoroughgoing and rapid reorganization of the countryside ever known in the world. In my view, this failure could be attributed to the disparity between the enormous land installations, particularly water installations, and the low increase in the production of chemical fertilizer. It is not very much use to concentrate on employing more labour, when there is too much of it already, unless the other factors for modernization follow. Additional reasons are the more casual attitude to work after the establishment of the people's communes and disappointment over the failure of the Great Leap Forward, which had unwisely promised 'ten thousand years of happiness for six years' hard work'.

No one can deny that China has made some progress in her agriculture[11] but not enough to keep pace with population growth. This means that she has to take immediate steps to check the expansion of her population. She will probably manage to do so before the rest of Asia. There is, therefore, a danger that by 1980 China will be the only country of South East Asia where the food situation is anything short of desperate. By that time, American food aid will probably not be large enough to cover Asia's requirements, particularly if it goes on encouraging corruption rather than development, and if the surpluses continue to decline.

If the present demographic policies continue, there is a grave danger that the population of India will have risen to 700 millions by 1980, the population of Pakistan and Indonesia to over 300 millions and that of Ceylon, Burma, Malaysia, Thailand, the Philippines and ex-Indo-China to 250 millions. With these 1,250 million people, the population of South East Asia may well be over 2,000 millions, even if China limits her population growth.

Let us return to our forecasts for agricultural progress, accepting the most optimistic hypotheses. It would seem that food production cannot possibly keep pace with this rate of population growth. If countries are to be equipped with machinery, and if the food deficits of this vast area are to be eliminated, production would have to be considerably in advance of population growth – which would mean a multiplication of food production by 2.5 between now and 1980. This is out of the question.

If the sparsely populated countries of Africa and South America launched a vast development campaign, they could just afford to wait for one or two generations before insisting on the general practice of birth control. South East Asia cannot afford to delay at all: it cannot continue with mere publicity for family planning, such

[11] 'According to western estimates,' P. Bairoch says, 'Chinese agricultural productivity increased by 2.7 per cent a year between 1946/50 and 1960/4. On the usual criteria, China is no longer in danger of famine.' But India is.

as India practises with little success. Pressure for birth control must be reinforced by economic measures penalizing all families with more than three children. China does this by making reductions in clothing and food rations and in private land-holdings. India is contemplating an increase in taxation for large families, but this is hardly likely to have any effect on the very poor. The world will never be freed from hunger unless the foolish are made to suffer for their lack of foresight. A preliminary stage will be necessary in which the most efficient methods of birth control and information about them are made available to all. Even the poorest countries could afford intra-uterine devices.

Compulsory birth control will not alter the fact that structural reforms must be undertaken to encourage the peasant to work harder. The former Director General of the FAO, Dr B. R. Sen, was surely thinking of India when he wrote in 1959: 'If agricultural workers improve their methods, much of the profit derived from the increase in production goes to the merchants and landowners to whom they owe money. Until these burdens are lightened, the work of agricultural advisers will fall on barren ground.'

6. DEVELOPMENT IN BACKWARD COUNTRIES IS CHECKED BY PRIVILEGED MINORITIES WHO DEPEND ON THE MILITARY

South East Asia must intensify its rice-growing; instead of the usual single crop, several crops must be grown each year on the same land; horticulture must be developed, as it has been in China. Top priority must then go to chemical fertilizer and to the completion of the present hydraulic installations before any others are embarked on. The area must then industrialize as quickly as possible, giving priority to tools for agricultural modernization but not forgetting craft industries and fishing. In brief, it must use every weapon in its armoury, checking population growth as far as possible at the same time.

If an expansion programme of this kind is to be put into effect, its directors must care more about the national interest than about their own individual privileges. This applies to the whole of the Third World where the beginning has been generally unsatisfactory. There has been no progress recently; for the administration bestows exorbitant privileges on itself[12] and relies on the army, an even more parasitic body, for support. The daily cuts taken out of the national revenue by the administration, in itself large enough to constitute a substantial check on development, are further increased by those for the army. If the army's takings become any larger (in Algeria, Morocco, Egypt, and Ghana), any chances of success are even further curtailed.

Army corruption has been the general pattern in recent years, in Ecuador, Ghana, Brazil, Dahomey, the Congo, Indonesia, Algeria, Pakistan, Upper Volta, Burma, the Central African Republic, Syria, and Thailand, not to mention the Dominican Republic and South Vietnam. Nevertheless, soldiers have done nothing to prove themselves to be competent agents of development. The situation in Brazil is deteriorating; no headway has been made in Burma; Dahomey's agricultural situation seems more disastrous than ever. The administration must set a better example of honesty, effort, and austerity if the peasants of Africa and Asia are to feel any obligation to try harder. The government must include real representatives of the peasantry, men and even women with hands roughened by work. And rural development policies must give them some basic economic and political training.

7. THE THIRD WORLD WILL NEED HELP

The backward countries could follow China's advice and try to be self-reliant, launching their own campaigns, investing their own money, and controlling their birth rate. It would be foolish to imagine, however, that the Third World, and particularly its more seriously handicapped, backward areas, will be able to achieve anything singlehanded in the next few years. It would certainly not be able to avoid the danger of starvation, latent in its population explosion and slow development. As P. Bairoch has shown, the problem of the present day is much more difficult than it was in

---

[12] Tradesmen and civil servants (and even landowners) all have useful functions; but the value of their services seems much lower than their income. In this way their earnings are supplemented by an unearned rent.

England in 1780, at the beginning of the industrial revolution. A concerted, world-wide campaign seems imperative.

India has been getting more food aid than ever since independence. Grave dangers are implicit in the Third World's lack of self-sufficiency and these may become apparent before many generations. We have tried to show that unless the present mistakes are corrected immediately, their outcome will be the most disastrous famine ever known. Even if the threat of famine were averted, the backward countries might easily become increasingly dependent on the aid-giving countries in the process, particularly on those giving food aid and most of all on the United States.

In order to avoid this neo-colonialism, the young states should put their houses in order, reduce luxury consumption, and cut the administrative budget. While public expenditure increases twice as fast as production (as it does in Tunisia), neo-colonialism[13] will surely triumph; all the quicker, as the population explosion will be its most faithful ally. In the absence of birth control, increased food aid would make the situation even more hopeless.

After a determined national campaign, a well coordinated world-wide drive will be needed. The Third World started to move towards unity at the Geneva Conference on Trade and Development (1964). After regional agreements have been established, it seems desirable to aim at a closer and closer common front of the poor countries against the rich; let us hope that the developed world will stop trying to divide them in order to increase its domination – by inducing a fear of communism, for example.

As we shall try to show in the last part of this study, we feel that it is vital for a substantial, immediate increase to be made in the amount of aid and cooperation given to the Third World; it is equally important for its markets to be widened and its terms of trade improved, but this will be more difficult. It will also be necessary to improve the effectiveness of aid: it should not be given on terms which are beneficial mainly to the giver. The Third World will not avoid the famine which threatens to become widespread around 1980, unless new, world-wide methods are found to combat

[13] Where domination by rich countries is economic rather than political (traditional colonialism), the poor countries are kept in a dependent position exporting raw materials and importing the vast majority of their manufactured goods.

the rising birth rate, idleness, the refusal to invest, and the squandering of public money.[14]

Hunger, our age-old enemy, will never be repulsed while we merely pursue policies which accentuate the young states' quickly growing food deficits. And hunger now could, in the future, lead to atomic suicide.

This chapter had already been written when we read P. Bairoch's[15] excellent work; he shows that 'most of the countries of Asia and Africa are below the hypothetical danger level for famine'. An even more horrifying fact: 'In the last fifty years agricultural employment in the Third World has doubled ... this has brought the law of diminishing returns into play ... between 1922–6 and 1960–4, agricultural productivity fell by about 20 per cent.'

While famine may have been worsening dramatically since 1959, it has been growing insidiously but unnoticed for half a century. According to Bairoch, agricultural productivity in Africa and Asia is about 50 per cent *per capita* lower than the level reached by the developed countries when they entered the Industrial Revolution. Most of the Third World will, therefore, not be able to follow the same road to development as Europe and the USA: they will need outside help of an entirely new kind. We must now turn to this theme.

---

[14] 'So far, many plans in Greece have never gone beyond the study stage, in the absence of any desire to put them into practice. The main problem is finding men who would be capable of putting them into practice.' And not only in Greece.
[15] 'L'evolution de la productivité agricole dans les pays économiquement sousdéveloppés de 1909 à 1964', in *Développement et civilisations*, March 1966.

PART FIVE World Solidarity

CHAPTER TWELVE
The stages of world cooperation

I. PREVIOUS RECORD: FAILURE

Around the beginning of the twentieth century, the bourgeoisie of Western Europe came to realize that widespread revolt among the poor constituted a serious threat to the rich. Though not afraid of running the risk of world war,[1] the bourgeoisie accepted income tax and then social security as necessary forms of redistribution designed to even out major injustices on a national scale. Wages were raised as a result of trade-union pressure and, together with periodic wars, this gave a new lease of life to the capitalist economy, though it was depressed by cyclical crises until 1938.

In addition to social inequality between individuals, there are now similar injustices between the more and the less developed nations. These international disparities are being dangerously accentuated: the advanced capitalist countries accelerate their development while the underdeveloped countries, under the strain of the population explosion, are hampered or checked in their economic growth. If the threat of famine to the Third World were to become a reality – becoming general by 1980 – the West might easily find itself increasingly isolated. Cut off from its main sources of food and raw materials (oil first of all) and a large part of its markets, it would also be in a very weak moral position. The attitudes of the United States and of Great Britain are hardly likely to halt this dangerous trend.

Faced with starvation, the Third World could either resign itself

---

[1] As a child, travelling by train in July 1917, I met a soldier on leave from the front and its horrors. He told me that 'War is an agreement between important people in all countries to massacre the unimportant ones.'

to its fate or revolt. Such a revolt might be led by China, whose atomic weapons would by then have become operational. The West has certainly given proof of its shrewdness: it has so far used its gifts to counteract progress. It did not think of building a united Europe until its world position (and its moral standpoint) had been weakened by two intra-European wars. This time, the danger threatening the future of Europe is so formidable that it would do well to undertake negotiations before widespread revolt or a common front of the poor countries makes it too weak and isolated: by then it would have its back to the wall.

Contemporary Europe has an enormous capacity for production, comparable to that of the two great powers; it, therefore, has good negotiating strength and concrete bargaining weapons, not least among these is its attitude to China. This country will become more liberal as it is granted more respect – when it is admitted into the so-called civilized group of nations, and given economic aid. There is no reason for this recognition to be withheld any longer.

Our 'cartieristes'* will remind us of our own needs and our own underdeveloped areas. Yet most such people probably call themselves Christians, and the funds of Pierrelatte (the French military nuclear plant) would provide the money to send many more workers and technicians to agronomic research projects in the tropics. If the socialists were truly socialist, and the Christians truly Christian, the moral idea of human solidarity could be used as a basis for discussion. But we must accept human beings as they are and point out the economic and political risks we would be courting if we abandoned the Third World. The principal aim behind this work is to do something to make people face the fact that the food situation and, in consequence, the economic and political prospects are more serious than ever before in the history of mankind.

New and unprecedented solutions must be found to meet this terrifying crisis: solutions which would traditionally be called utopian. The so-called realists have no right to protest: they have failed completely, since the gap between the rich and the poor grows ever wider. They have always led the battle against hunger under

* *A group in France following Jacques Cartier, opponents of aid to underdeveloped countries.*

other names; they lost the first battle on June 18, 1940. If we refuse to recognize the evidence before us and do nothing to correct our policy, we may well lose the fight against hunger even before 1980. Besides, the rich world could not go on developing peacefully in the midst of general poverty. L.-J. Lebret has appropriately called his book *Suicide or Survival of the West*.[2]

2. SUGGESTIONS FOR WAYS TO START A DISCUSSION

'What can we do?' ask the young audiences at our meetings once they realize both the scale of the dangers and our duty to stand together. Detailed outlines and utopian plans of the international institutions of tomorrow will not get us very far. Unfortunately, the most enlightened people too easily assume that everyone else thinks as they do. For example, Che Guevara, Cuba's Argentinian leader, wanted to create almost perfect human beings. Tomorrow's world will be in a constant state of change, influenced by different pressure-groups and sections of public opinion, different ideologies and interests, dictated by a reality far more complex than the schemes that dogmatic Marxists would have us follow.

No one can forecast the future in any detail: history does not move in a predetermined direction, bestowing victory on any one particular ideology. Everyone is free to put forward his ideas in the hopes of convincing the majority. We will, therefore, sketch out a list of hypotheses, making no predictions as to their fulfilment. Let us go further and state that the future will surely differ from our ideas in many respects. Nonetheless, if taken in conjunction with many other attempts, our suggestions could do something to help build the future; they need no further justification. Someone must take the first step and spark off discussion to make subsequent achievements more possible. Let us tell 'men of goodwill' the general direction towards which they should be moving; life is surely more worthwhile if one has an ideal to fight for.

Many other ideas may be put forward. Our suggestions are only intended to be very general, since details are irrelevant for the time being. We do not know which ideas will be put into practice, by

[2] *Suicide ou survie de l'Occident*, Les éditions Ouvriéres, Paris, 1958.

whom or at what time; until all these details are known, no more precise plans can be formulated. This will become possible when a large enough section of administrative and public opinion comes to realize that one of the steps we have outlined can actually be realized. Practical details will be of no use until there is some possibility of their being put into effect in the reasonably near future.

3. FOOD AID: EMERGENCY REPAIRS AND TACTICS

First we will draw up a list of the measures that seem most vital in the short and medium term. It will then be easier to describe the basic outlines of the institutions best suited to implement them. India is now the tragic victim of hunger. Aid must therefore be expanded to the full, whatever corrupt practices it may occasion and however irresponsible the administration. Ideally, however, aid should not simply take the form of the distribution of food, which offends the dignity of those who receive it, creates unemployment and apathy, and does nothing to solve the long-term problem; and usually it is not organized in conjunction with birth control.

In January, 1959, the village in the south of Madras which we have already mentioned had about 30 to 40 kgs of rice per head less than it required to feed the whole population adequately until the following harvest in June. If the workers had been strengthened by extra food rations, they could in the space of two or three off-seasons have dredged irrigation reservoirs and prepared a half-hectare ricefield for each family of five, to produce two harvests each year. This would be enough to produce 20 quintals of paddy per year, or 13 quintals of husked rice per family: 50 per cent more than the usual estimates of human requirements.[3]

Except in an emergency, rice could be distributed by contracts between the authority delivering it and the village community which would receive it and share it out – preferably under the people's control. The community would undertake to terrace a specified area of land as their contribution to reclamation projects set up by technicians of the irrigation service. One cubic metre of land for one

---

[3] In February 1966, the ration distributed in Kerala was 120, then 160 grammes per person per day.

kilo of paddy seems a fair exchange, given that one man can terrace about three or four cubic metres in a working day.[4] In some areas Indian employers will suggest lower rates of exchange, since the usual daily wage is often less than this.

Food aid without any sanctions of this kind would simply conceal the gravity of the situation while doing nothing to cure it. American aid could have been more constructive if it had been used to wipe out share-cropping and usury from the Indian countryside; this would have ensured that it did not merely make matters worse by discouraging agricultural production. It is difficult, however, to imagine the USA siding with the workers against the interests of the privileged minority, the faction it invariably supports.

Increased production should in any case be the principal aim behind the distribution of food aid. Its object should be to bring nearer the time when this kind of aid ceases to be vitally necessary and can be replaced by trade. It is not desirable for every country to be self-sufficient in food production, since additional trade could increase the advantages of the international division of labour. But it is often desirable for large countries to have a positive balance in their food trade.

The United Nations World Food Programme is working along the right lines but it distributes only 2 per cent of all the foodstuffs now sold on special terms. In view of the needs to be satisfied, it cannot do enough on a budget of $100 million for three years: it should have fifty times this sum. If commodity aid were increased, development projects could be financed on a realistic scale. Part of these funds would be used to buy the exported foodstuffs of developing countries. Sales at preferential prices by the United States obviously hold back Argentina's exports, but trade between underdeveloped countries ought to be expanded. Argentina suggested to the FAO that revenue obtained in import duties which restrict the export market for consumer goods, like coffee, should be handed over to the World Food Programme.

At the present time, the developed countries should be systematically increasing their production of surpluses of both agricultural

---

[4] Similar contracts have already been drawn up by the World Food Programme, FAO and UN, particularly in North Africa.

and synthetic foods, such as yeasts, without concentrating solely on profitable markets. The surpluses should be distributed according to the following criteria: to begin with, the relief of serious want – the improvement of the protein ration of pregnant or nursing mothers and of young children, so that they can achieve the mental and physical health essential for development. But the encouragement of land-improvement projects, above all of hydraulic installations, should soon become the principal aim. Extra fertilizer will be needed to make these projects more productive than they have been in China.[5]

4. FERTILIZERS – LESS COSTLY THAN THE MOON

As the FAO has reminded us, fertilizer is the key to agricultural development. Most agricultural progress for the last hundred years, and especially in the last fifty, can be attributed to widespread use of fertilizer. Mechanization reduces labour requirements, fewer men being needed to bring in the same sized harvest, thus increasing the productivity of labour; but fertilizer increases yields per hectare and consequently the actual volume of total production.

If we continue the present population and food-production curves into the future, we see that the Third World might have a deficit of 150 million tons of food grains by about 1980. The rich countries cannot produce surpluses of this size unless they are to go short themselves. It would, anyway, be impossible to transport the goods by boat, rail, and road, and to distribute and handle them. Even if it were to be done, at the cost of immense effort, the requirements will have tripled by the end of the century. Needs will continue to rise until the birth rate is lowered.

To produce additional good crops of a size comparable to its food deficit, the Third World would have to receive[6] each year about 30 million tons of the elements contained in chemical fertilizer. This means 16.5 million tons of nitrogen, 8.5 million tons of phosphoric acid and 5 million tons of potassium. As the Third World used about 4 million tons of fertilizer in 1965, imports and production would together have to rise by about 26 million tons. By 1970,

[5] Cf. *Chine surpeuplée, Tiers-Monde affamé*, by R. Dumont, foot of page 58.
[6] According to R. Ewell, Agricultural Adviser to President Johnson.

the equivalent of 10 million tons more in pure fertilizer could be given in kind, though some of this would be extracted in the countries themselves – potassium phosphate and, most of all, nitrogen, which can be synthesized with natural gas. With a ratio of two parts of nitrogen to one of phosphate and 0.75 potassium, this would cost about $1,500 million.

Most of the 26 million tons to be produced in 1980 could be manufactured in factories given to the Third World by an international equipment fund. For an investment of about $4,000 million, about $3,000 million worth of fertilizer, or 20 million tons, could be produced each year; the other 10 million tons would still be imported. As R. Ewell reminds us, $4,000 million is only a twelfth of the cost of sending a man to the moon. It is also one-fifth of the United States' expenditure on the war in Vietnam in 1965, and one-seventh of the figure for 1966.

5. GOOD CULTIVATION IN THE RIGHT ENVIRONMENT

In Chad, when the cotton crop is sown early it yields 800 kgs per hectare. Sown two months later, it yields 100 kgs. In either case, the right amount of fertilizer can almost double the crop. Thus the increased output from the use of fertilizer is eight times as high with early sowing than with late sowing. So in the one case the use of fertilizer is prohibitively expensive, but in other highly profitable. A number of conditions should, therefore, be fulfilled before fertilizer is used: the soil should be well prepared, the crop should be sown at the right time, the correct varieties should be used, the bushes should be well cut and there should be irrigation where necessary. In any case, the crop must be protected against disease. Until weedkiller can be used, this means early and frequent weeding.

Thus, before fertilizer can be used, all the materials and tools necessary for the protection of crops must be acquired: fungicides against fungi, mildew and rust; insecticides against all the worms, weevils, and caterpillars which destroy crops; and sprays and vapourizers with which to apply them. But these weapons must be used correctly[7]: an orchard can be destroyed by hormone weed-

[7] Cf. Jean Dorst, *Avant que nature ne meure*, by Jean Dorst.

killer intended for cereals. The Americans use it to destroy crops in Vietnam, and no objections are raised. They say they are Christians too. . . .

Though fertilizer is thought to save water, it only gives good results when the plants also receive the right amount of water: this means that water must be drained when in excess and supplemented by irrigation when there is too little; the high cost and numerous difficulties involved in these operations have already been mentioned. Fertilizer is only useful on good quality crops. To obtain the best results good organizers and overseers are needed to convince the peasants that fertilizer is useful and to teach them how to use it properly; the other preconditions include an efficient distribution network, credit loans and markets to sell the increased output.[8]

If these conditions are to be satisfied, large-scale plans must be adopted immediately for training, stimulating, and organizing the whole of the peasantry in tropical areas – no small task! The project must definitely be launched but if it is to be successful the difficulties involved must not be underestimated. Apart from machinery and factories for manufacturing the equipment in the places where it is needed, the developed countries should supply an increasing number of teachers, technicians, researchers, engineers, agronomists, organizers, economists, overseers, and so on.

Each specialist should work in conjunction with a colleague from the country concerned, who will replace him as soon as possible. European experts should make more effort to get on with the local officials. While acknowledging their authority the experts should nevertheless try to ensure that everyone is working towards the same end. From what I saw in July, 1965, in the Central African Republic, I realized that this is not always the case; production there was falling, while in the Northern Cameroons progress was fairly good.

6. PRICE STABILIZATION BY EXPANDING CONSUMPTION RATHER THAN BY RESTRICTING PRODUCTION

The EEC countries claim to protect their agricultural production from outside competition: thus the most productive agricultural

[8] Cf. *op. cit.*, Jean Dorst, chap. II, para 3.

workers are protected while the backward countries frequently have to sell at world market prices, which are often much lower than production costs. But their goods are very much in demand among the rich buyers in England and Germany; they exploit the tropical peasants, paying absurdly low prices for their raw materials. European protectionism, now coming to replace protection by individual nations, will probably soon give rise to a general stabilization of world agricultural prices and a corresponding drive to distribute food surpluses to the hungry through a suitable financial mechanism. The anarchy of economic liberalism destroys the peasant and makes the speculator rich. Besides, the coffee market has been 'planned' along traditional Malthusian lines: prices are protected by export quotas; in consequence production is reduced. Though this may not matter in the case of the coffee market, a similar policy would be disastrous for basic food products, since it would bring the threat of famine even closer. Want must no longer be aggravated in the interests of price protection; instead, consumption should be expanded, and the inadequate purchasing power of those who are underfed should be increased.

It is not the price of one particular raw material which should be protected, but the relationship between agricultural prices and industrial prices (of manufactured goods and machinery); both sides of the scale should be influenced. The capitalists and workers in the developed countries maintain that they can only benefit from increased productivity, but that is more necessary for their customers in the backward countries.

Another problem is the relationship between the prices of different agricultural goods. Coffee-growing – or rather gathering – in Betzimizarka on the eastern coast of Madagascar produces four or five times as much income per working hour as the irrigated ricefields on the high plateaux south of the capital in the Betsileo area. The groundnut growers of Casamance refuse to extend their ricefields, as was suggested in the first Senegalese plan, for rice-growing brings in only 40 per cent of the income from groundnuts.

As a result of the lack of market planning, foodstuffs, the most useful products, are the least profitable. If this state of affairs continues, food production will suffer. Of course all these relationships will be altered as the world approaches famine. Then planning will be even more essential to prevent black-market prices putting the goods even further beyond the reach of the poor. In the meantime, all peasants must be better paid, so as to place them on a more equal footing with the industrial and commercial sectors.

In a better planned economy it will be easier than it is now in a market economy to relate the value of a material to its production cost and utility, with less attention to its current scarcity. Peasants will then have more incentive to increase production. Production must then still be related to consumer demand, and this is the essential function of prices. It would be a grave mistake to think that this can all be settled by the mere stroke of a pen.

7. THE WORLD MARKETS FOR BASIC COMMODITIES MUST BE PLANNED

The underdeveloped countries' main source of foreign exchange and, consequently, their ability to purchase machinery is derived from the sale of the major basic agricultural commodities – coffee, cocoa, groundnuts, tea, sugar, bananas, and rubber – and also from minerals such as copper, tin, lead and manganese.[9] Groundnuts constitute more than 90 per cent of the exports of Gambia, Niger, and Senegal; coffee more than 80 per cent of Colombia's exports; palm oil three-quarters of Dahomey's; copper is equally important to Chile. These countries are extremely vulnerable, in that their balance of payments is wholly dependent on the volume and price of one, or perhaps two or three, exported products.

For a long time the uncontrolled markets for these major products have been particularly unstable. The prices depend on fluctuations in production resulting from climatic hazards, natural disasters, and various speculative purchases; they often vary considerably in the course of one year, or from one year to the next – far more than the variations in production according to the famous King's law.[10]

[9] Apart from petroleum, which we have omitted because of the exceptional nature of its production.
[10] Named after the English economist Gregory King, who was the first to note this fact at the beginning of the eighteenth century: that agricultural prices vary more than proportionally to the quantity produced. In other words, farmers' incomes are higher when there is a bad crop than when there is a good one.

Prices frequently vary by as much as 50 to 100 per cent of their average level.

With sugar, for example, a surplus or deficit of about 2 million tons, which is 4 per cent of world production and 12 per cent of the average quantity sold in the free market, can make the price fluctuate between 2 US cents and 12 US cents per pound. This often seriously damages the reserves of the underdeveloped countries, suddenly disrupts plans for importing equipment, and aggravates their weakness and economic dependence. Furthermore, the variations do not provide full compensation, since the profits from rising prices go to the exporters, foreign companies which repatriate part of their profit, or to local traders. When prices fall, it is the peasants or miners who immediately suffer, while the consumers in the industrialized countries are not very much affected.

There is one more phenomenon, again disadvantageous to the underdeveloped countries. A long-term view of these prices shows that most of them have been falling substantially ever since 1952, either absolutely or in relation to the prices of industrial goods. For example, in 1966 the state of sugar, cocoa and coffee prices became desperate. In consequence, the 'terms of trade', the relationship between the index of the prices of manufactured goods and that of the prices of raw materials, are constantly falling.[11] 'In 1954, we could buy a jeep for 14 sacks of coffee and it would now cost 39 . . .' a Colombian economist said in 1962.

This process is fairly similar to the fall in agricultural prices in industrialized countries and has much the same explanation: weakness of demand combined with badly planned supply. In industrialized countries, demand for staple products, food products in particular, grows very much more slowly than the economy as a whole. It is well known that as incomes rise the proportion spent on necessities falls (Engel's law). Between 1928 and 1955–7, world trade in primary products increased by only one-seventh as much as trade in manufactured goods.[12]

[11] In fact, from the terms of trade alone, which express the trend of the relationship between the prices of different products, one can form no judgement on this. We would have to be able to relate them to the factors used in producing these goods in order to take account of productivity changes.
[12] According to Guy de Lacharrière: *Commerce extérieur et sous-développement*. Coll. 'Pragma', P.U.F., Paris, 1964.

This trend is accentuated by the strong competition which synthetic products offer to agricultural products such as textile fibres and natural rubber. Similarly in minerals there has been a tendency for the proportion of raw material per dollar or even per ton in a finished product to decline.[13] The expansion of synthetic goods, the development of some crops such as soya beans, changes in eating habits, with meat, dairy produce, fruit and vegetables becoming more popular, reduce the dependence of the industrialized countries on the raw materials of the underdeveloped countries.

Such are the factors which have led to a deterioration in the terms of trade from the point of view of the underdeveloped countries. The actual structure of the markets is another factor. Far from being competitive, most of them are governed by large commercial firms working on an international scale, over which the developing nations have little influence.

The markets for raw materials, of vital importance to the income of Third World countries and thus to their possibilities of development, function extremely badly; this is one of the 'vicious circles' of underdevelopment. It alone absorbs much of the aid given to these countries by the industrialized nations. As in the case of the agricultural markets of the industrialized countries, a general reorganization would seem to be necessary. Reorganization should not merely be confined to the staple products, since the underdeveloped countries also face vigorous competition from the industrialized countries in the marketing of the few manufactured goods they are now starting to produce.

In answer to these problems, some people still preach the virtues of universal free trade as the principal way of disseminating economic development throughout the world, expanding trade through the law of comparative advantage and the rational international division of labour which results from it. In practice, however, this nineteenth century concept does not encourage economic modernization, still less the industrialization of backward countries.

The theory that international free trade stimulates growth does not seem to be, and cannot be, applicable when countries have

[13] In the United States this is probably happening at the rate of 1.8 per cent per year since 1940 (as above).

completely different economic structures – a situation which classical analysis did not even consider.[14] Gunnar Myrdal gave a very good explanation of why this is so.[15] Inside individual nations, the free play of market forces tends to encourage the expansion of those areas which are already developed; similarly, in international trade, it tends to favour the more advanced nations. And the phenomenon of continuous growth is naturally inclined to accentuate both internal and international inequalities. Technical skill and capital become concentrated in the most industrialized areas of the world: as their position becomes more dominant, all trade tends to favour their interests.

Unplanned markets, in theory governed by free competition, in practice controlled by industrial and commercial oligopolies in the developed countries, tend to turn the non-industrialized areas into backwaters, which are unlikely to be developed. This tendency is accentuated by the type of product sold by the underdeveloped countries – low-value raw materials – and by the structure of commercial markets, whose decision-making centres are not in the poor countries. It can thus be seen that though it seems necessary to intervene in the international markets for staple commodities, such intervention would never be sufficient.

8. FROM THE REORGANIZATION OF WORLD MARKETS TO THE FULL PLANNING OF INTERNATIONAL TRADE AND COLLECTIVE DEVELOPMENT[16]

This reorganization should be carried out with three different objectives in view. It should attempt to eliminate short-term fluctuations and to fix prices that are both equitable and remunerative; this will help to achieve the fundamental objective, which is both

---

[14] 'Valid for a free market economy such as that of most of western Europe before the Second World War, most theories of international trade are not perfectly applicable to the most developed economies of the present time, and may not be applicable at all to developing economies.' Gerard Macy, *Economie internationale*, Coll. 'Themis', P.U.F., 1965.
[15] In his book, *Economic Theory and Underdeveloped Regions*, London, 1957.
[16] See in particular, *Interdéveloppement et Organisation des échanges mondiaux*, special number of *Développement et Civilisation*, December 1965, in particular André Philip's articles and several FAO publications.

a medium- and long-term balance between production and consumption.

Accordingly world markets should be planned in gradual stages. In place of the present rudimentary type of commercial trade, in which production and consumption are erratic, trade should be regulated on a contractual basis. World agreements should, therefore, be worked out for products or groups of products according to a coherent overall plan and under the auspices of international organizations; they must be signed by interested parties, both producing and consuming countries.[17]

Careful study should be given to the future pattern of demand. It should increase as a result of growing contact with the socialist countries, which are still very small consumers of tropical goods. The underdeveloped countries should gradually build more trade between themselves. Demand could also be influenced by the suppression of fiscal barriers such as taxes on consumption.

Preliminary studies and agreements should be made, carefully distinguishing the various categories of products and types of markets. The problems and prospects are different for mineral goods on the one hand and for agricultural goods on the other; they are different again for agricultural goods which are in competition with agricultural or synthetic goods produced by the industrialized countries (such as cotton, rubber, sugar, rice and vegetable oils), and for those which still have no competition and will remain the monopoly of the tropical underdeveloped countries (such as coffee, tea, cocoa, bananas, spice, and some textile fibres). Still in the category of agricultural goods, different treatment must be given to food products and beverages (such as coffee and tea) and to raw materials for industry. Finally, some assessment must be made of the responsiveness of demand to price changes.

When the outlook for demand has been established, suitable agreements should be drawn up for purchase contracts at guaranteed prices for the groups of producers in underdeveloped countries;

[17] Three agreements affecting world trade in agricultural produce have so far been made. The international wheat agreement, signed in 1949, mainly affects the developed countries. The agreement on sugar, which was never very effective, has been allowed to lapse since the break between the United States and Cuba. The international agreement on coffee, drawn up by 57 exporting and importing countries, in force since 1963, was designed to make a long-term adjustment between supply and demand.

these should at least be medium-term contracts, based on sound economic principles. By setting up offices for international commerce, these countries should considerably improve their negotiating strength and consequently their prospects for obtaining advantageous contracts. These offices should succeed in controlling supply, thus avoiding periodic price falls.

Impartial commissions of experts, representing both buying and selling countries, under the arbitration of international organizations, should carry out economic studies as a basis for price-fixing. The prices would be guaranteed by the possibility of intervention by an International Fund charged with studying and assembling information on the markets and regulating and directing production and trade. It should be possible for temporary surpluses either to be stored and used to stabilize the market or to be used for economic aid programmes.

But the reorganization of international trade should not stop here. If it is necessary to control the chaos of world markets, then, contrary to the view sometimes held, interventions of this kind are bound to be completely inadequate. They might even be harmful in that they might perpetuate the existing structure in the same way as agricultural price-support policies sometimes do; above all, they might confine the underdeveloped countries to their present role of providing raw materials for the industrialized countries. If this remained their sole function, it would represent the greatest barrier to real economic development, which implies diversification – in particular, the modernization of food production and industrialization.

At present, as we have already seen, foreign trade will be unable to stimulate expansion, even when it is planned in the interests of the Third World. Economic development may stimulate the expansion of trade, as it has between the industrialized countries, but the converse (that trade stimulates development) has never been proved. It is, therefore, insufficient to influence prices and markets without completing the process by changing the basic economic structure of the underdeveloped countries. This raises the whole problem of international trade.

The problem has never been fully understood, even by the underdeveloped countries. At their conference on Trade and Development

(UNCTAD) at Geneva in 1964, they made the stabilization of the prices of staple products their principal demand. Thus trade was discussed at length, but development was scarcely mentioned.

We should give some thought to the meaning and purpose of trade.[18] We are too accustomed to thinking that trade must be unequal by definition, one side losing and the other gaining (and in international trade, it is usually the same side which loses all the time). Now, as the whole concept of trade implies, each side should obtain some goods or services which it cannot provide for itself in exchange for goods which it has in relative abundance. The difference in resources between different countries is its starting point. 'It begins and ends with the realization that different resources can be exchanged.'[19] As trade creates more general satisfaction, it should logically benefit both parties at the same time. This proposition, generally valid in the economic and cultural spheres, is the basic justification for international cooperation. As J. Austruy points out, in order to increase general satisfaction, trading partners must assess and exchange their different resources: 'greater communication, involving increased specialization and organic interdependence'. Now, in present conditions, with enormous inequality between trading partners and their access to information, the goods exchanged tend to be wrongly valued. Furthermore, the West with its very high propensity to save tends to pay too little attention to the values and requirements of the future. 'It is clear that if natural endowments are destroyed, in the interests of an already outdated industrial society, the wealth of many societies and the endowment of mankind will be diminished.'[20]

The formation of a progressive idea of development – the task of our generation – is synonymous with the attempt to give world resources their true value by renewed or intensified trade between clearly distinct but allied human societies for the greater benefit of all. A completely new meaning can then be given to economic aid by industrialized countries to less industrialized or non-industrialized

[18] Particularly after reading Jacques Austruy's article 'L'échange, l'information et l'interdéveloppement', in the special number of *Développement et civilisations* referred to above, without which the following passage would not have been written.
[19] Jacques Austruy, *Le Scandale du développement*, ed. Marcel Rivière et Cⁱᵉ., Paris, 1965, p. 298.
[20] Jacques Austruy, *op. cit.*

countries. It can be seen both as a 'measure to conserve world capital' by forecasting 'future shortages' and also as a factor that could be used to initiate a movement towards mutually beneficial development. This definition goes much further than one which refers only to trade in immediately profitable markets. But such trade cannot be eliminated, since development demands both greater trade and also that, in helping the non-industrialized countries to 'take off', the industrialized countries should be prepared to enlarge future trade, especially of a commercial kind.

Genuine development in the Third World will require an efficient productive system, above all for progressive agriculture, obtained with the aid of international cooperation. But, as we have already said, both the vital modernization of agriculture and the establishment of a cumulative growth process are closely connected to a policy of industrialization. Industry will not only allow the undermechanized countries to improve their standard of living directly but will also enable them to sell less raw agricultural produce and minerals and more manufactured goods, thereby improving their trading position.

In view of the poverty of Third World countries, experts and politicians agree that they can only be given the necessary stimulus if efficient planning and large-scale intervention in the economy are undertaken by the government. But since many of the countries are small, since their resources are limited and their markets for industrial products are narrow, development programmes cannot really be effective unless they embrace large geographical areas. Widespread economic cooperation, initially at a regional level, becomesivitally necessary for the co-ordination and implementation of policies for intra-structural investment, industrial development and trade.

This kind of genuine cooperation between underdeveloped countries, in contrast with the present national cooperation, could make international aid much more effective; it would then be more acceptable to public opinion in the industrialized countries, with the result that it could be extended. This would also facilitate a change in direction in cooperation between developed and underdeveloped countries under the stimulus and supervision of international organizations: a concerted campaign for development, planned for large, multi-national economic areas and linked to agreements on specific products – in particular by making provisions for the gradual substitution of finished products for raw materials.

One formula for 'interdevelopment' seems particularly attractive: this is 'international co-production', as recommended by Maurice Byé,[21] after a searching analysis of the evolution of international relations. The necessary build-up in the underdeveloped countries of modern productive and commercial concerns could then go forward rapidly thanks to 'the association of decision-making units, both private and public, from different nations in a single productive venture'; in other words, through the creation of enterprises within what is in two senses a mixed economy – financed by both public and private capital[22] from at least two different countries.[23]

Co-production is already being practised by consortia of private firms, principally for the exploitation of oil and mineral deposits. The governments of developed countries also have agreements of this kind to enable them to combine their resources, which would be individually inadequate, to undertake large-scale ventures. The socialist countries of eastern Europe do this to exploit metallurgic deposits and complexes. The same thing happens between the countries of Western Europe, in some technologically advanced sectors, such as aeronautics and atomic energy. In the past few years agreements for industrial co-production with mutual benefits have also been drawn up between private capitalist companies – particularly German firms – and East European states or socialist enterprises. The one provides technical skill at a high level and specialized equipment, the others, skilled labour and markets; the profits are shared.

As these examples show, the industrialized countries are finding it increasingly necessary to continue their growth by undertaking joint projects, and thus to strengthen the economic ties between

[21] In two articles in *Le Monde diplomatique*, November and December 1965, entitled 'Les formes nouvelles de la coopération internationale'.
[22] With strict controls, these could be guaranteed by an international mutual assurance body and could eventually benefit from interest rebates permitted by an international institution.
[23] Why not international funds as well, as soon as the international solidarity tax is introduced?

them. This is surely infinitely more necessary for those countries which still have their whole development before them and which can offer a large labour force and progressively widening markets in return for technical skill and machinery.

One of the first such achievements is the cooperative association set up between Algeria and France[24] in 1965 for oil production and for Algerian industrialization. In the words of the agreement it is 'founded on the community of interest of a producing country still in the process of development and a developed consuming country'. This agreement represents an important new departure in relations between industrialized countries and the countries of the Third World. Its achievements and its development should be closely watched.

By paying attention to their geographical and economic location, these cooperative projects set up in underdeveloped countries can become poles of multi-national development; in other words complexes able to stimulate economic growth by large-scale 'spread' effects. The manufacture of various means of production necessary for agricultural progress, such as chemical fertilizers, could become 'industrializing' industries, as Gerard de Bernis calls them. Other factors should also be regarded in this light, such as those which will effect a sizeable increase in food resources or food transport facilities: firms for processing agricultural and fishing produce or for making new foodstuffs.

During the period of industrialization, tariff preferences and quotas must be introduced to favour the goods manufactured in the Third World, in the most appropriate way for each individual case and according to the level of development of the various national industries, as is explained, for example, in the Brasseur Plan.[25] Similarly, at the end of an initial period of economic construction, these countries should still protect their new industries by special tariff measures, but only on a temporary, selective and declining basis.[26]

[24] By the Franco-Algerian oil agreement signed on July 29, 1965; see Maurice Byé, 'L'association coopérative et les accords pétroliers franco-algériens', in the number quoted above of *Développement et Civilisations*.
[25] Named after the Belgian minister who proposed it.
[26] The case for protectionism is not new, having been formulated over a century ago in Germany under the stimulus of Friedrich List, to promote economic 'take-off'.

9. BILATERAL AID AND DOMESTIC EFFORT: BOTH ARE INADEQUATE

Governments give aid to those countries which they approve of and which support their policies; this is particularly evident in the case of the United States. France is more to be commended for granting aid to socialist Algeria in 1966 than for abandoning 'rebel' Guinea in 1958. But though she did not support Fulbert Youlou, she did restore Leon M'Ba to power, since her interests in Gabon are more important. French aid still places more emphasis on social expenditure and infra-structure than on industrial equipment.[27] Presidential palaces, assembly halls, and ministries are built; private accounts in Swiss banks flourish. Even so, bilateral aid of this kind is not entirely useless, especially in the agricultural sector; all the same it is inadequate, above all in the industrial sector.[28]

The Third World will have to make greater efforts if it is to reach 'take-off' quickly enough. The peasant of the African forest or savannah often devotes only five hundred or a thousand hours per year to direct agricultural production, when he should be working at least fifteen hundred hours; to achieve this will involve reorganization in some places.

Africa as a whole probably invests 15 per cent of its gross production, according to a recent calculation by the Economic Commission for Africa (which puts the figure higher than in previous estimates). But a large proportion of this investment comes from abroad – almost the whole amount in some countries; and 60 per cent of the investment goes into building, a completely disproportionate amount, since it is not directly productive. It would be logically desirable for investment to rise to 20 and then 25 per cent of the gross product in the next few years. National resources should provide at least half the money, partly in the form of work; 40 per cent should be the maximum allotted to building.

Algeria devotes 35 per cent of her total national income to public spending, and Tunisia 28 per cent; the proportion seems to be equally high in many other tropical African States. Given the

[27] As I pointed out in *False Start in Africa*.
[28] We have already drawn attention to the recent petroleum agreements between France and Algeria.

present structure of budgets, this figure should be reduced to 25 per cent or perhaps 20 per cent at some later date. But this depends largely on the way the money is used. Congo (Brazzaville) devotes 78 per cent of its total budget to civil servants' salaries, not leaving very much for other current expenditure and equipment; 40 per cent should be the absolute maximum.

We have now given a rapid summary of a few simple, basic rules of sensible economic thinking, but have not embarked on a much more difficult problem – the practical application of the rules and the imposition of sanctions against those who refuse to accept them. We will return to this point in our study of the even more difficult question of making food aid dependent upon the adoption of a more rigorous birth-control policy. This will soon become absolutely vital if we really mean to conquer world hunger. Each new state will, however, tend to demand complete respect for its newly acquired sovereignty – this could be incompatible with any move towards a united world. If unity is to become a practical reality, rules established for all will have to be respected. National sovereignty will have to be transformed into supra-national sovereignty.

Any young state which wishes to maintain its independence as far as possible should be primarily self-reliant, as advised by China. But primarily does not mean solely, and does not rule out cooperation or international solidarity. But it does imply that foreign aid, however great, will not enable the Third World to cover the enormous distance it has to go, without the backing of greatly and rapidly accelerated internal effort. The war against hunger may never be won if the interested parties do not organize an enormous increase in work, training, and saving. Otherwise, foreign aid would become similar to charity, encouraging in some countries neo-colonialist paternalism with an element of contempt, and in others the mentality of the subsidized – blithe indifference.[29]

---

[29] 'We have always lived in a state of unconcern; do not worry us with your development,' a young man said to me at Antsirabe (summer 1958); in that case, do not ask for independence.

CHAPTER THIRTEEN
A world economic development organization: the only way to avoid famine

I. GRADUAL ENLARGEMENT OF COMMON INTERESTS

At the same time as the perfection of productive techniques and the development of units of production, wider and wider areas of economic solidarity have been growing up irreversibly in human society through trade and the exchange of skills.

The narrow unit of the village, in which at one time the peasant and the artisan were mutually interdependent, gradually expanded to embrace a larger region, involving the manufacturer and the merchant. Too limited for the development of large industrial firms, this closed regional unit had to make way for trade within the nation as a whole. The nation is now becoming too limited to stimulate and support the enormous industrial complexes of the modern technological age or to provide its members with all the goods and services they require.

At each stage of this process, the framework and institutions of society have been correspondingly altered and enlarged, though always with some delay. Social units have developed from the family to the village, from the village to the feudal domain, from the feudal domain to the province, from the province to the most recent stage, the nation.

It is with the progressive widening of economic units that collective management and administration have become necessary. Similarly, wider social units have also come to be accepted. As autonomous economic zones have expanded, so human communities have become larger. When the common interests of the members of the community gradually overcome their differences, a unified human society is set up with larger social and political organization. Thus, in the new unit, justice instead of violence is used to solve conflicts, through arbitration based on recognized laws. Moreover, the members of the new group also allow a proportion of their work or income to go to the community to finance communal services or to support the most needy members of the group – children, the sick, the infirm, the old, the poor, etc.

But since the structure of societies is so inflexible, these two elements which bind them together – completely dominant in the family unit – usually only emerge in larger societies after open conflict between social groups, sometimes as violent and extreme as revolution. Such conflicts usually give rise to a new, wider social contract, sanctioned by new rules.

The intermediate period, between the formation of new economic units and that of a suitable socio-political framework has often been a difficult one. When a society is governed by laws made for an earlier stage of development, it cannot solve the problems which arise in a wider context and in different social conditions.

Of particular significance here is Western Europe's period of industrialization, which took place in the socio-political framework of a provincial, artisan society. It was not until a century later that the most pressing social problems of the time – working-class conditions, in particular – even began to be seen as important. Similarly, in most countries of the world today, social legislation and policy are not keeping pace with the economic facts of large-scale industrialization and urbanization.

In the past, violence has usually been used to remove the contradictions between dynamic technological and economic progress and backward social organization. The process can also be carried out by deliberate negotiation, as with the international agreements drawn up after the last world war – a great improvement on armed conflict.

'In the course of a few generations all sorts of economic and cultural links have been forged around us and they are multiplying in geometric progression. Nowadays, over and above the bread that to simple neolithic man symbolized food, each man demands his daily ration of iron, copper and cotton, of electricity, oil and radium, of discoveries, of the cinema, and of international news. It is no longer a simple field, however big, but the whole earth which is required to nourish each one of us.'[1] Because economic interdependence has become world-wide (although we are still divided by the barriers of a bygone age) we know that some day we must establish correspondingly universal forms of social organization, and introduce general arbitration and collective responsibility for the whole world. The nations of the twentieth century are reminiscent of the French provinces of the eighteenth century, before national integration. At that time some areas were allowed to suffer from serious want in spite of food gluts in other areas.

If the most serious upheavals of the transitional period are to be avoided, we must take deliberate action now to build a universal socio-political unit transcending the nation – an historically necessary development. Internationally as well as nationally we must substitute structural reforms for mere acts of charity, and establish solidarity with, rather than give assistance to, other nations. And we must start with the most urgent problem – that of food.

The time has now come when we should profit from the lessons of history and build the world of tomorrow, for the 'future is not only what may happen or what is most likely to happen. It is also, and to an increasing extent, what we want to happen.'[2]

2. THE PROBLEMS OF WORLD GOVERNMENT

As the first and most acceptable step towards world government, we should attempt to reduce social injustice not simply on a national but on a world scale.[3] In order to do this, there must be a large and rapid increase in international cooperation, so that more food may be distributed to India and all the other places where people are in want. In the next stage, absolute priority should be given to providing these countries with means of production, machinery for example, and to sending them teachers and technicians of all kinds

---

[1] Pierre Teilhard de Chardin, *The Phenomenon of Man*, Collins, London, and Harper, New York, 1959.
[2] Gaston Berger, *Phenomenologie du Temps et Prospective*, P.U.F., Paris, 1964.
[3] Thomas Aquinas wrote in *Summa Theologica*: 'In case of necessity, all things are common.'

(this has already begun but not on a realistic scale). If public opinion in the affluent countries put sufficient pressure on their governments, this second stage could soon be accomplished.

If the United Nations were extended to include all nations, including China and her neighbours, it could as a really universal international body gradually assume more power and become more effective. It could begin by increasing the resources of the World Food Programme, which was set up under the auspices of the FAO.

The setting up of a world government will be a long and arduous task, fraught with setbacks and disagreements. It seems almost impossible to try to build it by direct union between all the nations of the present time, with no intermediate stage. In 1964 we wrote that African states, still proud of their newly acquired sovereignty, would be more willing to abdicate some of their autonomy to the Organization of African Unity than to a world organization. Recent conflicts within the OAU make this intermediate stage seem even more difficult to realize at present.

The road towards progressive integration, starting at the level of individual countries, could very well begin with agreements for economic cooperation. For the time being, it would be very useful if the various states of one geographical zone adopted complementary plans for investment and the reduction and eventual abolition of trade barriers – as a temporary measure before common markets are set up. We are doing our utmost to promote this plan at the United Nations Economic Commission for Africa at Addis Ababa.

With economic co-operation, adjacent small states would become more unified and, with progressive integration, would be able to reduce some of their general expenditure (on the army and the foreign service) and embark on development with more chance of success. As a result of the first negotiations now being undertaken about plans for the Maghreb, Central Africa, and Central America, and about proposals for economic co-operation made by Chile, these countries are creating a climate in which political difficulties may be more easily resolved. The recent conflicts between Algeria and Morocco, and between India and Pakistan, place such an intolerable burden on the countries involved that they jeopardize any hope of accelerating development to deal with the population explosion.

Let us not underestimate the difficult problems ahead, ranging from the vested interest of the armaments manufacturers to traditional patterns of thought, prejudices, and behaviour. It would be best to make several different approaches at once to bring about the necessary world rapprochement. As a vital preliminary, public opinion must be convinced that all present conflicts, the worst of which is the Vietnam war, must cease. Then the idea of peaceful coexistence could be elaborated and realized through constantly increasing economic and cultural ties. China could certainly be incorporated if she is given respect and aid. At the same time, bilateral, multilateral, and regional agreements should be increased.

International bodies, by this time universal and reorganized, should receive steadily increasing resources. If the World Health Organization did more to sponsor birth control, it would be able to reduce the rates of death and disease without fear of the consequences. If the budget of the FAO were first doubled, then increased fivefold, and later tenfold, it would be more able to give instruction on recent technological discoveries and take part in the actual application of the projects which its experts are now devising.

At the same time, propaganda for a united world should continue: 'world citizens' should press for 'the election, on a trans-national basis, of delegates responsible for defending human rights, for expressing the wishes of the people of the world and finally for drawing up laws for a peaceful and civilized world.'[4] Jean Jaurès reminds us to work for the ideal and understand the real. The campaign for the ideal of world unity in no way exempts us from taking immediate short-term action, both as individuals and as members of a community. But we must keep the inadequacies and limitations of this kind of action in mind, as an incentive to further effort.

[4] Campaign for World Citizenship, 55 rue Lacépède, Paris 5eme (Jean Rostand, Danilo Dolci, Lord Boyd Orr, Mme Rjan-Nehru, Bertrand Russell, Linus Pauling, Josué de Castro, Abbé Pierre, Shinzo Hamaï, Hromadka, Arthur Koestler, Ivan Suprk, Hans Striving, etc.). The appeal adds: 'In the absence of a supranational law, nations have to resort to force to defend their interests. The consequence is war, either intentional or accidental, which since the splitting of the atom and the development of bacteriological warfare is becoming the absurd "final solution" of complete genocide by the whole human race. In the absence of world institutions to ensure the satisfaction of universal, basic human needs, the human individual is oppressed. While vast wealth is wasted, two thirds of the human race endure hunger.'

3. THE POLITICAL DIMENSIONS OF CHARITY

'I have adopted a little Korean girl and so I have done my duty towards the underprivileged peoples,' a worthy Swiss bourgeois said to me. 'I have sent a donation to the Catholic aid society and we have sent tool boxes to Africa.' The young members of the Quebec Red Cross showed me some woollen garments they were making to send to Upper Volta, where the climate is very hot. All this is very touching and can be useful, so long as everyone admits that it is quite inadequate to solve the most colossal problem that human society has ever had to face. Minor acts of generosity should not become a cheap way of salving the consciences of all those who claim that they want to help others. They should give daily proof of their good intentions through increasingly frequent and effective actions.

The most attractive feature of communal projects, such as 'Yocotan' (Guatemala) at Verviers in Belgium or 'Operation Cameroun' run by the lycée in Montargis, is that they are really helping to make people, and particularly young people, realize the extreme gravity of the problem. Let us hope that the members of these projects will become active militants who will give their neighbours, families, fellow students, friends, and acquaintances no peace until they all make their own contributions; let us also hope that the young people who are being mobilized will eventually become active citizens who expect their representatives to make more energetic and effective demands upon the resources of their country to help the Third World to develop. The poor were once our immediate neighbours; before 1914, people made an automatic habit of throwing them a couple of coins on the way out of church. Later the poor were our most underprivileged citizens; even when they are not our immediate neighbours, we help them indirectly, through taxation and social security and family allowances. We have now come to realize that the destitute are so numerous that we cannot take individual responsibility for them. They live so far away from us that we are unable to make direct contact with them.

After Father Maillard had heard my lecture at Laval University in Quebec, he talked of the political dimension of charity; in modern times political action is the only useful expression of charity. Public opinion should bring pressure for increased world solidarity and for the founding of organizations to safeguard it. But we must try to improve our existing methods, rather than merely to substitute vague or unrealistic plans; we do not know when these plans will become practically possible.

4. FROM BILATERAL AID TO WORLD COOPERATION THROUGH GUARANTEED MARKETS

With increased pressure from a better informed public, both bilateral aid[5] and European aid could be increased. At the same time, every effort must be made to see that aid is more productively used[6] – for industrialization projects and for sending more teachers and technical advisers to the underdeveloped world. First of all, as we have already said, prices of raw materials must be stabilized and guaranteed markets must be created. It would be useful to introduce preferential tariffs to make the rich countries accessible markets not only for the raw materials but also for the manufactured goods of the backward countries.

In brief, we must do the opposite of what we did to Japan between the wars, when our attitude forced her to take up an aggressive position. We could begin with simple articles such as textiles, oils, leather, shoes, furniture and other wood products. Gradually halting their production of these goods, the developed countries would concentrate on more advanced technology (specialized metallurgy, machine and automated tools, synthetic chemical goods and electronics). As soon as they are ready, the backward countries should also embark on these complex industries, which will be necessary for their future development. But on the whole their best policy would be to begin with the more simple manufactured goods; they will then make faster progress.

[5] In *Le Monde*, March 6–7, 1966, G. Mathieu shows that French aid to underdeveloped countries dropped to 1.56 per cent of the gross national product in 1964 as opposed to 1.92 per cent in 1962. Net aid would, therefore, be less than 1.35 per cent. In 1965 budgetary aid probably fell by 11.4 per cent.
[6] In *False Start in Africa* we pointed out the wastage or under-use of FIDES and FAC money: we will merely remind the reader of the palace of the National Assembly and the airfield for jets at Bangui, the latter being more costly than the training of all the peasants of Central Africa.

When pressure for world unity becomes sufficiently influential, it will be able to emphasize the supra-national aspect of the co-operative projects.[7] As we have already suggested, a substantial extension in the World Food Programme could be made as a beginning. Multilateral cooperation could also be gradually increased, at first in addition to and later in place of bilateral aid. Measures must be introduced to ensure that this new, universal, international organization does not place any political pressure on the countries receiving aid from it, as happens with the existing, and all too often neo-colonialist bilateral aid. After this stage has been completed there will still be much more ground to cover and so resources for this purpose must be correspondingly increased.

5. A PROGRESSIVE INTERNATIONAL SOLIDARITY TAX

At the Trade and Development Conference in Geneva in 1964, it was proposed that every country should spend 1 per cent of its national income on aid to the backward countries. The measure was opposed by the USSR among others and was not adopted; and yet even this was not ambitious enough. Even more money is needed to avert the threat of famine by 1980. One per cent of national income would only be a suitable contribution from semi-affluent countries, such as Italy, which still have large underdeveloped areas. At least 2 per cent would soon be required from the other EEC countries, since France gave almost as much as that in 1962.

The slightly richer countries (such as Switzerland, Sweden, Australia and Canada) could give 2.5 per cent; the United States and Kuwait would have no difficulty in giving 3 per cent. This scheme cannot be put into effect without concerted pressure from a large (and growing) section of the world's population, who genuinely believe in the value of unity. If the United States continues its shameful wastefulness and its policy of military destruction, it must be harshly censured by this section of the population. Our scheme would raise forty to fifty thousand million dollars per annum. It would require this amount of money to initiate real

[7] According to G. Mathieu, the proportion of French aid which is channelled through international bodies dropped from 8 per cent in 1962 to 1 per cent in 1964; it is likely to increase again slightly in the future.

development in the backward countries by the early seventies. We must not forget that time is pressing.

The funds thus collected would be handed over to the existing international bodies who would use them to provide loans without security, to finance infra-structure, and to give interest-free credit loans for machinery; traditional loans are putting the countries so much in debt that soon all their available resources will be spent on paying interest and amortization, leaving nothing over for industrial investment.

When the World Solidarity Fund has collected the forty or fifty thousand million dollars referred to above, it will set up a world organization to fight hunger and promote international economic cooperation. This organization should eventually become a world development agency, designed to make interventionist policies more rapid and efficient. The contributions made by the developed countries would be granted partly in the forms of goods (food, fertilizer, machinery, etc.) and partly in currency to finance the transportation and distribution of the goods and to send teachers and technical advisers to give instruction on how the goods should be used. Details can be filled in when the plan comes nearer to being adopted and has been discussed more widely.

When schemes for professional training are set in motion, the backward countries will be able to make good use of more resources and more machinery. The percentage of national income exacted from the rich countries should rise with the course of time. They will not have to deprive themselves of anything, since they will only be giving up a proportion of their future accumulation of wealth, and slowing down the rise in their standard of living slightly. Even that is not certain, since the resources of the Solidarity Fund may enable them to avoid crises and solve many of their economic problems. It will broaden the market for all forms of production, both agricultural and, particularly, industrial. The countries of over-populated Western Europe cannot allow the exponential increase of private motor-car production to continue. By contrast, demand for machine-tools in the backward countries will be extremely high for some time to come.

It is frequently argued that the United States' economy is dependent on constantly growing military expenditure. Industrialists with vested interests exert pressure on the Pentagon to carry through the escalation policy in Vietnam. This can only lead to world suicide; whether or not the prosperity of the United States is dependent on arms industries, this dynamic country must find other less dangerous methods of expansion.

The mechanization of the Third World countries will increase demand to a level where the only restraining factors will be the world's productive capacity and the size of international aid. Finally, on the (pleasant) hypothesis of general disarmament, aid could gradually be made equal to former military expenditure: that is, $140,000 million officially but $200,000 million in fact.[8] Thus even the United States would find that generosity was in her own interest; it would have to be explained, however, that different companies would be making the profits. The government would itself have to redirect a certain amount of production. Suggestions of this kind could lead to the development of a really democratic movement in the United States; unless this happens, aid to the Third World will always be inadequate.

The Solidarity Tax should discourage the rich from excessive consumption (their health should benefit as excess weight is a constant hazard!) and it will also arrest the dissipation of the limited riches of our planet – forests, mineral reserves, flora, soils that are in constant danger of erosion, and fauna that have been decimated by thoughtless hunting. People reading the Sunday newspapers in New York forget that African children do not even have paper with which to learn to read and write. People who buy American cars can be accused of causing starvation if not murder: in Africa and Asia, the peasants cannot obtain enough steel for even the simplest tools. In India I have seen ploughs on which the share was so worn that they could not function properly; but they could not be replaced on account of lack of steel or money. Money can buy every service, even that offered by prostitution. We have no reason to be proud of our

---

[8] The encyclical, *Mater et Magistra*, mentions this: 'On the one hand we are shown the fearful spectre of want and misery which threatens to extinguish human life, and on the other hand we find that scientific discoveries, technical inventions and economic resources are being used, often extensively, to provide terrible instruments of ruin and death.' (Para 198, Catholic Truth Society Translation.)

scale of values or of the civilization based on it. We should think a little more of the world's underprivileged and we should not forget the needs of future generations before we multiply the human race to infinity. Life on the earth may continue for a great many generations and our dissipation of natural resources now may cause a great deal of suffering in the future.

With the possibility of erosion becoming more and more dangerous, the food situation in 1980 may prove even more serious than anticipated. And soon more and more countries (from Egypt to the United States, from the Maghreb to Europe, even Western Europe) will have a shortage of water, the most vital of all natural riches and the source of all vegetation. Soon, even humid countries, such as Belgium, will have to desalinate seawater at great cost.

6. THE DISTRIBUTION OF RESOURCES, BASED FIRST ON NEED, AND THEN ON POTENTIAL

As soon as possible the affluent countries should provide the modern means of production, first in addition to and later in place of food aid. They should also provide industries to satisfy demand for the most important consumer goods and to make it possible for the underdeveloped countries to export manufactured goods. The next priority[9] will be factories in which these forms of production and other manufactured goods – either consumer goods or machinery – can be made. The next question is how to distribute the (rapidly growing) product of the international Solidarity Tax suggested above.

We should first of all help those countries where suffering is most serious: these are probably India and, once peace has been re-established, North and South Vietnam. Otherwise the copies of the plan that was proposed for South Vietnam in Honolulu in early 1966 would look like empty propaganda.

The population of Indonesia, most of all in Java, has been suffering from hunger at least since 1963, and their agricultural problems have not been helped by more recent massacres. A large part of East

[9] The Soviet model, giving priority to heavy industry, is not suitable for these small backward countries. With a few exceptions they should start with agriculture, then light industry.

Africa is regularly ravaged by drought. Surpluses from the Andes should be sent to the neighbouring plains, though this would be costly. Production should be diversified in the Caribbean islands, with more food crops added to the sugar-coffee-cotton group; money for this must be provided. Some priority should be given to the north-east and north of Brazil, to North Africa and also to all of South East Asia, Southern China, tropical Africa and most of tropical America.

During the first stage, the World Solidarity Fund could be allocated according to this criterion of urgency, the acuteness of need. However, the criterion of efficiency should not be overlooked. It has two aspects: economic potential and the standard of political administration. Efficiency will be vital; for resources are strictly limited and needs virtually unlimited. All resources should, therefore, be used to maximum advantage.

In the second stage (starting at the same time as the first in the less destitute areas), attention should be concentrated on places with the highest potential for increased production. They will be given equal consignments of new resources. It is better to concentrate on cultivating the most fertile and best watered areas of the south and centre of Brazil than to devote enormous but inevitably much less productive effort to the drought-ridden dry *sertão* of the north-east. It is more worthwhile for the Mossis of Upper Volta to plant oil palms in the Ivory Coast than to allow them to remain in over-populated conditions on infertile land.

Agricultural potential is often so limited as to raise the question of the usefulness of work. Potential is not only dependent on physical environment but also on the economic system (infra-structure, markets, etc.) and the social system (ability to accept new ideas, breadth of knowledge, etc.). In brief, if we succeed in making our governments declare universal war on hunger, we should proceed through three basic stages:

1. The international fund would buy surpluses from rich countries by contract. All surpluses would be sent abroad and, for a generation, food aid would be very much increased, going particularly to children, and financing investment work.
2. The fund would accelerate 'take-off' in backward countries,

by providing them with factories (making fertilizer, etc.), set up in a system of co-production; in this phase, aid would concentrate particularly on industrialization.

3. The fund should give a new stimulus to research into non-agricultural foodstuffs, so that large quantities could be produced rapidly. Priority should go initially to fish-flour, oilcakes, and yeasts for human consumption – until now, these proteins have been consumed by animals. It should then encourage research into synthetic amino-acids, which would represent an economic way of wiping out protein deficiencies, and into improving the protein content of the major agricultural foodstuffs.

7. SANCTIONS AGAINST LACK OF FORESIGHT: ABSOLUTELY NECESSARY BUT DIFFICULT TO ENFORCE

The human element will always be the most important factor in any society. The existence of corrupt, privileged minorities is the main hindrance to development in the backward countries. As soon as the World Organization for Economic Cooperation is respected by public opinion it will be able to stipulate conditions for efficiency before granting the means of development. It could then propose (being in a better position to do so than the former colonial powers) the formation of economic and political organizations to receive and administer the aid; through them it could be better used for economic progress.

Between 1953 and 1963, Japan increased her production by about 10 per cent per year; her budget expenditure is equivalent to only 16 per cent of her gross production.[10] According to Samir Amin public expenditure in Algeria is about 35 per cent of production; and between 1960 and 1964, production probably fell by about 36 per cent. These two facts are not unrelated.

Our proposed World Organization for Economic Cooperation could be directed by an international management committee comprising equal numbers of both donors and beneficiaries. Arbitration would be entrusted to highly qualified independent members, chosen by mutual agreement between the backward countries and the

[10] Paul Fabra, *Le Monde*, March 1–5, 1966.

developed countries. The socialist bloc would, of course, be given the place it deserves. This body, responsible for the mitigation of world hunger and the promotion of 'inter-development', would soon acquire high status; it could then relate its grants of aid to the internal effort made by each country requesting it. As we have shown in Chapter XII, several different factors could be studied in order to establish the correct order of precedence: for example, the government's standard of responsibility;[11] reduction in public spending, particularly luxury spending; the increase in employment, saving and investment; fairness in income distribution.

The peasant's working year must be extended and consequently new agricultural systems and new reclamation projects will have to be introduced in some places. Countries with full, regular employment should be granted most aid; this would give other countries an incentive to mobilize the peasants (in the off-season) and the unemployed from the shanty towns into land-improvement projects.

Decisions on the criteria for grants and allocations will give rise to bitter arguments and conflicts. Experts of international standing[12] could be brought in to arbitrate. It will be impossible to establish a world order with universal peace and harmony – there are more likely to be many 'tears and gnashing of teeth'.

If we try to lay the basic foundations of a more unified society, we must be prepared for all the hindrances and difficulties that will be put in the way by privileged minorities motivated by their own interests, passions, and ideologies. Che Guevara did not succeed in creating perfect men. Tomorrow's world will not be an easy one and will have no place for the indecisive. The world will not vanquish hunger by aggravating its general food deficit and economic failure, nor by merely appealing to the better nature of one particular ruler, trade-union leader or politician, nor even by public charity. The

[11] Galbraith says: 'All support, not only moral but also material, should be withdrawn from non-productive ruling classes in the underdeveloped countries.'

[12] Prebisch from South America, Mahalanobis from India, Gunnar Myrdal from Sweden, Oskar Lange from Poland, Gardiner from Ghana, Kollontai from the Soviet Union, Samir Amin from Egypt, Bairoch from Belgium, Tibor Mende from France, Balogh from England, etc. This list is a suggestion for the kind of people who would be appropriate. There would have to be more experts from the socialist bloc, China included, and from the underdeveloped countries.

world order of the future will undeniably need a new mechanism to penalize mistakes such as luxury spending by the privileged class, idleness, insufficient saving and investment. This raises at least two major problems: birth control and the choice between reform and revolution.

8. THE MOST URGENT AND MOST DIFFICULT TASK: CONTROL OF THE POPULATION EXPLOSION

The following measures seem essential: (1) an enormous, immediate increase in the aid granted by the industrialized countries, (2) greater efficiency in international cooperation with most effort on the part of the backward countries, and (3) sanctions to penalize mistakes. But the population explosion contains by far the worst danger; if it overtakes economic progress, as it already has in most of the Third World, it will swamp or sweep aside any attempt at improvement.[13] We may then be finally defeated by hunger and all the misery it entails; our children will inherit a world in which life is impossible – ground fertile only for nuclear disaster.

India has been issuing propaganda for birth control ever since independence, but so far with little result. Japan and the People's Democracies have, however, succeeded in substantially reducing their birth rates and China seems to be making rapid headway in the same direction. If agricultural and industrial production are accelerated, birth control need not be such an immediate priority in tropical Africa and South America as it is in North Africa, the Caribbean and, above all, South East Asia. A world organization would find it quite impossible to help the backward countries to develop without imposing sanctions on rising birth rates. International aid to any country which continues to allow its population to grow faster than its production should, therefore, be cut or, if necessary, stopped altogether. Rules on birth control could only be introduced if they are made applicable to all – to rich and poor, affluent and backward countries.[14] Information, education, and

---

[13] And food aid could help to prolong it to a dangerous extent.
[14] On the whole the rich have already adjusted themselves to strict control of the birth rate. The World Bank is now making its aid to Morocco conditional on the adoption of birth control.

publicity on contraceptive methods must be given first of all. There is no alternative to strict rules on birth control; the human race will not survive unless it controls its numbers. We cannot discuss the way in which sanctions should be applied until the idea is more widely accepted. The problem is urgent: the vast majority of people still refuse to face the true facts of the situation. Catholicism and Communism have been the main obstacles to any progress; and the Catholic Church has refused to change its views.

The fear that a reduction in the birth rate will raise the average age of the population does not constitute a valid objection. The possibility of a higher average age is not wholly disadvantageous; it would then be easier to recoup the cost of the 'upbringing' period and, still more important, of the training period, which is becoming longer and longer. It will soon probably seem vital, for the sake of both mental and physical health, for older men to continue to do some form of work, although perhaps for shorter hours. Basic structural reforms of this kind, however, inevitably invite opposition. Formidable political problems will be unavoidable.

9. REFORM AND REVOLUTION

Will the privileged class now holding political and economic power – for example, the monopolists, the 'beloved' heads of state, and the bureaucracies – ever accept a policy by which their excesses of power will be removed? When the personal interests of a tyrant – Haiti is a good example – are the sole factor behind government policy, there is no alternative but to force a change. The upheavals of the last fifty years, however, have resulted in an overwhelming number of lost opportunities for social progress.

Is there any chance of success for revolutions inspired by the common good and by the interests of the poor? Must they be perverted towards a questionable ideology, designed to conceal the interests of a privileged power-hungry class? This class might be the Stalinist old guard, or the military landowning oligarchy of South America, or the Indian bureaucracy, with its mixture of pride, inefficiency and laziness. Guided by their own interests, they will never relinquish the privileges of power without a struggle.

Some factions claim that they safeguard liberties, in the sense in which they understand the term. In particular, they defend the privileges of wealth.

In consequence, they refuse economic independence to South American countries and resist the will of the majority in Vietnam. They claim to uphold Truth and seek to impose on the world a life-style dominated by waste. This way of life must not be allowed to become universal.

At the opposite end of the scale, in the east, the communists believe that they are holders of another Truth, which they wish to impose on the world in their turn. Fortunately, Marxists are now expounding various different theses, which weakens their unity and their pretentions to a revealed, dogmatic and unitary faith. The confrontation between the various interpretations may prove a constructive way of provoking discussion and argument.

In theory, the principal aim of communism is to prevent one man from exploiting another. But the communists make this ideal subservient to their bureaucracy, the only organ entitled to interpret the sacred dogmas, forgetting those that are inconvenient. They maintain but do not prove that collective ownership of the means of production is the cornerstone of the society of the future. Not all communities, however, have reached the stage of evolution at which they are fit to manage the means of production in the best interests of the nation and its citizens. Besides, all decisions are immediately referred to the Party, which regards itself as omniscient. In consequence, the Party can become all powerful and is free to abuse its dictatorial powers, while maintaining that it represents the proletariat.

We are unable to formulate an absolute and universal political Truth because no such concept exists; we cannot even say which economic system is the most efficient. Capitalism seems to have a clear lead in developed countries, for example in the United States and Japan as compared with the USSR, and in Western Europe as compared with Eastern Europe; even when some allowance is made for the Eastern countries' late beginning, the West still leads. Capitalism has only been able to flourish, however, in a small part of the world. After forcing colonial domination on the rest of the world, it then abandoned it to underdevelopment. Such is the ugly reverse side of the glittering medal of Western profit.

The essential elements of development, on the other hand, can be defined: they are investment and increased employment, more schooling and professional training. The merits of a country or a government can, therefore, be assessed by the extent to which they try to obtain these results; they can also be judged by the value they set on human dignity as shown in struggles against the most flagrant social injustices and support for freedom of expression. Now that these conditions have been defined, it should be easier to specify the principal obstacles to growth inherent in given economic structures and political systems. Once the obstacles have been recognized, should an attempt be made to negotiate a way through them, as it is by reformists such as Frei, or should they be overturned by revolutionaries such as Castro?

Only one thing is definite: the developed countries must not take the backward countries' decisions for them. Any such interference would be dangerously close to neo-colonialism, which is always detestable, even when practised by *pieds rouges*.[15] The decision must be taken by those who are living in the country under the existing system, by those who will eventually pay the price of their own errors; they should not be made to suffer from our mistakes as well. We may, however, show them the lessons to be learned from past revolutions. Some revolutions produce economic recession (as in Cuba), others deprive the people of some of their essential liberties (as in China and the USSR). This in no way alters the fact that they do have some extremely positive aspects.

A brief appraisal of the history of the last few centuries shows that no single, clearly defined, direction exists. No one with any pretentions to a scientific approach can say that he is moving in the direction of history or forecast the victory of a particular form of socialism. Socialism may still have a chance, in spite of its lack of success in recent years, if it can adapt itself quickly enough: in other words, if it makes revisions – just as Marx and Lenin did in their time. The

---

[15] In Algeria, some of Ben Bella's revolutionary advisers were called *pieds rouges*, by analogy with the *colons*, who gave themselves the name *pieds noirs*.

charge of revisionism bears the stamp of communist dogma, and is used to defend unrealistic principles.

Development cannot be accelerated unless the oppressive privileges of the élite are destroyed and with them the inhuman misery they cause. The poor, both individuals and nations, must be given more part in decision-making, more economic power and political influence both on a national and an international level. Every time a privileged minority appropriates some productive resource necessary for growth, a revolution becomes necessary as a preliminary to a period of reformism: nineteenth century liberalism was the outcome of the French revolution. Even if revolutions do not achieve all their objectives, they sweep aside the insidious and reactionary forces of apathy, as can be seen particularly clearly in China. But the abuses of revolution must be resisted.

Liberalization then is a vital remedy for the infant diseases of the revolutionary state. The process of liberalization, fairly advanced in much of Eastern Europe, is now being consolidated in the USSR, in spite of all the reactionary resistance to destalinization, which, if successful, could have dangerous repercussions.* The attitude which right-minded people should adopt must depend on the extent to which the privileged classes in the backward countries (and their supporters, above all the United States) try to maintain their indefensible position. What will make them understand that changes are inevitable if development is to be possible? Without some revolutionary pressure they will never give up their privileges at all. The United States has committed some serious political mistakes – when, for example, at the end of April, 1959, it repelled Castro's overtures of friendship, the invasion in April, 1961, of the Bay of Pigs in Cuba, and the interference four years later in the Dominican Republic. They have not yet paid the full price for their mistakes – indeed they are committing a far more costly blunder in Vietnam.

10. THE COMMUNITY AND THE INDIVIDUAL

The eradication of hunger can be taken as the primary objective of the last third of the twentieth century. It would, however, be very

* *This was written before the Soviet invasion of Czechoslovakia.*

inadequate as the sole objective – man lives not by bread alone.[16] Of course we give the highest importance to the fight against hunger and the methods best designed to stimulate development. By suppressing the worst excesses of capitalism, however, the way should not be left free for totalitarian oppression of the Stalinist or even Maoist type. No one particular political standpoint can be recommended to the backward countries as valid in all situations and at all times.

As we have seen in Cuba, and as Samir Amin would have us believe in Africa, collectivist socialism (in the communist sense of the word) cannot be considered until after a certain level of development has been reached. This does not mean that the backward countries must go through all the stages of mercantilism and capitalism, tolerating their abuses, oppressions, and delays. Some minimum of planning seems vital, in order that the scarcest resources may be allocated to those places where their efficiency will be highest. Obviously this is much easier said than done.

Maximum planning would be dangerous as it would make the whole system tend towards centralization, curbing initiative and, in consequence, enthusiasm among the mass of the people, and such planning is often impossible with the present state of production techniques. Some flexible form of planning, therefore, seems most desirable but we cannot yet tell which economic or political system will be best when development has begun.

The assumption that collective ownership under state control of the means of production is an essential precondition of socialism is a limitation, even a distortion, of all that is contained in this great idea on which a large section of the human race has pinned its hopes. In our view socialism is better defined as a particular conception of society in which the common good is supreme, social barriers are eliminated, and each individual is treated with the respect that human beings deserve. In brief, socialism emphasizes the dignity of man as much as it does a particular economic system.

The best form of society is one which can evolve at the same rate

---

[16] 'Feed men, care for them and give slaves their freedom,' as François Perroux puts it in *Guerre ou partage du pain*, vol. 3 of *La Coexistence Pacifique*. Education and instruction should not be forgotten. It is not enough to feed them; they must learn how to make their own bread or rice.

as its level of development and general education; the one should complement the other. In a backward economy the technocrat might prefer a form of enlightened despotism in which he would put himself at the service of the people, the common good, and the future. Could there ever be a despot who was sufficiently honest and disinterested, as well as sufficiently competent and capable? It is far from being proved. Even if someone assumed such a role, with the best of intentions, he would soon be corrupted by power, as has been shown by many recent cases.

Rivalry between several different political parties can easily degenerate into mere competitive demagogy, to the neglect of any investment for the future. This rivalry would seem more desirable if the principal demands of the people ever reached the government, and if a real dialogue could be established between the leader and the peasant and between the various factions within the Party. A leader like Fidel Castro, who enjoys high prestige, should also be a teacher: he should try to explain in simple terms the reasons behind the government's economic, social, and political decisions. It is always dangerous for one leader to hold absolute power. When this does happen, there should be continuous discussions and exchanges as a safeguard against despotism; and the answers should not be suggested to the people, as they so often are.

Reformism is an efficient policy for countries that have already reached a certain standard of living and level of education.[17] The case for reformism is well exemplified by a parliamentary system on the English or Scandinavian model, which allows the people to voice their views. The parliamentary system has not been so successful in most underdeveloped countries. Revolt is justifiable when dictatorship benefits the interests of a minority or of a dominant foreign economy, as in many South American countries. Revolution is absolutely necessary for development when one social class refuses to permit effective use of an essential factor of production, as with the huge neglected *latifundia*.[18]

Revolution should, moreover, be organized in such a way as to

[17] The French and Italian communist parties, for instance, now accept the possibility of a peaceful transition to socialism.
[18] Michel Bosquet, *Le Nouvel Observateur*, March 9, 1966, on Francisco Jalião and Father Francisco Lage.

favour both economic development and human fulfilment, while at the same time respecting international laws; these will have to become more rigorous if overpopulation continues. As a structure for development, revolutionary socialism should show greater concern for the means of development – for example, savings, investment, equipment, the training of all kinds of staff and teachers. As a means of attaining personal fulfilment, this more humane form of socialism pursues a double objective, at once communal and personal. Neither aspect should be neglected. By placing exclusive emphasis on its communal aspect, the state may sacrifice the individual to the community; this would encourage authoritarian tendencies, soon leading to totalitarianism, which is useless in the long run. By concentrating on the personal aspect, self-interest might be encouraged, leading to various anarchist and terrorist deviations. Man cannot fulfil himself unless he has freedom of expression. But his predominant concern must be for his fellow citizens, for the poor in particular, not forgetting future generations to whom we are responsible for leaving the world in a fit state to inhabit.

11. TOWARDS A WORLD ECONOMY?

It would be extremely useful if we could disseminate the knowledge which has been acquired about the world's economic evolution, pointing out the major successes and failures and trying to establish their causes. Simple economic forecasts could then be drawn up to show where intervention is most needed, research could be carried out to establish a more sensible distribution of world production, and the outline of a world plan could be drawn up in successive stages. It would have to be a flexible plan, which could be corrected and improved as it is put into practice. The outline would only give the general overall direction to be followed, without going into detail. The plan would make it easier to assess the potential of each part of the world as determined by natural resources, equipment, level of development, etc. The international division of labour could then gradually become more clearly defined and more logical.

The economy will not improve its organization unless public opinion is made to realize that it is essential that it does so. The economy should be at the service of the people, designed to satisfy their principal needs in order of priority. Priorities imply political choices.

As A. Chominot reminds us, any attempt to graft modern economic methods on to traditional (tribal, feudal, latifundiary) or neo-colonialist structures is doomed to failure. Hunger will not be wiped out if priority is given exclusively to agriculture, since universal education and industrialization are equally important factors for general agricultural progress. The allocation of the correct proportion of resources to each sector will present the most difficult problem, one which we cannot solve with any degree of certainty. More experiments, whether they fail or succeed, will have to be carried out before we come any nearer to a solution.

Concerning the detailed practical application of the plan for each sub-region, producers' organizations (management committees) and consumers' organizations (cooperatives) should be allowed to give their opinions and express their wishes. The most difficult step will be forming consumers' bodies: voluntary cooperatives have not been successful outside Scandinavia and England. Unprotected, the consumer is an easy victim for advertising. It should not, however, be impossible to make advertising less immoral or to impose sanctions against abuses.

In view of the recent difficulties in both socialist and capitalist countries, we favour a mixed economy, with planning and a free market, which should try to avoid over-emphasis on the profit motive on the one hand and over-dogmatic planning on the other. This concept is now fairly generally accepted. Research should be done into both systems to discover how the two mechanisms can be combined to the best advantage, with national characteristics taken into account and every choice made on rational grounds. If this branch of research is to move forward, there must be competition between all aspects of established systems, including their economic and, therefore, political principles. Freedom to criticize might remove both the abuses of capitalist exploitation and the totalitarian suppression of freedom of expression and economic progress. This line of thought might lead to impossible utopian visions and we will therefore follow it no further. The longer one looks forward into the future, the more difficult it becomes to make any predictions. The outlook soon becomes very uncertain. We do not feel there is any point in looking beyond 1980. We do not claim to solve the problems of the modern world in this book. We have confined ourselves to stating some of the most fundamental ones, hoping to stimulate greater awareness of them.

CONCLUSION
A new world?

The world's food resources will, of course, increase steadily with the course of time. We now know, however, that in the Third World as a whole food production has virtually never risen faster than 2 per cent per year. P. Bairoch says that the productivity of the African and Asian peasant has probably fallen by about a fifth in the course of the past fifty years. Since 1959, even the world average has not been above 2 per cent; in 1965, world population growth reached the same level of 2 per cent for the first time in human history; and the population growth rate has been rising steadily for centuries.

What will happen if the population explosion continues; if the developed countries continue their selfish monopolization of the benefits of the industrial revolution; if they do not stop bickering over every penny of aid and every single advantage given to the backward countries – as was still the case in Geneva in June, 1964; if the socialist countries, whose successes in the cultural and industrial spheres are indisputable, continue to impede agricultural and economic growth with their dogmatic preconceptions; and if the privileged minorities continue to stress the paramount importance of their own interests to the neglect of general development and the standard of living of the mass of the people?

If all these conditions remain unchanged, and at present it seems likely that they will, the world will be threatened by the most terrible disaster in its history. What will seem most surprising in the future is how few people realized this when the evidence was so strikingly obvious. The more we know about the hunger, poverty and ignorance of half the people of the world, the more horrifying it seems. If all the countries of the world combined their efforts, these conditions *could* be changed; and yet they deteriorate constantly.

If hunger and poverty are to be eliminated, agricultural and industrial development must be promoted throughout the world. This does not mean that every area should try to achieve the same degree of expansion. Success will be most easily obtained if various poles of development are used as centres for the areas around them, irrespective of national frontiers. People will then be able to migrate to the areas which are the easiest to develop and responsibility will be collective and universal: there must be total mobilization in the fight against poverty and hunger.

If world solidarity is to be positive and effective, the term 'peaceful coexistence' must take on a deeper meaning, and all countries must disarm in order that all available resources may be devoted to the only battle worth fighting. Owing to its size and complexity, the problem is first and foremost political. The various campaigns against hunger would be failing to live up to their charitable intentions if they stopped at mere charity. Valuable as a means of stimulating the public into awareness, charities are bound to fail if they go no further than individual or communal acts of generosity.

We should not be afraid to say it: the time has come when a new world must be built and preferably *before* the old one collapses. It will be easiest to do this while our present institutions – many of which are excellent – can still be used as a foundation. Socialists, Buddhists, Christians, Muslims, Hindus, Animists, Humanists – should all remember their international, unitary, humanitarian, and communal responsibilities. The reawakening of Asian Buddhism, the consequences of the twentieth Congress of the Communist Party of the USSR, the second Vatican Council, and many other developments are the first auguries of a better future.

We must all try to adapt our socio-economic structures to suit the requirements of development. We must, therefore – and this is another reason why this book has been written – try to make our own governments feel genuine concern, which is usually easier than changing them. In July, 1965, I explained to President Dacko and his entourage that when a social group ceases to justify its dominant position, by ignoring the common good, it invariably falls from power. I did not realize how quickly this would happen in the Central African Republic; dictators often manage to stay in power longer –

as if they were trying to justify, before it happens, the violence that will ultimately overthrow them.

'How can I influence the future of the world?' dedicated militants always ask after my lectures: they are right-minded people, who are aware of their own weakness. If everyone gave up all hope of achievement the world would be lost; but if we are really convinced and determined each one of us can have a real influence over our common destiny. We discount those who live only for the pleasures of the moment (they should now be making best use of the little time left to them); of the others, many belong to trade unions, clubs, political parties, professional associations, sports clubs, or religious sects. All of them can at least influence their neighbours, families, children, friends, and acquaintances. When I go to a meeting by train, I seldom miss the opportunity of talking to my fellow passengers and I do not often feel that I am wasting my time – although results vary.

It may seem pessimistic to forecast world catastrophe even before the year 2000; it may even discourage possible supporters. But they would be wrong to be discouraged: we are by no means without defence. We should increase tenfold the resources of the World Campaign against Hunger; then small projects (like the vegetable growing at Pointe-Noire in the Congo Republic) would spread with enormous speed. Under the stimulus of outside pressure, North Korea, Formosa, and Israel have undeniably obtained good results.

The rural organizers trained in Africa by IRAM (Institut de recherche et d'action contre la misére mondiale), the project run by Goussault and de Chaponay, have started to arouse the peasantry of Africa. In January, 1966, I was very critical of the Tunisian economic planners' complacency and I am, therefore, all the more pleased to see how successful they have been in spite of difficult circumstances. The Ivory Coast is making constant progress, though it may soon find that it has exhausted its immediate possibilities. The vast country of China is beginning to develop more harmoniously now that the mistakes of the Great Leap Forward have been corrected; it is doing so with no foreign assistance whatsoever. It could still improve its chances by curbing population growth.

Thirty or forty thousand million dollars in foreign aid by about

1970; a hundred thousand million by 1980. These sums should not be hard to find. They would promote rapid mechanization and industrialization in the Third World if these countries made more effort. We should attempt to give so much aid so efficiently that the growth rate of the backward countries overtakes that of the developed countries.

If scientists ceased to give priority to military and space research, they could concentrate on biological questions, such as the mechanism of chlorophyl assimilation, and agronomic research, with special emphasis on tropical agriculture; and in addition on the new foodstuffs, such as petrol yeasts and synthetic proteins. We must create preferential markets with fixed prices for the agricultural, mineral, and industrial goods produced by the Third World, and above all, we must launch a more determined campaign for birth control. Japan should be an example: it halved its birth rate in ten years (from 32 to 17 per thousand between 1947 and 1957).[1]

The outlook, therefore, is still hopeful, as long as we do not underestimate the difficulties nor the scale of effort that world development will require. The exploitation of the conquered is not the worst aspect of colonization, though it certainly occurred. Far worse is the fact that the colonial powers prevented the subject peoples from deciding their own fate, thereby reducing them to the state of irresponsible children. The conquerors monopolized the most exalted and economically profitable positions, the offices of government and economic activity in the secondary and tertiary sectors. This situation is, to a large extent, perpetuated in the international division of labour, a slave economy in a neo-colonial framework. To break free from this tradition we must concentrate on industrial progress paralleled by agricultural progress. Though banks may be an absolutely vital part of modern life, there is no reason why they should be so concentrated in London and New York. Scientific research is indispensable but need not be confined to the temperate regions of the Northern hemisphere.

[1] The population of Japan will of course go on growing by about 1 per cent per year until 1980. And it took her a long time to settle down to this rate. The population of China can be forecast to reach over 1,000 million in the near future and India will probably reach the same total at the beginning of the twenty-first century. A vast campaign to increase production will be needed.

Some day, the new world order must recognize that the rights to food, health and education are universal. A world community guaranteeing these rights can then be seen to be justified, indeed necessary. The world of the future may be magnificent to live in; but it will never be secure. Life will demand more civic courage and a greater sense of responsibility. Inactive members of society are guilty of all the evils which their passivity permits. With universal solidarity, the little rag-girl of Shanghai,[2] the families living on the pavements in Calcutta, the Congolese, the people of the Andes, and the peons of the *zona da mata*[3] and the *sertão* of Brazil, will be the concern of all of us.

Disaster can only be averted if we are prepared to risk our safety, by denouncing prejudice and inequality, and by trying to mitigate these evils, for it is impossible to suppress them altogether. The attitudes of most human beings are to a large extent determined by heredity and environment, but not so much so as to deprive them of responsibility (or the ability) to dissent. Life would be less valuable and challenging if this were not so. However imperfect men may be, they will always be perfectible – slowly. If future generations are brought up in an environment of increasing waste and luxury, wealth will still be regarded as a matter for pride, though it is mainly the result of the work of our ancestors and of the people of the underdeveloped world. Political, revolutionary, and moral standards would sink. Let us show people the alternative possibility of devoting part of their lives to the *political* campaign against hunger, disease, ignorance, and poverty. Let us explain the futility of privileges that can only lead to their own destruction, a desirable result on condition that it did not give rise to other injustices which could be more oppressive for the mass of the people.

Revolution remains a route to progress: on the whole, China and Cuba are more seriously concerned for their future than most African and Latin American countries. Revolutions must not, however, be allowed to decrease the freedom and personal responsibility, the duties and dignity, of the citizens of the Third World or of anywhere else. Life on this planet must be improved for everyone,

---

[2] Cf. *Chine Surpeuplée, Tiers-Monde affamé*, p. 182.
[3] Cf. *Living Lands*, chap. III.

not only the people of the Atlantic bloc and the privileged minorities in the backward countries. This tenet is emphatically revolutionary.

I am frequently asked the same question at the end of my lectures: do you believe that your ideas are at all practicable? Apparently they only seem valid to a few powerless idealists. Others regard such ideas as utopian, if not dangerous. There is a serious risk that they will not be accepted until it is too late for them to be really useful.

Conflicts between nations, tribes, classes, interest groups and ideologies will no doubt produce solutions which are quite different from our suggestions. But the most urgent cause at present is to make as many people as possible realize the gravity of the situation.[4] Provoking discussion may be the best way of finding coherent and valid solutions. The problem is that of world development; it is too vast and complex, we repeat, to be solved by charity. Food aid without birth control will aggravate future difficulties; and support for corrupt, privileged minorities may strengthen the obstacles to development.

The new generation will find itself faced with difficulties such as the human race has never known before. We want to help it to solve them but are not satisfied with the contribution we have made. The reader is, therefore, invited to take part in a constructive discussion.[5]

In conclusion, I should like to acknowledge that widespread famine and terrible poverty do seem difficult to avoid. This should make us all the more determined to reduce their magnitude, since we are collectively responsible for our common destiny.[6]

[4] 'Even here in Madagascar, the growth of poverty is alarming, and we are still a privileged class', Père Boltz wrote from Ambositra.
[5] You are invited to send us your criticisms, reactions, ideas and counterproposals. Those who are dogmatic or inflexible could hardly participate, since any dialogue with them would be completely useless.
[6] 'Basic dialogue between peoples unfortunately takes the form of war. Though I approve of your point of view, I still feel anxious about the practical steps to be taken.' (G. Severac).

A NOTE ON WEIGHTS AND MEASURES

Weights and measures have been left in their metric form. There is a conversion table below. *'Tonne' (or metric ton) has been translated throughout as 'ton'; in fact a metric ton is equal to 0.984 of a long ton—(2240 lbs).*

WEIGHT	1 metric ton (1,000 kgs)	= 0.984 long tons (2,240 lbs)
		= 1.102 short tons (2,000 lbs)
	1 kilogramme (kg)	= 2.20 lbs
	1 quintal (100 kgs)	= 1.97 cwt
AREA	1 hectare	= 2.47 acres
CAPACITY	1 litre	= 1.76 pts (UK)
		= 2.11 pts (US)
	1 hectolitre (10 litres)	= 2.22 gallons (UK)
		= 2.67 gallons (US)

'Corn' is used throughout in the general sense of 'grain' and not in the restricted American sense of 'maize'.

SELECT BIBLIOGRAPHY

AUSTRUY, Jacques, *Le Scandale du développement*, éd. Ouvrières, Paris, 1965, with commentary by G. Leduc and L.-J. Lebret and an analytical and critical bibliography by Guy Caire, 535 p.

BAIROCH, Paul, *Révolution industrielle et sous-développement*, SEDES, Paris, 1963, 360 p.

BARRE, Raymond, *Le Développement économique*, analyse et politique, ISEA, Paris, 1958, 82 p.

CÉPÈDE, Michel and LENGELLÉ, Maurice, *Economie alimentaire du Globe*, Librairie de Médicis, éd. M.-T. Génin, Paris, 1953, 649 p.

CIPOLLA, Carlo, *The Economic History of World Population*, Penguin Books, London, 1962, 117 p.

FANON, Frantz, *The Wretched of the Earth*, MacGibbon and Kee and Penguin Books, London, 1965 and 1967; Grove Press, New York.

FURTADO, Celso, *Development and Underdevelopment*, University of California Press, Berkeley and Los Angeles, 1964, 171 p.

HIRSCHMAN, Albert, *The Strategy of Economic Development*, Yale University Press, New Haven, 1958, 217 p.

JACQUOT, Raymond, *Les Facteurs d'efficacité alimentaire, les aliments*, Imp. Leconte, Marseille, 1958, 290 p.

LACOSTE, Yves, *Géographie du sous-développement*, Coll. 'Magellan', P.U.F., Paris, 1965.

LATIL, Marc, *L'Evolution du revenu agricole*, Centre d'études économiques, Lib. Colin, Paris, 1956, 368 p.

LEBRET, Louis-Joseph, *Suicide ou survie de l'Occident*, Coll. 'Economie humaine', Economie et humanisme, éd. Ouvrières, Paris, 2ND ed., 1962, 406 p.

MENDE, Tibor, *Un Monde possible*, éd. du Seuil, Paris, 1963.

MYRDAL, Gunnar, *Economic Theory and Underdeveloped Regions*, London, Duckworth, 1957, 164 p.

MYRDAL, Gunnar, *Asia Drama*, Penguin Books, New York and London, 1968.

PADDOCK, William Paul, *Famine 1975! America's Decision: Who will Survive?* Little, Brown and Company, Boston, 1967

PERROUX, François, *La Coexistence pacifique*, P.U.F., Paris, 1958, 3 vols., 666 p.

ROSTOW, W. W., *The Stages of Economic Growth*, Cambridge University Press, Cambridge, 1960, 179 p.

SAUVY, Alfred, *Malthus et les deux Marx*, éd. Denoël, Paris, 1963, 353 p.

JOURNALS AND PERIODICALS

FAO, The State of Food and Agriculture (annual) Rome.

Développement at Civilizations.
Tiers-Monde.

Index